From Preschool to Grad School:

Strategies for Success at Any Level of Competitive Admissions

Kim Palacios

Copyright © 2012 Kim Palacios

Distributed By Luxe Publishing, P.O. Box 190697, San Francisco, CA 94119

Visit our website at www.luxe-press.com

Visit the official book website at www.getintoanyschool.com

ISBN-10: 0985798300

ISBN-13: 978-0-9857983-0-7

Printed in the United States of America

Edited by Jill Bailin Rembar

Design by Frank Parker, A Creative Experience:
www.acreativeexperience.com

May all your admissions dreams come true!

- Kim Pei

May all your admissions

dreams come true!

To Mom and Dad,
for sacrificing so, so much
to give me a great education.

TABLE OF CONTENTS

INTRODUCTION

I was a "C" student in high school. A "B" student in college. My test scores were good, but not great. I'm not a piano virtuoso and I've never rescued kittens from a burning building. So, how did somebody so ostensibly mediocre manage to get into so many prestigious schools?

I'm joking. But just a bit. I know I'm not mediocre. I know that I was qualified to attend most of the schools that I've ever applied to. But I also know that acceptance to top schools seems nearly impossible, almost as if it's reserved for the godlike few with a long list of superhuman qualities.

You know who I'm talking about. The four-year-old who's applying a year early to kindergarten because she can count by tens to a million in English, Swedish, and Cantonese. The thirteen-year-old high school applicant whose science project even a chemistry Ph.D. couldn't replicate, and frankly, which you wouldn't understand in a hundred years. Even saving kittens from a burning building pales in comparison to an application I once read in which a former Marine told of risking his life to save other men during combat. Whenever I applied to private schools, I never had credentials like any of those.

The truth is that although I have ended up attending some of the finest institutions in the world, I haven't always been successful in getting offers from all the schools on my target list. What I know about the admissions process comes not only from serving on the admissions committee at a #1 ranked business school, but from the sting of many past failures and rejections.

But, that's not my whole story. After so many years spent applying to, and attending private schools...after spending two years as an admissions officer...after starting the process of researching private schools for my own child, something big—really big—clicked.

It was all the same.

It hit me while standing in the gymnasium of a prestigious private K-12 school, sipping lemonade from a plastic cup at a Saturday open house. Though I was attending the event as a prospective parent, my retired admissions hat slipped on clandestinely when certain things became hard not to notice. Like the family with two fidgety children in tow, conspicuous not only because the children behaved rambunctiously, but because the school had firmly requested that children be left at home; like the few parents who arrived late (some very much so), and families who were dressed inappropriately, and those who made inquiries that seriously called into question whether they had done any research about the school at all. I also saw parents who behaved impeccably, speaking, acting and representing themselves in ways that were certain to bolster their chances of getting their children into the school. I was experiencing déjà vu. I remembered these people, or at least caricatures of them. I'd seen this behavior before.

> *Most competitive schools, regardless of education level, rank candidates in similar ways.*

As an admissions committee member who attended countless debriefs after similar open houses, I recalled candid conversations about attendees who made the best—and worst—impressions. In subsequent weeks (because, by then, I was really paying close attention) I saw the same polarity of behaviors at two other prestigious private schools. It made me want to test a theory I had, the results of which led to the writing of this book. I set out to learn whether private school admissions are really all that different, from one learning level to the next.

After researching the matter, the answer was clear: most competitive schools, regardless of education level, rank candidates in similar ways.

THE ONLY PRIVATE SCHOOL ADMISSIONS BOOK YOU'LL EVER NEED

What if the best advice for improving your child's chances of getting into a great preschool and improving an adult's chances of getting into a great graduate school were the same? Certainly, the prerequisites are different, and the selection criteria seem dissimilar. But what happens when we take a closer look? A detailed review of private school applications, from the earliest to the highest education levels, reveals similarities that cannot be ignored.

This book exposes patterns found across application processes and deconstructs the vital role that common elements play in candidate success. In illuminating these patterns, it answers that critical and elusive question: what are the best schools really looking for?

SOME THINGS NEVER CHANGE...

Consider the following questions found on the admissions applications of four world-class private schools:

- Please tell us what attracted you to our school. Why do you feel it may be a good match for you?

- Describe yourself as a person. What qualities do you like and value most about yourself? What would you like to improve?

- What kind of role do you hope to play in our school's community?

- Discuss a time when you faced a challenging interpersonal experience. How did you navigate the situation and what did you learn from it?

Now, I'll ask you to take a guess: which one of these questions appeared on an MBA program application? A middle school application? A preschool application? Which of these questions appeared on a high school application? You can't really tell—not without the names of individual schools, or language showing whether it was the parents or the children who were expected to answer the question.

There's something else you can't tell from these questions: what year they are from. In this case, I pulled all of those questions from applications for students entering target schools in 2012. Yet, when I applied to top business schools exactly ten years ago, I was asked all four of these more than once.

The fact is that most schools, regardless of education level, rank prospective students around a core set of values. They want to know the same kinds of things about a six-year-old applicant as they want to know about a twenty-six-year-old applicant. Therefore, improving your chances of admission starts with understanding the fundamentals of what every competitive school admissions committee cares about. We will make a foray into the inner workings of competitive schools to reveal not only what they care about, but why.

Commonalities across applications are seen not only among short answers and essay questions. A thorough look at interview practices, the way test scores are regarded, and the very structure of the admissions cycle itself reveals that, across the board, competitive school admissions committees show more similarities than differences. This book will present fact-based, time-tested insights that will help readers be competitive in private school admissions beginning right now, and for the rest of their lives.

...OTHER THINGS DO CHANGE...

What schools are looking for might not be changing, but the admissions process is. Economic woes and trouble in public education have influenced who, when and how many students wish to attend and are willing to pay for private schools. Successful applicants must be doubly attractive to admissions committees, showing polish around the fundamentals while also sailing through tests specific to applying to school today. These include:

- a larger number of qualified applicants competing for a relatively static number of spots
- the diminishing ability of families to predictably afford private school education
- essay and interview questions relating to emerging trends and social concerns (e.g., innovation, critical thinking, design, and globalization)
- the widespread emergence of cheating (facilitated by the Internet) and the role of ethics

This book will discuss contemporary issues that admissions committees are compelled to consider and show readers how to gain an advantage by responding appropriately to the current environment. It will teach candidates how to tailor applications to the individual challenges and circumstances of any year's admissions cycle. It will build upon proven strategies and show candidates how to be more competitive using advanced tactics. It will supply up-to-date, practicable advice that will allow you to make your application stand out.

...AND ONE SIZE DOESN'T FIT ALL.

Perhaps most importantly, this book will relieve you of any misconceptions you have about right or wrong answers, passing or failing interviews, or about your test scores being good enough to get you in. Admissions committees are not the punitive, sadistic, narrow-minded types they are sometimes made out to be, and the application and interview process is not designed to trick you.

> *Your authentic answers—not unachievable "right" answers—are always best.*

Admissions officers typically love meeting and interacting with candidates, and the committee's greatest task is to elevate you beyond the two-dimensional being you are on paper and help you come alive as a whole person. This book will teach you why your authentic answers—not unachievable "right" answers—are always best.

I will be honest with you. Lessons about being authentic in your application are the trickiest ones to learn, but also the most important. This book fully addresses making choices and statements that are authentic to you. We will explore issues such as:

- applying to the right schools for you (not the right schools according to Newsweek, the Joneses, or anybody else)

- personal reflection and the critical exercise of identifying why you are really interested in a particular path or a particular school

- how to stand out, even when everybody is being asked the same question and many people will have the same authentic answer

- how to stop trying to seem so perfect and let your human side show; writing a balanced application

- how to use storytelling and personal anecdotes to help your application come alive

◆ candor and communicating difficult or taboo information effectively

Admissions committees read hundreds, if not thousands, of applications each season, so in order to be successful, candidates must be memorable. This book will teach you how to make choices that will allow you to achieve two difficult goals: being authentic (even if the truth isn't terribly exciting) and also standing out.

BUT SERIOUSLY...COULD ADMISSIONS FOR ALL EDUCATION LEVELS REALLY BE THE SAME?

Yes. But if you're skeptical, I get it. Different school types are different. That won't go unaddressed. Though each chapter will focus on the mastery of general process elements, specific examples highlighting various education levels are peppered throughout the book. The education levels addressed will be preschool, primary school (K-8), secondary school (9-12), college (undergrad), and masters-level graduate school. By reading the general sections, as well as those most pertinent to the next school level to which you will be applying, the combined insights will tell you much of what you need to know.

WHO AM I?

And what makes me qualified to write a book about getting into any school? Let me introduce myself.

◆ **I am an alumna of two prestigious private primary and secondary schools and two world-renowned universities.** I have personally experienced the pressures, joys, and disappointments of the admissions process several times. Over the years, I have written more than 100 short answers and essays, sat in dozens of interviews, and waited for approximately twenty admissions verdicts. I have attended competitive schools in three different states and one foreign country, and even when enrolled as a full-time student, I was compelled to apply for competitive programs requiring separate admission, including exchange programs and special status courses.

◆ **I sat on the admissions committee at a top university.** As a student at the University of Chicago Booth School of Business, I participated as an application reader during my first year, before being selected to be one of four admissions committee co-chairs in my second year. That appointment made me a member of the committee with full "accept/deny rights," on par with full-time admissions committee staff. During my tenure as an admissions committee co-chair, I spent 10–15 hours per week reading applications, interviewing candidates, and coordinating and participating in admissions events. I read hundreds of applications, interviewed dozens of candidates, and made the tie-breaking admit/deny decision numerous times. I was party to closed admissions committee meetings during which waitlist or borderline candidates or event attendees were candidly discussed. During my two years of service, played a large role in influencing outcomes. I know what is said behind closed doors.

- **I have volunteered as a long-term coach, mentor, and career advisor to more than a dozen individuals applying to schools.** As a successful corporate professional, I was sought out to mentor colleagues considering different career and educational paths. To those applying to school, I became a coach, giving candid feedback and insider tips throughout the process. Of those who pursued school admissions, all were successful in attending their program of choice.

- **I am a professional writer and editor who has critiqued and supplied editorial advice on numerous application essays and resumes.** The ability to articulate oneself using the written word is critically important to applicant success. I have supplied coaching and editorial advice concerning how to refine voice, tell stories, and create structure to enhance written application elements from essays, to short answers, to resumes.

- **As a student, my grades were always mediocre at best, and my test scores were never at the top. I got accepted to great schools because I knew how to highlight my strengths and address my weaknesses. As time went on, I got better at applying to schools. I can make you better, too.**

IS THIS BOOK FOR YOU?

This book will be of the greatest benefit to applicants or parents of applicants:

- planning to apply to any school with a competitive selection process, from preschool to graduate school

- possessing broad familiarity with the admissions process and entry requirements for target programs

- who have applied to competitive schools previously, with mixed or disappointing results

- very familiar with the private school application process and looking for an extra edge to extremely competitive schools

If you are totally unfamiliar with the competitive school admissions process, this book should not be your first read. If you have no awareness of the key components of the application process for the school to which you plan to apply, such as the month in which most applications are due, what standardized tests are required, whether interviews are customary, etc., consider starting with a more basic book. Though this book will discuss all application elements, including testing and timing, the discussion will begin at an intermediate level.

This book is ideal for somebody who is committed to applying to private schools but who has never personally undergone the process or has never done so on behalf of a child. It is also appropriate for application veterans looking to update their strategies by learning what schools are currently seeking. This book is also highly recommended for those who want to write world-class applications for extremely competitive schools.

GETTING THE MOST OUT OF THIS BOOK

From Preschool to Grad School: Strategies for Success at Any Level of Competitive Admissions is not the kind of book that must be read from cover to cover. If you are genuinely confident about a particular area, or if a topic does not seem to apply, do not be afraid to move on.

That said, a little extra curiosity may go a long way. Just because you aced your entrance exams doesn't mean you wouldn't benefit from reading the chapter on testing in order to learn how admissions committees view test scores, and how far good ones will really get you. The stakes are high, here. You can't really be over-prepared.

Finally, go beyond the book. A web site dedicated to this volume can be found at www.getintoanyschool.com, and you'll also find a blog in which I will discuss emerging topics and answer reader questions.

PART I:
GETTING GROUNDED

CHAPTER I

UNDERSTANDING THE MARKET

Here are two questions for you:

   1. Is a 16 oz. Starbucks espresso drink *really* worth $4.25?

   2. Are public schools *really* failing?

Hint: there are no correct answers. And, for practical purposes, all that matters is the market.

Here's what I mean: a cup of coffee doesn't cost $4.25 to produce, but millions of people are willing to pay that price. If you want that brand of coffee drink, that price—the market price—is what you will have to pay to get it. If fewer people were willing to pay that amount, the price would drop to a level that people were willing to pay. If more people were willing to pay that amount, the price might actually rise. Ultimately, the price you pay for this cup of coffee may have little to do with the actual cost of getting it to market.

Competitive school admissions operates in a similar fashion—the "cost," in this case, is the baseline standard admissions criteria the school sets forth—things like academic aptitude, personal achievement, and fit. No candidate who doesn't meet the baseline (i.e., who can't pay the cost) has a chance of getting in. Yet the "price" of admission is set by the number of students who are at or above the baseline. The more candidates who come in at or above baseline, the harder it is to get into a school. Like the price of a cup of coffee, "price of admission" is determined by the market.

This question of whether public schools are failing shows how school admissions are like markets. If your goal is to get into a competitive school, it doesn't really matter whether public schools are actually failing—what matters is how many people believe that public schools are failing, and therefore how many above-baseline candidates enter the competitive school market based on that belief. The market can also become less competitive. During a recession, families with children in K-12 schools may be less inclined to pay hefty private school tuition fees—in that case, many above-baseline candidates may exit the market, lowering the price of admission for those who remain.

> *The more candidates who come in at or above baseline, the harder it is to get into a school. Like the price of a cup of coffee, "price of admission" is determined by the market.*

In this sense, your chances of getting into a school will have less to do with whether you are qualified to attend than how saturated the market is with qualified candidates, and how well-positioned you are in that qualified pool. Being successful in admissions comes down to understanding, and playing to, the conditions of these ever-changing markets.

SCHOOL ADMISSIONS AND MARKETS

The price of admission is always changing. Consider a competitive high school that sends fifty acceptance letters per year and prefers to admit students with a 3.5 or higher GPA and standardized test scores in the 95th percentile. Now suppose that school receives one hundred applications and only thirty meet the aforementioned preference. In that case, the school would probably choose to admit several students who fall short of its preference, but who can still do well at the school. In such a year, the price of admission—and the number of offers made—is lower than average.

Fast-forward to the following year: suppose the same school receives 120 applications and 110 of them meet the preferred criteria. In that case, the school has so many qualified applicants that it can choose to ratchet up its standard. It may decide to accept only those students with 3.8 or higher GPAs who have test scores in the 98th percentile. A stronger applicant pool raises the price of admission.

> *Though the process itself is well-defined, decision-making is not linear and there is no precise formula for getting into a school.*

This may sound obvious. Yet even applicants who feel they know this may lose sight of it at some point during the process. This is because most overheard discussions of admissions frame it as static and unmoving, despite the fact that it is moving constantly.

In that sense, there's only one true answer to the question of what you have to do to get into a given school: be better than most other applicants. But "better" isn't a simple matter of showing perfect grades, perfect test scores, or a list of world-class accomplishments. "Better" is about showing that you will succeed inside the school's ecosystem while helping to strengthen the ecosystem itself. Getting into competitive schools is a matter of choosing targets for which you meet or exceed the baseline and making a strong case for why you will not only succeed, but thrive.

THE WISDOM OF NO GUARANTEES

In order to navigate markets like this, you must make peace with ambiguity. Though the process itself is well-defined, decision-making is not linear and there is no precise formula for getting into a school. Great interview + great test scores + great application essays or

short answers ≠ an offer of admission, at least, not every time. Meeting all of a school's published criteria is no guarantee that you'll get in, just like *not* meeting the same criteria is no guarantee you won't.

Even many students currently attending the most elite competitive programs didn't get into all the schools they applied to. A student who is accepted by Harvard might not get into Stanford. A Princeton admit may fail to get into Brown. Most people think that if they can swing an offer of admission from the #3 ranked school in a certain category, they will probably also get an offer from #4, #5, and #6—but this is simply not the case.

This is where market dynamics come in. Conditions are always changing. The applicant pool will vary from school to school, and year to year. Rankings and other factors influencing public opinion are always shifting the environment. The broader economy, from state and local funding to public policy, determines whether people can afford private schools, and to which ones they are likely to apply. And the schools themselves may adjust what they are looking for, a little from year to year, and possibly a lot over time. Even if the evaluation process stays the same, the outcomes are bound to be different.

Since there are no guarantees, the best way to maximize your chances is to cultivate an understanding of all the stakeholders, their incentives, and the complex environments within in which they operate. Being savvy about admissions market dynamics is essential to targeting and applying to individual schools.

CURRENT MARKETS AND COMPETITION

Who is the competition and what does that mean for you? This section will explore why, more than ever, students are driven to apply to competitive schools. It will supply the latest facts, figures, and trends, but also deal with popular opinions and social beliefs that drive behaviors, but that may or may not be substantiated by fact. Finally, it will broadly describe the admissions committee perspective, showing how market dynamics impact decisions makers. These themes combine to provide critical insights about how competitive private school admission really is.

Even as recently as twenty or thirty years ago, preschool was seen as an alternative to the norm. For some progressive minority of families who believed strongly in early education, it was a mechanism to cultivate intellectual curiosity and a love for learning. Programs like Montessori,

Reggio Emilia, and Waldorf have been used since the early- to mid-1900s among families who valued education and had the means to send their three- and four-year-olds to such schools.

Back then, whether children attended preschool was also influenced by whether both parents pursued careers. Some families with the inclination to have one parent serve as a full-time caregiver preferred to raise their children from home until it was time for kindergarten. Facilities geared toward working parents were more commonly thought of as day care centers, places where children went to play, and be cared for, while parents went to work. Now—for both practical and academic reasons—preschool has become the norm—practically an academic necessity—and even the public sector has gotten into the game.

A 2008 article in the *American School Board Journal* reported that thirty-nine states participated in public funding to educate three- and four-year-old children. A 50 percent rise in spending took place over a six-year period— from $2.4 billion in the 2001-02 academic year to $3.7 billion in 2006-07 (a rate that surpassed growth in K-12 spending). At the time of the study, 25 percent of the nation's four-year-olds (approximately a million children) attended public pre-kindergarten programs. Despite restricted budgets, public institutions have undertaken large investments to address the serious problem of children entering kindergarten being underprepared. To this extent, preschool is no longer viewed as much an option as a necessity; widespread belief in the importance of early education has flooded the market with parents seeking academic enrichment for children as young as two years old.

What this means, naturally, is that private preschool enrollment is on the rise, and that the number of preschools has skyrocketed in recent decades and continues to grow. Working families who would have paid out-of-pocket child care expenses are now willing to pay a premium for programs that are academically enriching. Even families with at least one parent available to care for children until kindergarten often choose to send children to preschool to add rigor and structure to early learning. It is no longer uncommon for families to think of preschool as directly correlated to a child's success in all future academics. The fact that the Association of Waldorf Schools of North America proudly advertises that 94 percent of Waldorf graduates attend college confirms this increasingly-held belief.

With increased interest has come increased competition. A 2008 documentary, Nursery University, reported that there were fifteen applicants for every open seat at top New York City private preschools. Following the progress of four families with high hopes for their three-year-olds, the film portrays the admissions cycle as intense, emotional, and high-stakes. A 2012 article in *New York Family* magazine suggested, with only a hint of sarcasm, that it may be easier to get your child into Harvard than into a great New York City preschool. Though most markets for preschool aren't as tough as the New York market, many other intellectually-charged geographies (i.e., places where highly-educated adults live) make getting into preschool a serious game.

Preschool admissions is further complicated by the fact that comparing two- and three-year-olds to one another is difficult to fathom. Children at this age are inconsistent from day to day, and it's difficult to stomach the idea that your child will be assessed in a single meeting. The assessment criteria can also be difficult to get behind. Parents wonder how to demonstrate their children's developmental readiness and potential in ways that can be measured, let alone replicated.

Public vs. Private Schools: Pre-K through 12

Enrollment in private U.S. primary and secondary schools is substantial, with overall enrollment and performance tracked by the U.S. Department of Education's National Center for Education Statistics. Nearly 5.5 million students from pre-kindergarten through 12th grade are enrolled in nearly 35,000 private schools, according to a 2009-2010 study. Of that number, only 13 percent of students (about 700,000) were enrolled in non-sectarian institutions, with the remainder in religious schools, primarily Catholic.

Eleven percent of kindergarten students entering school in 2010 attended private institutions. The mean reading scores of private kindergarten students had a 3.6 percent higher baseline than those of public school students; in math, the gap was wider at 4.1 percent.

By fourth grade, 89 percent of private school students demonstrated grade-appropriate math skills at a basic level, compared to 82 percent of public school students. By eighth grade, basic math proficiency at private schools had dropped four points to 85 percent, yet at public schools it dropped a full ten points, to 72 percent.

The reading gap was even more pronounced, with 81 percent of private school fourth graders showing basic skills compared to just 66 percent in public schools. By eighth grade, the private school figure climbs to 90 percent while the public school population fails to rise above 75 percent. An older (yet telling) study of writing skill differences conducted in 2007 showed 96 percent of private school eighth graders demonstrating basic skills, while the public school figure halted at 87 percent. Science, history, geography, and civics saw even greater discrepancies, with proficiency gaps that had a 15 percent to 20 percent range.

Most people who are aware of public school underperformance haven't bothered to dig into the details of statistics like these. But they didn't need to—not with sound bytes about the state of public education pervading local and national news media. Even opinion pieces—films like *Waiting for Superman* and *The Lottery*—and public warnings issued by thought leaders like Bill Gates have placed Americans in a position to hear the same bleak messages about the poor state of public education. Such messages are even more prevalent during election years, when political rhetoric stokes the fire.

The numbers may change slightly from year to year, but the message remains the same: on average, our nation's public schools aren't educating our children as well as private ones are. Certainly, some public schools are excellent, while other private ones perform below average. But for the purpose of private school admissions, individual cases rarely matter. What matters to you, if you are applying to private schools anywhere on the spectrum from pre-kindergarten to twelfth grade, is that the worsening reputation of public schools has prompted more families to explore private education.

Undergraduate Program Admissions Trends

College is the new high school. That is, more entry level jobs than ever require college—not high school—degrees As recently as the 1980s, high school graduates were competitive for jobs that would place them in the middle class, while those without high school diplomas were relegated to low-wage jobs. Things have changed—increasingly, individuals need college degrees to secure the same middle class positions that were once filled by high school graduates, and those with high school diplomas are ill-positioned to rise above low-wage positions.

This means two things for admissions: first, that the applicant pool is growing, with more students than ever before eager to pursue a degree; and second, for students who were already college-bound, the stakes are higher to get into a great school. After all, more college graduates means more competition for a pool of highly coveted jobs. From there it becomes important to have not just any college degree, but one on par with the desired position.

A November 2010 study conducted by the National Association for College Admissions Counseling found that public four-year colleges and universities saw a 47 percent increase in application volume between 2001 and 2008; private not-for-profit colleges and universities saw a 70 percent increase in application volume during those years. The same study showed that the proportion of applicants accepted to private not-for-profit four-year schools decreased by 2 percent each year, an overall decline of 10 percent during the same window. The public sector acceptance rate declined by 7 percent.

There's another reason why college admissions are tougher than ever: graduate school enrollments are on the rise. For individuals seeking the most prestigious, highly paid jobs, graduate school is increasingly a prerequisite. Students who plan to pursue professional degrees must choose programs that will help their chances for grad school. With this added pressure, it becomes increasingly clear why college admission stakes are so high. Finally, to the extent that college is a greater financial commitment than ever, applicants have become more serious—and circumspect—about the process. New behaviors on the part of applicants have also changed the game.

Graduate School Admissions Trends
Graduate programs across the country have reported double-digit application growth. Ivy league schools like Cornell (whose law school saw a 44 percent rise in applications in 2010), Brown and Princeton (who saw

27 percent and 20 percent jumps, respectively, in applications across all grad schools in the same year) confirm trends of heightening interest and competition among the best schools.

Yet it's not merely the best schools that are seeing jumps in applications—a widening applicant pool shows a farther-reaching trend at schools across the board. An August 2011 Council of Graduate Schools report showed that foreign student applications increased 11 percent over the previous year; it was the sixth consecutive year of foreign application growth, and a subsequent April 2012 report from the same council confirmed 2012 as the seventh consecutive year of such growth. The greatest rise has come from emerging economic powers such as China, India, and Brazil, which are seeing more demand for citizens with a globally sophisticated education. Yet even U.S. neighbors Mexico and Canada are applying more widely to U.S. graduate schools.

Standardized tests saw an uptick as well. Between 2009 and 2010, the number of students taking the Graduate Record Examination (GRE) rose 13 percent to 670,000. Between October 2008 and October 2010, the number of people taking the Law School Admissions Test (LSAT) grew by 20 percent, with an unprecedented 60,746 candidates taking the exam. The Graduate Management Admissions Council (administrators of the GMAT) reported a 4.9 percent increase between June 2008 and 2009, bringing the total number of 2009 test-takers to 173,441.

These trends are somewhat complex and, at times, curious. For one, it is common to see recession-year jumps in application volume. In addition to finding a place to wait out the recession, jobless-workers-turned-students often look to grad school degrees to help land them better jobs. Similarly, the number of graduate school applications sometimes fall during economic bubbles, when most workers are disinclined to leave secure, well-paying positions. Other factors—such as employers subsidizing graduate school education—are also tied to the economic cycle. Tuition reimbursement programs are more prevalent when the economy is good than when it is bad.

Though several well-publicized studies speculate that the ROI on a graduate school education may not be as high as previously believed, this viewpoint has done little to slow graduate school application growth, despite graduate programs' prohibitive cost. The fact that hundreds of thousands of older students—often ones with families to support—are willing to forgo income for two or more years to attend full-time graduate program remains a testament to the high perceived value placed on graduate degrees.

OTHER MARKET DYNAMICS

Beyond fluctuations in the total number of people applying to competitive schools, other supply and demand factors impact the market. Increased demand caused by things like changes in rankings and press coverage, as well as lowered supply created by things like application caps, early admissions, and rolling admissions will have a tangible impact on applicants' prospects for success. Most of these will be out of your control, but understanding them is important to targeting and gauging your chances of getting into a given school.

The Impact of Rankings

Society conditions many of us to try for the "best" schools we can get into, which leads to an overemphasis on rankings. Though I don't recommend this approach, the reality is that many candidates use rankings as the main criterion to determine where they will apply.

Because of this, a school moving up or down a few spots from one year to the next can have a large impact on application volume. Some candidates (illogically) react to year-over-year changes instead of looking at net change over time, which tends to find schools trading positions with the same competitors over and over, but remaining in the same tier.

This is mixed news for candidates choosing schools based on fit. It can be frustrating when a school that is a great fit for you climbs up a few spots in the rankings the year that you apply, because it will be harder for you to get in than it would have just one year earlier. Conversely, if the same program falls in the rankings, applications may drop a bit, and in that year, it may be a bit easier to get into that school.

Press Coverage and Other Hype

A number of other external factors can place an individual school (or set of schools) under the spotlight. Traditional media coverage, such as a major newspaper or magazine article, can have a large impact on the school's reputation. The University of Michigan, for one, received ongoing national media coverage regarding affirmative action law suits for more than six years. Yale has struggled with bad press around issues of gender and ethnic discrimination. Penn State's reputation has suffered in the wake of the Jerry Sandusky child molestation trials.

Beyond news media, the public might learn about schools through documentary films such as the aforementioned *Nursery University*. Popular films like the 2001 comedy *Legally Blonde*, set at Harvard Law School, or the 2002 film *Orange County* which features a protagonist obsessed with attending Stanford, or even 2010's *The Social Network*, a biopic of Facebook founder Mark Zuckerberg, influence the reputations of schools.

Whether discussions of these schools are editorialized or dramatized, they do affect public opinion, and contribute to how some people feel about individual schools. The portrayal of Harvard in *Legally Blonde* glorifies the school, while *The Social Network* insinuates a culture of fierce competition, backstabbing, and lack of ethics.

Caps on Applicant Volume

Certain schools (particularly at the preschool and prep school levels) have "first come, first served" policies for the distribution of applications. In these cases, the school itself (and therefore the school's admissions staff) is so small that it wouldn't be able to process the applications of 100 percent of the candidates who might want to show their interest. In these cases, candidates or their families must first secure one of a limited number of applications before throwing their hats into the ring. Certain candidates (such as siblings of current students) may make an application shortlist, but most newcomers without some affiliation with the school will be on their own.

If you are lucky enough to obtain one of the coveted application spots, such a policy improves your chances of getting in by virtue of narrowing the number of applicants to whom you will be compared. In cases like this, it's possible that some superstar candidates were shut out of the process, which is good news for you (even if you are a superstar yourself).

If you're not lucky enough to get an application, and you are indeed a superstar, policies like this will be prove to be frustrating and disappointing, particularly if you get shut out of a school that is an exceptional fit, one you know you may have had a great shot at getting into.

Similar to the application cap issue, some schools without the staffing capacity to treat a whole pool of applicants the same may default to a lottery system for certain elements of the application. Interviews are a good example of an element that is sometimes chosen by lottery at schools. Lotteries and other arbitrary processes that determine whether, and to what extent, you can fully engage in the process go far in determining the market for admissions.

Early Admissions
Early admissions applications are also on the rise, with new demographics choosing this avenue in droves. Higher rates of traditional applicants (e.g., those from elite private schools), as well as a critical mass of new entrants such as international students and minorities, have rendered earlier perceptions of early admissions unrecognizable. With some schools admitting up to 45 percent of incoming classes from early applications, disruptions in this pool create ripples throughout.

At Duke, early applications nearly doubled between 2005 and 2012 (compare the current 2,700 to 1,482 seven years before). In 2011, the University of Chicago received 8,698 applications, up 130 percent from 2008's 3,776, and up 214 percent from 2,774 in 2005. Pomona College saw a 33 percent jump from 2011 to 2012. Compounding competition from the applicant side has been a scaling-back on offers from some schools. Expecting higher offer acceptance yields, some schools have reduced their number of offers, while some schools temporary suspended early admissions programs altogether.

Specific trends include higher acceptance rates for minorities (Harvard reported that 20 percent of its early admits were black or Hispanic in 2012, compared to 15 percent the year before); Haverford College and Duke University have reported an influx of applications from California students in the wake of problems in the University of California system. A New York Times article suggested that foreign students applying early were not only opting in at higher rates, but might also have an admissions advantage given a higher ability to pay than American students who typically qualify for aid.

Rolling Admissions

Schools offering rolling admissions create a unique market dynamic because they value students differently at different points in the admissions cycle. As with every other element of the process, how competitive you will be depends on how you compare to other students after you have cleared the basic requirements—yet with rolling admissions, how you compare will change over time. If you meet the requirements and seem like a good fit and you've applied early in the cycle, you have a better chance of getting in than if you wait until later. By the end of the season, competition may be more fierce, and schools may be hoarding spaces for straggling superstars.

Priority Treatment

The number of candidates receiving priority treatment will also determine your prospects for admission. For example, if you are applying at the preschool or K-12 level, whether siblings have attended the school usually gives families a leg up for subsequent children. Other factors like legacy, feeder schools, and other close ties to the school may also play a role in which candidates are made offers.

> *As you choose your targets, it's a good practice to think of the number of open spots as a factor of total open spaces minus those likely to be awarded to applicants with some sort of priority.*

These topics will be discussed in detail later in the book. However, as you choose your targets, it's a good practice to think of the number of open spots as a factor of total open spaces minus those likely to be awarded to applicants with some sort of priority. So, if the kindergarten you are applying to has a classroom that seats twenty children, find out how many of those seats are likely to go to siblings versus the children of brand new families.

WHAT ADMISSIONS COMMITTEES THINK OF COMPETITION

The schools themselves manipulate the competitive climate through active (and often fervent) management of their reputations; and most competitive schools make attempts to improve their reputations, even if their reputations are already quite good.

In some sense, a school's constant focus on bolstering its reputation is an act of self-preservation. It's desirable to have a reputation strong enough to consistently and effortlessly retain talent who will enhance the school's status and its financial health. Well-funded schools are in the best position to provide excellent education to current students by hiring top teachers and maintaining cutting edge facilities—they can expand their scope to include important academic or social work, and in so doing serve a larger community or a greater cause.

Consider a school like Johns Hopkins University, which is well-known for its medical programs and which hopes to attract the very best medical talent in the world. By drawing the best medical talent to its school and later its research centers and hospital, it positions itself to remain a world leader in patient care and medical innovation. It can attract such talent by showing said leadership and garnering positive recognition. From an admissions perspective, it also achieves this by marketing the idea that Johns Hopkins is a highly exclusive, highly desirable choice.

> *The price of admission is getting higher and higher, even if the basic cost of admission (e.g., basic aptitude levels) hasn't necessarily changed.*

That's right—I said marketing. Schools want to signal to prospective applicants (and the general public as well) that they are highly selective. In an immediate sense they are hoping that the perception of fierce competition will compel top candidates with offers to attend. Admissions committees are aware that a truly impressive candidate in its offer pool probably holds matching acceptance letters from competitors. To that extent, marketing materials for applicants are geared toward providing information, displaying aesthetically impressive views of campus and student life, and inviting experiences that make the school seem as attractive as possible.

APPLICATION INFLATION AND THE VICIOUS CYCLE

So, what happens in markets when demand outpaces supply? Prices rise. When prices rise over time, inflation occurs. For our purposes, that simply means that the price of admission is getting higher and higher, even if the basic cost of admission (e.g., basic aptitude levels) hasn't necessarily changed.

The full cycle can be seen in a phenomenon described by the Chronicle for Higher Education and *the New York Times*. In a joint article published in November of 2010, "application inflation" is said to arise when candidate behavior and school behavior combine to create a vicious cycle.

Here's how: candidates, perceiving greater competition, apply to a longer list of schools, but still only attend one. This floods the market with extraneous applications. It also means that schools lose some ability to predict yield because it's not clear how many applicants would genuinely attend if offered a spot (versus those who applied only to hedge their bets). The less that schools can predict yield, the more complicated the admissions process becomes—certain schools at lower grade levels guard against this by recommending a "first choice" letter at the application stage as a show of high commitment. At the collegiate level, early action and early decision are designed to help schools manage yield and to de-clutter the market early in the cycle.

Still, some of the volatility in the admissions market cannot be accounted for by such shows of commitment, which causes admissions committees to adopt policies and practices (e.g., more complex waitlisting) that make the environment more competitive. From there, it becomes less and less clear to candidates what is actually needed to gain an offer of admission, which restarts the cycle as those candidates apply to an even longer list of schools.

However bleak this may seem, there is hope—and lots of it. Millions of students are admitted to top schools every year. You can be, too. And by taking a conscious, informed approach you will avoid hours of insecurity, wasted time, and frustration. Your main task as an applicant will be to tell cohesive stories about yourself that show admissions committees why you would be a great fit for their schools. The next section explores what every admissions committee wants to know about you and why.

PART II:
WHAT EVERY SCHOOL IS LOOKING FOR

CHAPTER II

ALL SCHOOLS
WANT THE SAME THINGS

There's a reason why a book promising to help you get into any school is feasible. It's because every competitive school you have ever (and will ever) apply to cares most about these two crucially important things: your ability to thrive during your time as a student, and your potential to become an alumnus who positively impacts the school's reputation.

Assessment of these qualities (which trump all others) is the driving force behind all components of the application. The main elements—transcripts, test scores, essays and short answers, interviews, interactions at open houses and orientations—combine to allow admissions committees to predict whether you will be capable and happy as a student, engaged as an alumnus, and become somebody whose opportunities or actions after graduation improve the school's image. Schools need successful alumni in order to attract the best student talent, charge a sustainable tuition, and show a return on investment. After all, most competitive schools cost tens of thousands of dollars per year—money most people aren't willing to invest without some evidence that the school's benefits outweigh the costs.

As you can see, it's not just students and parents who are looking for a return on investment. The schools themselves must make strategic investments that will help sustain and, ideally, elevate their status. Attracting top teachers and administrators, earning reputations as centers of research and innovation, and engaging in other activities that raise the schools' profiles are top priorities for administrators. Feeding this virtuous cycle of dually beneficial goals is an effective admissions process. Good admissions decisions lock in a school's desired position in the market.

> *The admissions process is a school's first line of defense when building (and protecting) its reputation.*

For example, a private high school that wishes to maintain a top three ranking in its region must attract and retain students who can score better on the SATs and other college admissions tests than students at competitor schools.

It needs Advanced Placement or International Baccalaureate classes, high graduation rates, and an impressive list of colleges attended by alumni of the school. It will want to keep tabs on its alumni, tracking how many obtained graduate education, and a list of institutions attended. It will also want to see its alumni go on to do impressive things—things notable enough to bolster the image of the school.

Suppose you received offers from two private high schools that both charged $20,000 per year in tuition and claimed high academic standards — is there any question which of the following you'd choose? One boasts a 100 percent graduation rate, average test scores in the 95th percentile and Nobel Prize- winning alumni. The other has an 85 percent graduation rate, average test scores in the 75th percentile, and its most notable alumnus was convicted of a white collar crime. Most people would choose the first school because of the perception that its overall standards are higher and that it has a better track record of graduating high-achievers. The admissions process is a school's first line of defense when building (and protecting) its reputation.

But admissions is not just about risk management. Schools need to safeguard their ability to deliver consistently superior results. The application process is an extension of schools' need to sustain or improve current standards. By viewing the admissions process as a custodian of the school's best interests, it's easy to see what they're really looking for.

THE TRUTH ABOUT BASELINE REQUIREMENTS (A.K.A. "DEAL BREAKERS")

Most candidates won't be offered admission to a school if they don't meet certain baseline requirements. In general, these baseline requirements, or deal breakers, are about weeding out what schools don't want.

Essentially, schools mitigate their own downside risk by eliminating candidates who may cost the school excess money, effort, or reputation. Baseline requirements go much further than test scores, and relate directly to what's at stake for the schools. Failure to meet a single baseline requirement can be enough to take you out of the running for admission. Yet, since they relate to risk management (and not desirability), meeting all baseline requirements is rarely sufficient to get you in. For this reason, even students who are confident that they meet all published requirements may not be granted admission.

Deal Breaker #1:
Schools Don't Want Students Who Can't Keep Up

Students who can't keep pace with the academic curriculum are costly on many levels. They may slow down the learning pace for the rest of the class, create extra work or frustration for the talented teachers that schools are eager to satisfy and retain, and require increased attention from other administrators.

Students who fall behind (particularly if they can't catch up) are doubly undesirable to private schools. Academic troubles may translate into lackluster achievement after graduation, which could tarnish the overall reputation of a school. It's no wonder, then, that schools care so much about academic aptitude. They want evidence that—at the absolute least—the candidate can do the work.

Two elements of the application process work best to help schools filter candidates in furtherance of this goal:

- **Aptitude tests** indicate whether a candidate meets an academic baseline that places her or him on par with other students. Depending on the focus of the target program, aptitude in some areas may be more important than in others.

- **Transcripts, report cards, and teacher recommendations** help admissions committees understand how well students did at previous schools; in some cases, the committee will be able to compare the rigor of past programs to target programs as a gauge of how well a student is likely to fare. Candidates will also be evaluated for their ability to excel in a class of their peers (as an indicator of relative academic commitment and personal perseverance).

Deal Breaker #2:
Schools Don't Want Bad Ambassadors

Private schools view you as more than just a learner and academician—if admitted, you will become a walking advertisement for the school and its values. Failure to present yourself in a positive manner during the admissions process may discourage the school from wanting its good name associated with your potentially questionable one.

Signs of good ambassadorship take on different forms at various education levels. At the college and grad school levels, this may be a matter of personal presentation. Are you well-groomed? Polite? Professional? Well-spoken and polished? If you arrive at admissions events late, unkempt or ill-prepared, admissions officers might fear that you will also present yourself poorly to other audiences who are aware of your affiliation with the school.

Similarly, most exclusive preschools and kindergartens would be loath to admit a child who is seen hitting or in any way abusing other children. Most schools at that age level want to build reputations as programs that produce bright, well-adjusted children who know how to behave. These schools don't want the parents of highly qualified and desirable children to pass on looking at their school because it has a reputation for disciplinary problems.

This concern is illuminated further when considering the types of policies private schools create for their students. When I was a student at a private high school, I remember a rule that any student seen smoking off campus in her uniform would be subject to disciplinary action, and another saying that the skirts of our uniforms could be tailored, but hems could fall no higher than our knees. Both rules existed, no doubt, to maintain the school's clean-cut image. Only by screening out prospective students who display questionable behavior can schools avoid being frowned upon by association.

Admissions committees use the following mechanisms to judge ambassadorship:

* **The interview,** in its basest form, permits admissions officers answer a simple question: "Do I want this person, or family, representing my school?" This is not a particularly rigorous or formal test (most people pass without a problem), but some small handful of applicants show qualities in interviews that simply are out of alignment with the school's values.

* **Open houses and meet and greets** give admissions officers a chance to experience applicants in a social setting; for many schools, social grace is an important indicator of a candidate's fit within the school community.

Deal Breaker #3:
Schools Don't Want Students Who Lack Positive Ambition

Schools favor students (or in the case of younger children, families) with their sights set on lofty goals. This means they want to admit students who view the target education as the means to a greater end, and not the end itself. This may sound obvious, but many applicants are so focused on getting in to the "right" school that they fail to demonstrate any meaningful (or, in some cases, genuine) goals for after graduation.

Why is ambition so important to schools? For one, they want to admit students with personal goals that will drive them to work hard. Unmotivated people are difficult to teach; schools want students who are there for the right reasons, ones whose energy for the curriculum will spread, helping to propel their entire class forward and helping to raise the overall standard of the school.

And of course, students with positive ambitions self-select into meaningful careers that later reflect well on the school. Finally, students who do well after graduation will be in better financial positions to contribute funds to the school later in life.

The following elements of the application process correlate to ways in which admissions committees gauge ambition:

- Essays and short answer questions: All private school applicants will be asked one or more questions that inquire (directly or indirectly) about ambition. Direct questions may be "How would a degree from our school benefit you?" or "Where does an education from our school fit into your future plans?" Other versions of this question, such as "What makes our school a good match for you?" don't directly point to ambition, but rather leave the door wide open for you append your answer with comments about future plans.

- Interview questions: Ambition questions may be asked in any interview, especially if the interviewer feels that the subject wasn't sufficiently answered elsewhere in the application. It may come in the form of classic questions like "Where do you see yourself in ten years?" or "What are your plans after graduation?"

Ambition questions are less obvious at lower grade levels, where the next step in the student's education is readily known.

RISING ABOVE THE BASELINE (A.K.A. "DEAL SWEETENERS")

Since many applicants to a given school will meet baseline requirements, getting in becomes a matter of showing as many other desired qualities as possible. The students who can demonstrate qualities that will help a school achieve its goals will have the clear advantage. Though the matter is rarely framed in such terms, the potential to get a school closer to its own goals is, very simply, the only important quality that an applicant needs to show.

So, let's go back to what schools really want: candidates who can thrive during their time as students and later become alumni who positively impact the reputation of the school.

Let's examine qualities that signal a student will be a school's ally in reaching these goals.

Deal-Sweetener #1:
Schools Want Future Evangelists

Schools don't want you to collect your diploma and never look back. They want you to rave about the great education you received at their fine institutions forever—or as close to forever as possible. This relates to the elusive "great fit" that admissions committees are fond of referencing. Schools want students who have the intellectual capacity to do well, the social temperament to fit in, and cultural values in harmony with the school. It's not lip service—admissions committees favor candidates who they feel can truly be happy at the school. Happy students perform better than unhappy ones, and those who enjoy their student experience become evangelists as alumni, spreading good will.

> *The potential to get a school closer to its own goals is, very simply, the only important quality that an applicant needs to show.*

Evangelism is far-reaching. It relates not only to what you are willing to proactively tell people about your alma mater—friends, neighbors, employers, and countless other people in your network will learn of your educational connections and may ask you, whether casually or formally, about your experience. Therefore, schools favor candidates who they genuinely believe will have positive memories. Applicants must make a convincing case for why they can see themselves at the target school, and why it would be a great fit.

Application elements that speak to this:

* Essays and short answer questions may ask directly "Why are you a good fit for this school?" The more effectively a candidate can prove that she or he will be a great cultural fit for the school, the more convinced the committee will become that the candidate can be happy there and will ultimately become a great promoter of the school.

- Interviews also help admissions committee members gauge how well a candidate will fit in. Candidates who show temperaments and other intangible qualities similar or complementary to current students may reveal themselves to be a good fit.

Deal-Sweetener #2:
Schools Want Students Who Balance Out a Class

To the extent that competitive schools will see more qualified applicants than there are spaces available, admissions committees have the luxury of engineering the student mix to form a "balanced" class. This entails admitting students with a diverse set of complementary skills, backgrounds, or perspectives in order to populate classrooms with different strengths or points of view.

This desire for balance extends beyond institutions with a commitment to gender, ethnic, or cultural diversity; even schools with demographically homogenous student bodies will seek to balance incoming classes on some valued level. As always, the desire to create balance relates to the incentives of the school, and its core objectives: students who will thrive and alumni who will build the reputation and financial stability of the school.

Think of a student body as an orchestra. The admissions committee may "audition" many outstanding violinists, but, ultimately, a large group of violinists does not constitute an orchestra. Accepting too many violinists, no matter how stellar their technique and musicianship, would come at the expense of including other instruments, creating an ensemble that sounds imbalanced and incomplete. Yet, the orchestra's reason for being is to create the fines music that it can, gaining increasing recognition for its excellence and continuing to attract the most talented musicians. In order to fulfill its goals, the orchestra must remain committed to the correct balance of members: that means accepting the players of strings, brass, woodwind, and percussion instruments in proportionate measure.

A school's sights for balance may be set on short- or long-term goals, including academic excellence in certain areas and/or strategies to attract a particular type of student. For example, a middle school that has seen its average math aptitude test scores go down in recent years may seek to admit more students with strong track records in math in order to help bring those scores back up. A school that has not previously focused on gender balance may seek to change its student mix in order to align with the latest research findings about the importance of gender balance to effective learning.

Such tactics are pursued by schools in order to make them better, or to position them to tout features that will be desirable to applicants. More candidates applying to a school makes the school itself more competitive, and to be more competitive is what most schools want.

Application elements that speak to this:

* Essays, short answer questions, and interviews offer a fantastic opportunity to showcase skills that may be desirable to admissions committees seeking some sort of specific balance. However, since balance objectives are not always stated openly, it can be difficult to anticipate whether you have something in particular that the school is looking for. If you are aware of, or can guess at, a quality or characteristic you have that may be appeal to schools, and it would be tasteful to work them in to essays, short answers, and interviews, it is advised to do so. For example, if the school to which you are applying is investing in a historically underserved theater program, and you are a thespian, by all means, work it into your application.

Deal-Sweetener #3:
Schools Want Current Fundraisers and Future Donors

Consider the economics: furnishing high-quality education costs a lot of money. Excellent teachers, administrators, facilities, and materials come at a hefty price. Beyond tuition and fees paid by students or their families, private schools rely on endowments and private fundraising to maintain desired standards. Consequently, alumni are a critical source of funding for private schools, which makes schools invested in admitting students who are not just academically apt, but also a good fit. Not only do happy students make alumni evangelists—they also make generous donors.

Does this mean that you need to proactively donate to the school of your choice, or somehow show during the admissions process that, if admitted, you will become a faithful financial contributor? The answer is an unsatisfying "maybe". No school will tell you the truth about how much financial contributions matter; if it were openly admitted that donations do help a candidate's prospects for admission, the school in question would come under scrutiny for "selling" seats.

If you want to answer this question for your list of target schools, look for clues that signal financial expectations. The following (sanitized) text appears on the web site of a prestigious San Francisco Bay Area K-12 school on the "Tuitiion & Fees" section of the web site:

"Each year, families are asked to make a tax-deductible, unrestricted contribution. These donations are used to help the school fund the difference between the tuition and the actual cost of education. We strive for 100 percent participation by our families each year and ask that everyone give at a level that is comfortable for them. All gifts, large and small, make a positive difference in the annual operations of the School and we are deeply grateful for each contribution."

A statement like this sends a very strong signal that financial participation matters, and its placement on a sub-section of the admissions site suggests that demonstrating a willingness and ability to fundraise is preferred.

However, there is no specific element of the application that is designed to test this, and in most cases, you won't be questioned about this at all. But, if your target schools rely heavily upon donations, and you could see yourself giving to, or fundraising for, your target school, it won't hurt your chances to subtly signal your values on the matter. Don't mention it so blatantly that you seem to be insinuating that you expect to "buy" a spot. But, if you have experience fundraising for other organizations, or a track record of supporting previous schools, mention it. There's nothing wrong with mentioning that you support communities to which you belong.

OTHER MAKERS AND BREAKERS

Certain schools hold a special emphasis or value a special mission that becomes a major focus for admission. Ultimately, these special considerations boil down to fit; yet some schools emphasize these elements so strongly that they can become deal breakers for applications.

There are also deal-makers: things that an applicant brings to the table that are so extraordinary and sought-after that schools are willing to look the other way if a baseline requirement isn't met. Applicants like these are few and far-between, but for the sake of thoroughness, we'll devote some effort to their discussion.

Maker/Breaker #1:
Community-Focused Schools

Schools with a focus on serving specific communities (e.g., economically disadvantaged communities, faith-based communities, or any other highly targeted affiliation) may have additional criteria for admission. Faith-based schools may prefer students from families who are members of the related congregation; schools designed to serve a specific need may want applicants to demonstrate alignment with the profile of the target student.

For example, a private high school focused on providing a better education to at-risk students in impoverished communities may not care at all about a student's ability to pay or fundraise, but may care very much about parental commitment and engagement. If your target school has a special community focus (or some other affiliation), take some time to think about (and ask about) how the school is funded, how it operates, and what its goals and challenges are. Recognizing and responding to the bigger picture of a given institution will always help you get into that school.

Maker/Breaker #2:
Schools Focused on a Specific Academic Subject or Talent

A number of factors, from general academic potential to social behavior, may be less important than usual when a target school focuses on a specific academic subject or talent. The rarer or more extraordinary the applicant's talent, the less some of the other factors will matter. And if the talent is promising enough, it can often neutralize other baseline areas that may otherwise be viewed as lacking.

For example, a student applying to undergraduate film school may be asked to submit work from her portfolio alongside the standard grade transcripts, aptitude test scores, and essays. In this case, a very strong film portfolio may be enough to cause admissions committees to overlook weaknesses in other areas (such as general academic aptitude).

Exceptions like these are more common at the collegiate level when basic academic skills have already been established. Talent-focused schools may be inclined to overlook weaknesses in certain areas if the applicant shows enough aptitude to complete the program and seems poised to be very successful after graduation.

Maker/Breaker #3:
Superstars

Prodigies, geniuses, extraordinary talents—anyone with truly standout capabilities—can be thought of as a "superstar." In certain cases, schools are willing to make exceptions for them. These are the Mozarts of the world—individuals with such extraordinary talent or intellect, schools are eager to work with them, regardless of age, personality, temperament, or weaknesses in other desirable areas. In these cases, schools take calculated risks, accepting that superstar students may not be poised to thrive in every respect, but mollified by the excellence the student is likely to display in her areas of extraordinary strength.

An example of this is the very bright preschooler who cannot get a public kindergarten to accept him at the age of four because of governmental regulations, but who may be accepted at a private kindergarten willing to overlook his behavioral underdevelopment for the sake of providing a challenging environment in which the little genius can thrive.

IT ALWAYS COMES BACK TO INCENTIVES

Is it really all that simple? Will avoiding the three deal breakers + adding the three deal sweeteners = gaining admission to the school of your choice? In many cases, yes, but don't lose sight of the real lesson: schools are driven by incentives. The best strategy for getting into any school will always begin with understanding what the school is and what it aspires to be, and then making a case for how you, the candidate, can help said school to reach its own goals.

Most competitive schools want the flexibility to offer the best programs, therein attracting the best students, whose actions as alumni will bolster the profile of the school. This, in turn, will only help the school's ability to continue to offer the best programs (by attracting the best faculty, building the best facilities, and fundraising from successful alumni), creating a virtuous cycle that repeats itself in a loop. Other competitive schools do not operate in this ecosystem and may be driven by slightly different things. Boost your chances of getting into any school by looking for clues to that school's motivations and incentives, figuring out its deal breakers and deal sweeteners, and responding appropriately.

CHAPTER III

THE ONLY TWO QUESTIONS THAT MATTER

Forget test scores. Forget pedigree. Forget your impressive list of redeeming qualities and talents. None of those matter if you can't answer two simple questions. Your responses will serve as the foundation of your entire application, giving it critical context and personal insights essential to the admissions committee. The answers to these questions will shape the lens through which your candidacy is viewed.

These questions, of course, are:

- Why are you on this path (e.g., of pursuing a private school, or higher education)?
- Why are you interested in this school in particular?

They may sound obvious to you, but you'd be surprised by how many people don't give these enough thought. Bad answers fall into two categories: those offering lackluster reasons, and those with good reasons clouded by shoddy packaging and poor presentation. We'll review both, but first, let's talk about why these questions are so important.

WHY THIS PATH?

Schools want to hear their candidates' excellent reasons for pursuing a certain path, because they are eager to become a partner in the success of truly promising students. If a veterinary school candidate tells of a lifelong career ambition that started with healing her stuffed animals' "injuries" as a child, schools want to hear about that passion. Parents applying on behalf of a child who is becoming bored and unmotivated in the public school system may make a case for pursuing private school education in order to find a more challenging program to revitalize their child.

There are also some terrible, truly awful reasons to pursue a course of study. Schools want to know why you are on a given path so they can be sure you're not in it for ignoble reasons. Consider the high school student forced to apply to strong pre-med programs by overbearing parents, or the business school applicant whose singular goal in pursuing the degree is to earn more money. Schools want to screen out candidates who don't have a genuine enthusiasm for the curriculum or a good understanding of what they're getting themselves into, as these types will make neither good classmates nor long-term assets to the program.

The "why this path" question serves another function, that of a measuring stick for consistency throughout the application. Are the applicant's stated reasons for pursuing the path in question supported by the applicant's past choices? For example, can an applicant to a performing arts high school be considered credible if she opted out of many performance-focused activities offered at her middle school? Inconsistencies surrounding the answer to this question can cast doubt on the entire application.

In extreme cases, the "why this path" question can also expose disclosure problems. Suppose that you are applying to a new school because you were expelled from (or failed out of) a current one. Checks and balances elsewhere in the application make it likely that admissions committees will learn of any stains on your record. Full disclosure of any such circumstances in the "why this path?" section sends the signal that you are forthright, ethical, and gives you the chance to take ownership of the story.

WHY THIS SCHOOL?

Admissions committees have several reasons for asking about your specific interest in their school. For one, they are looking for evidence that you understand distinct program features as well as the school's values and culture. It is a test of effort and circumspection: your answer's level of detail will reveal the thoroughness of your research, your dedication to the admissions process, and your level of interest in the school.

The "why this school?" question is also test of an applicant's abilities to self-reflect and to articulate his thoughts. Its unspoken question is: *Have you thought meaningfully about whether we are a good fit for you, and if you believe we are, can you logically and convincingly articulate why?* Admissions committees want more than just a list of generic reasons why anyone would find their school desirable—they truly want to know about you. They want your story to be well-crafted, persuasive, unique, and to ring true. They want to know that, were you to attend their school, you would have a clear notion of whether, and why, it would be a good fit.

Mediocre answers to this question are common. Many applicants simply aren't specific enough. This question isn't about listing the school's most redeeming qualities or giving an answer that implies "who wouldn't want to go to a school with so many wonderful things to offer?" It is about showing a connection between specific program's features and what you, the individual, want and bring to the table.

There are also bad answers. Believe it or not, I've read quite a few applications that listed the wrong school's name in the "why this school" response. The behavior of applying to too many schools and not giving all applications adequate time and attention is, unfortunately for all, alive and well. This is part of why admissions committees are looking for highly specific answers to this question. They want to weed out applicants who are lazy, or inattentive to quality and detail. Applicants will lose ground on this question by raising points that bear little resemblance to target programs.

BAD VS. GOOD VS. GREAT ANSWERS

Suppose you arrive at an ice cream shop and ask for a double scoop of Dutch chocolate ice cream. Before serving it to you, the attendant asks why you want ice cream, and why Dutch chocolate.

- **Bad Answer:** Everyone wants ice cream, and doesn't everyone love chocolate?
- **Good Answer:** I'm hungry and I like the taste of chocolate.
- **Great Answer:** I want ice cream because I have a sweet tooth, and I prefer Dutch chocolate because my mother used to make homemade Dutch chocolate ice cream. Besides, cocoa is rich in antioxidants.

The example above may seem facile, but you might be surprised at how often admissions committees hear some version of the bad answer. To illustrate this, let's replace the question with a real school admissions question geared toward parents looking to enroll a child in private kindergarten. The question is: *Why are you choosing private kindergarten for your child, and why this school in particular?*

- **Bad Answer:** Every parent wants her child to have a great education, and this school is the very best.
- **Good Answer:** We're concerned about overcrowding and budget cuts in local public schools and are looking toward private schools to help our child reach her academic potential. We believe this school is right for our child because of its track record in helping students exhibit their art.
- **Great Answer:** We (her parents) are private school alumni, and having witnessed firsthand the benefits of smaller class sizes and a challenging academic environment, we want the same for our child. We believe this school is right for our child because of its focus on the visual arts—our child's favorite activities are painting and drawing and we know this school's art program is strong.

So, what is the difference between the Great, Good, and Bad answers?

Bad answers may be logical, but are indistinct, supplying no real evidence that the reply is not a stock answer being given on applications to multiple schools; they are bad because, even if they are true, they offer no substantial information about the candidate and give no evidence of serious, deep thought. The aforementioned answer is bad because admissions committees already know that parents want their children to have a great education, and that many candidates are attracted by a school's good rankings. If your draft answers to these questions don't offer any personal information about you or say anything unique about the school, they are probably bad answers.

Good answers are logical and personal, but may not reach greatness if they are overly generic. They may provide evidence that you have given a school individual consideration, but they're not really great if any applicant could come up with the same answer. Most people struggle with taking answers from good to great. This may be because it seems strange to enhance an answer that is authentic. Maybe public schools are overcrowded and you are attracted to a school because of its visual arts program. The trick with good answers is to take them a step beyond logic and make them even more personal.

We'd be able to elevate the example above to "great" status if it articulated exactly how school budget cuts have impacted or will impact your family (e.g., fifty teachers in our district got pink slips last year and music and art programs have been reduced to once a month). Being more specific and personal will add color and heart to your application—this type of connection is key in making your application stand out.

Great answers are in a class of their own. They are memorable and they ring true. Most importantly, they form a connection that compounds logical reasoning with personal insights that help admissions committees understand the applicant.

> *If there is no human element to your application— no note of authenticity—you will fail to make a critical emotional connection with your audience.*

While the "good" ice cream shop answer conveys an unextraordinary love of chocolate, the "great" answer paints a rich picture of fond family memories and the reconciliation of a guilty pleasure with a value for health. Similarly, the "great" kindergarten admissions answer paints a picture of a child who loves art and parents who understand the value of, and are committed to, private education. These answers are great because they transcend the anonymity of the applicant pool, allowing the contours of a real person to take shape. Yet, they are not empty—behind the personal stories is evidence of good, logical thinking.

YOUR AUTHENTIC ANSWERS

If there is no human element to your application—no note of authenticity— you will fail to make a critical emotional connection with your audience. That's why there are no right or wrong answers to the two basic questions. The best responses come from honest reflection on reasons that are true to you or your family. Authenticity is important for another reason: self-confidence comes from self-knowledge. If you are not clear about the answers to your own questions, you will never persuade anyone else.

Start with a List

The advice to sit down and write a list may sound too simple to actually do. But there is value in getting your thoughts on paper, if for no other reason than to facilitate numerous elements of the application, specifically:

- Most schools will ask one or both questions directly in the application; if you've listed your reasons before tackling each application, you'll have the building blocks of masterful responses.

- At open houses, meet and greets, and, eventually, interviews, these topics will come up as you meet members of the school's community and even other applicants; you'll want to have considered your answers deeply and thoroughly enough to respond instantly with a well-crafted response.

- With respect to the "why this school?" question, mapping out the pros and cons of each school on your list will serve as the foundation for customizing each application. This is discussed extensively in the chapter about how to choose a school.

- If you are fortunate enough to end up with multiple offers, having an existing list of what you initially liked about each school will help you compare programs. Answers to the "why this path" question will keep you grounded to your true intentions and help keep you on track.

But perhaps the best reason to write a list is that you are likely to surprise yourself. Brainstorming tends to lead us to insights that our minds don't consciously acknowledge. Understanding your own thinking will become an invaluable asset to you, despite the fact that some of your true reasons may sound selfish, or even crass, when you see them in writing. Ultimately, understanding your true goals and motivations will position you to make the best decisions.

MAKING AUTHENTICITY DISTINCT

Admissions officers read hundreds of applications each recruiting season, and may read upwards of a dozen every day. Most people applying to a given school have similar motivations, which naturally means that there is tremendous potential for applications to look the same. The two key questions are particularly susceptible to commonalities among answers. This section will guide you through a method that allows you to be truthful and authentic in your answers while also standing out from the crowd.

Surface Reasons

The first reasons that come to mind when you ask yourself the two core questions are probably superficial, obvious reasons, reasons that are true not only for you but also most other applicants. For example, most people apply to private schools because they generally believe the quality of education to be better than what can be found at public counterparts. Similarly, a surface reason why many people apply to law school involves the wish to eventually take the bar exam and become attorneys.

While surface reasons may be among your most important reasons for pursuing a specific path, when undressed, they can sound generic. "I want to go to law school because I want to become an attorney" is a pretty dry answer. The reason itself is fine and may be true, but it's not memorable or exciting. Most of the time, it makes sense to mention such reasons strongly, but briefly, making way for other more memorable points. In a small number of cases, it may make sense to speak at greater length about surface reasons, but only if there is a relevant personal story or deeper meaning.

The only time to focus on a surface reason is when you can go deeper with a personal story, such as, "I have wanted to be a lawyer since I was five years old and I used to hold mock trials with my teddy bear as the judge and my other stuffed animals as the jury," shows commitment and self-knowledge on the applicant's part, and gives an opportunity to showcase personality and humor.

Common Reasons

Common reasons are less universal than surface reasons, but still may be true for many applicants. For example, parents applying on behalf of a second child to the same preschool as an older sibling will say that they want their children to attend the same school. Similarly, many families applying to parochial schools choose that path over public or private school because they favor faith-based education.

As with surface reasons, it is appropriate and you are encouraged to mention common reasons on your application. Again, state them strongly and unequivocally, but avoid spending too much time on them unless you can relate a meaningful personal story. These reasons may be good and logical, but the admissions committee doesn't need them explained at length—they've seen them many times before.

Unique Reasons

Unique reasons are those that apply only to a small number of applicants, or, in rare cases, only to you. It is important to dig deeply and learn whether any of your authentic reasons for applying to a school or for taking a certain path are unique. Perhaps there is a single program characteristic or course offering that appeals especially to you. Perhaps there's a compelling reason to pursue a certain degree at a specific point in your life.

For example, a former Wall Street banker may find herself so financially secure that she finally feels free to pursue a Master's in Fine Arts with a specialty in creative writing. A family raising a child bilingually may be attracted to a specific private school that already emphasizes the second language they are teaching their child. Schools want to hear your unique reasons because meaningful and personal responses are most compelling to read, adding humanity and heart to applications.

Finding unique reasons that connect you to a particular school or path also act as solid confirmation that you're on the right track. If you have truly engaged in self-reflection and taken the time to list your reasons—

but you can't find any unique ones, it may be a signal that you lack a deep, personal connection to your target path. In the absence of credible personal elements that connect you to what you say you want, your candidacy may not be successful, no matter how attractive the other areas of your application are.

> **Schools want to hear your unique reasons because meaningful and personal responses are most compelling to read, adding humanity and heart to applications.**

Tricky Reasons

What if some of your authentic reasons feel too candid for polite conversation? What should you do if you feel that your real answers might portray you in a bad light? Suppose that you're only applying to Harvard because of its name cachet, or that your decision to send your child to private school is prompted by struggles the child is having in his current environment. I, for one, applied to graduate school when I was underemployed during a recession. So, should we mention reasons like these on applications? And if so, how should we go about that?

Believe me when I tell you that the mindful presentation of tricky reasons can be a tremendous asset. Applicants who only portray themselves favorably may seem too good to be true, or worse, come off as stiff and overly polished. Yet an applicant who can handle a taboo subject adroitly reveals refreshingly human qualities, as well as evidence of effective communication skills. If there's something you're unsure about writing in your application, it's worth digging deeper to considering whether the motivation behind the reason is really so bad as to create apprehension.

This requires real reflection. Packaging tricky reasons is not about stretching or sugarcoating the truth—it's about digging deeply enough to find out what's underneath. A cynical way to view the parents with a struggling child is to assume that if the child is struggling there must be something wrong with him, his parents, or the whole family. A more balanced way to view parents' motivations is to recognize that by applying to private school they are looking for a better situation for their child, an environment in which he can thrive. If anything, this shows the Admissions Committee parents who are committed to their child's education and are more aware, and maybe even more invested than other parents in finding a great fit. The truthful, balanced handling of possibly problematic motivations can carry any application a long way.

Similarly, consider the applicant to Harvard, who may not honestly believe it's the right fit, but who would seriously consider going if he got in. It would not be disingenuous for him to answer the "Why Harvard?" question by saying that in addition to receiving a well-regarded education, he is attracted by the prospects of reaping the lifelong benefits of a strong alumni network. This answer is truthful, but tactful. It finds the author admitting that he is interested in Harvard because of the school's reputation and lifelong networking opportunities. However, it's not blunt or crass—it reads as carefully worded, but honest. Such an answer shows candor, pragmatism, and savvy. That applicant is also much more credible than anyone who fails to mention a desire to go to Harvard because such a pedigree would benefit him. Admissions committees know that applicants view private education as an investment and, if worded carefully, it's always fine to mention the returns.

THE 5 SITUATIONS IN WHICH YOU MUST KNOW THE ANSWERS
Though subsequent chapters deal with each of the following situations at length, commenting on them now in conjunction with the two questions should underscore their importance. In fact, it is because you will have to answer these questions in so many settings that I have distinguished them as the two most important ones.

The following shows examples of when, and how, you may be asked to respond to these questions. Notice that two of the five situations are informal and don't fall within the confines of the official process. However, your behavior in each of these situations may influence your success.

Open Houses, School Fairs, and Meet and Greets
Any event designed to let prospective students or their families get to know a school will be swarming with admissions committee members, student volunteers, and other staffers. While the primary role of those individuals is to help and inform prospective students, it is very common

for interactions with candidates in these settings to come up in admissions decision meetings.

This isn't to say that open houses are a test—generally speaking, they're not. However, if your behavior stands out, you will be remembered— whether it's for your extraordinary polish, for a faux pas, or for showing a general lack of preparation. Even if you are still learning about a school, it behooves you to have done some research and thinking about fit prior to an open house. If somebody asks you why you're interested in ABC University or XYZ Academy at an open house, "That's what I'm here to find out" is a bad answer... but one I've heard several times.

Informational Interviews

Informational interviews are informal one-on-one meetings that you might seek out with a current student, alumnus, or parents of other children in the school. Suppose your co-worker has the degree you're looking to earn, or has some connection to a school you're interested in. When you offer to buy him a cup of coffee if he'll take time to tell you about his experience, you're inviting him to an informational interview.

Despite being informal, these types of meetings are important because the better your contact understands your motivations and goals, the more tailored the insights he can share about the school. Walking away with information that speaks directly to you will help you refine your application in ways that are likely to make you more successful. Also, the ability to cut to the chase during an informational interview may quickly carry the conversation toward insights that challenge whether the school is a good fit after all—or confirm the idea.

Finally, an informational interview with a school community insider may play a more direct role in your admission to the school, should you ultimately choose to apply. Such a person, if he or she comes to believe you may be a good fit for the school, is in a position to recommend you, either formally or informally. However, you are less likely to be recommended if your interest in the school and your motivations to be on the path are not well-understood. These ideas can only shine through if you are prepared to share well-packaged information about your motivations during the meeting.

On the Application

Though both questions often show up on applications, it's important to note that sometimes they don't. That makes it even more crucial to know and understand the answers to the two key questions because, if they're not asked forthrightly, you must find a way to work the answers into other interactions. Suppose that neither is asked as an essay question on a college application. In that case, you must deconstruct what the answers to these very important un-asked questions say about you (e.g., what qualities and values of yours they show), and make sure that the same qualities and values that you want to shine through can be incorporated in your answers to other questions.

The Application Interview

If the admissions process includes an interview, you must be prepared to answer both questions directly. Similarly to the application short answer or essay questions, if the two questions are not asked directly, find ways to weave key points into other answers.

Follow-Ups and Thank Yous

During my days as an admissions committee member, I sometimes interviewed five or more candidates a day. Receiving a thank you note was always a nice touch, and I especially appreciated it when I received one that articulated key points an applicant wanted me to know, or any other points discussed during the interview. Having a few lines in your back pocket that succinctly summarize your two answers will make for robust thank you notes that punctuate personal interactions.

It's also appropriate to send thank you notes to anyone who granted you an informational interview. Using e-mail is usually fine.

COMMON MISTAKES

It is my belief that most competitive school applicants truly have logical, respectable motives for applying and that good answers lurk somewhere, deep down. Regardless of how good the true, heartfelt motives of an applicant are, there is often a disconnect between what an applicant wants and feels and what that same applicant actually communicates.

There are reasons for this: some applicants struggle with candor, stripping their answers of personal details in order to make them "safer" (that is, closer to what they think the committees want to hear). Other applicants simply don't give questions enough thought, stopping at obvious answers and not bothering to go any farther to understand their own true motives. Yet what it comes down to for most applicants is that they don't yet grasp one of the most important keys to success: finding a way to be both truthful and memorable. The common mistakes listed below highlight some of what admissions committees frequently see, and show how not to fall into the same traps.

Answers That Fail to Make a Connection

Answers that state a general fact (usually a desirable motive) that is not later connected back to the applicant or what she wants is a very common mistake in applications. For example, if the parents of a preschool applicant answer "Why this school?" with a statement like "We're interested in XYZ Academy because of its strong focus on music," and say nothing more, they are missing the opportunity to mention why a strong music program is important to their child.

Though it is implied that a strong music program is desirable to the family applying, this answer is not great for two reasons: 1) it says nothing particular about the family applying, and only states a fact about the school (thus missing the point of the application process—to tell the committee about yourself or your family); and 2) by merely stating a fact, it supplies no logic—no insights into the family's thinking.

These may sound identical, but they are different. Suppose the family had answered "Why this school?" with a statement like "We are interested in XYZ Academy because we have a track record of investing substantially in our child's musical training." This is also a bad answer that doesn't make a connection, given its lack of logic (but not lack of personal information).

A better answer to this question would have been "We are interested in XYZ Academy because we believe that its excellent music program would be a fantastic complement to the ongoing music training we have furnished for our child." In addition to completing the logic, the answer itself is more complete, and the statement is stronger, and more polished.

Applicants sometimes forgo supplying logic for reasons of word count or space, but I advise strongly against this. It is always convincing to overtly finish the logic of any question in order to crystallize your motives, even if the logic seems obvious. And it is always most desirable not to skimp on good writing: express complete thoughts in clean, well-structured sentences.

Answers That Are Not Specific Enough

Answers that are logical, understandable, and authentic, yet that speak very broadly may not be specific enough. Admissions committees receive many beautifully written responses that reveal applicants to be smart and polished, but that lack enough substantive reasoning to truly help the application.

For example, the question "Why are you pursuing a college education?" is not significantly helped by an answer like "It is well-documented that individuals with college educations report higher earnings, greater personal satisfaction, and more interesting careers than people who do not attend college; my desire to pursue a college education is driven by my desire to be personally, professionally, and financially fulfilled."

Because it is so well-composed and draws a logical connection, this may seem like a great answer, but let's get down to brass tacks. It basically says that the applicant wants a college education because people who go to college do better in life than people who don't. Logical? Yes. Understandable? Yes. Authentic? Yes. Is this a good answer? Yes. This answer won't hurt the application, and, depending on the caliber of the school, may even help it a little bit. But it's not a great answer that can elevate the application to the top of the pile since it's nothing that every single candidate who is applying to college isn't also thinking and doesn't already know. .

A great answer would pass the following test: it would say why you, specifically, are applying to college, not why you—and everybody else— are applying to college. If your most authentic answer is the good answer, let the answer you provide briefly state that good answer before integrating something personal and great. A great answer to "Why are you pursuing a college education?" might be "I am attracted to pursuing college not only because people who go to college do better in life, but also because I am

passionate in my desire to continue studying biology, and at a higher level."
This answer is great because it tells of a specific, personal motivation to
attend college, and reveals an important and unique goal.

The Answer You Think They Want to Hear (a.k.a. The "Right" Answer)

There's a scene in *Miss Congeniality*, a well-known movie about a beauty
pageant, in which contestants are probed for what they would request,
if given just one wish. Each supplies the same answer: world peace. Of
course it's the right answer (if the right answer is one that showcases as
many virtuous qualities as possible), but trust me when I tell you that
admissions committee members have heard the "world peace" response
to short answer and essay questions a thousand times. Not only is the
"right answer" unoriginal—in most cases, it's not true. More effective than
stock answers are personal, authentic ones.

For the "Why this path?" and "Why this school?" questions, some
applicants gravitate toward grandiose goals and noble intentions. "Why
are you interested in medical school?" may yield many answers like "I
want to find a cure for cancer," while similar law school questions might
yield answers like "I want to be a Supreme Court justice."

There is nothing wrong with these goals (in fact, they show qualities like
ambition and good citizenship—ones that I have readily admitted that
schools like to see) and some percentage of medical and law school
applicants may sincerely hold these aspirations. Still, there is a problem
with answers like these: for some large percentage of applicants who
express such thoughts, they simply aren't true, and all answers along
those lines may be viewed with skepticism.

So, even if you do truly want to cure cancer, sit on the Supreme Court,
or create world peace, the expression of your true intention may still be
read as pandering. Therefore, it behooves you to choose an answer that
won't make you sound like you are politicking. If you absolutely must use
a "right answer," be sure to check your tone and include enough personal
detail to ensure that it does not sound empty. Ask trusted friends who will
be candid with you to read it and give feedback as to whether it sounds
too good to be true.

Answers That Other People Will Give, Too (I Mean a LOT of Other People)

There are common answers to open-ended questions that are authentically shared by many. Of course, during a competitive application process it is extremely important to be memorable. So important, in fact, that Chapter 4 will be devoted to this issue.

While considering your answers to the two key questions, ask yourself whether the main reasons motivating you to pursue a particular path and a particular school could be shared by many others. I can already guess your answer: it's *yes*. That's because many of the best reasons to pursue a path or a school make so much sense that they truly are shared by many. Applicants should honestly express their motivations—even ones that may be shared by others—but must also be prepared to weave in facts and ideas that create an aura of distinctiveness.

Suppose you are applying to an academically rigorous high school in order to help your child be more competitive in college admissions. Undoubtedly, all families applying to the school share this motivation. Expressing that fact won't hurt your application, but that discrete sentiment alone is unlikely to elevate the application to a level that makes it more competitive. In order to be *more* competitive, you need more information that will help bring your individuality to life.

The best way to handle this is to briefly acknowledge the common reason and use most of your response to say something more personal and interesting. After all, the admissions committee does not need common motives or reasoning explained to them at length—they have heard it all before and already understand and accept common reasons.

So, a better answer to "Why are you applying to a private high school?" might briefly acknowledge the aspiration to be competitive for a top college, but would go on to discuss secondary and tertiary motivations uncovered during brainstorming. Maybe you crave smaller class sizes, more interesting electives, richer field trips, a better choice of extracurriculars, or single-sex education. This is why the brainstorming stage is so important. It forces you to think past your common reasons and recognize your own unique, personal motivations. Only these deeper truths will make your application come to life.

Cut-and-Paste Answers

It is very common for admissions committees to receive applications from candidates who seem to have cut and pasted their answers from one application to the next—sometimes this is done in error and at other times, candidates deliberately write "transferrable" answers, presumably to allow them to save time. This can be a big mistake, particularly if a cut-and-paste strategy diminishes the quality of answers and reveals undesirable qualities (such as laziness or inattention to detail). Also, even if a cut-and-paste strategy is <u>not</u> used, this issue can be a problem for applicants who craft broad answers that appear as though they can be used in multiple applications, even that hasn't been done.

I know what you may be thinking: shouldn't the answer to the "Why this path?" question be the same for any school that asks it? Good point, and, yes, it should be. Candidates who lose points for cutting and pasting on this question may not pay attention to detail in the act of the transfer. This usually manifests as a proofreading issue, revealing that a candidate has not changed key details from one application to the next, such as the name of the school. (Do not let that happen in your application materials!)

Cutting-and-pasting problems are more prevalent in the "Why this school?" section. Fundamentally, candidates should not be trying to write an umbrella answer to this question, and it can be a total deal breaker if it is obvious that a stock answer has been submitted. The very reason for this question is that schools are different and it's necessary to clarify what, specifically, you like about an individual school. Transferring answers for this question from one application to another completely misses the point and sends an unflattering message. It says: this candidate does not care enough about this school to invest the time necessary in making a case for himself to earn a spot.

This cutting-and-pasting issue further highlights why specific, unique answers are so effective. Top applicants are so meticulous in making their case for a specific school that, by contrast, it is clear when other applications are generic and nondescript. Admissions committees can tell the difference between original copy vs. existing copy edited for resubmission. The way to avoid this, of course, is to have done your homework and listed out what you like about each school. If the lists of what you like about each school are identical, you're not looking closely enough.

THE CONSEQUENCES OF BAD OR MEDIOCRE ANSWERS

I won't mince words: bad answers to the two core questions will probably take you out of the running; even perfect grades, test scores, and other favorable elements are rarely enough to save an application from a poor showing in this area. No school wants to admit a student who can't legitimize the education he says he wants to pursue, or the place where he says he wants to pursue it. The fastest way to take yourself out of the running for a spot in the school of your choice is to answer these questions in a way that:

- is vague and shows little serious thought

- shows naivete about the path

- reveals a lack of specific understanding of the school

- makes no connection to future goals

- fails to draw logical connections

- demonstrates undesirable qualities (e.g., shallowness, arrogance)

- contains errors

> *Remember: selective schools have far more qualified candidates than spaces to offer. This means schools will see many good candidates, but only great candidates will get offers.*

Clearly, most people don't set out to write inferior applications, but applications can come off as deficient if the applicant is not conscious of how certain omissions of information will be viewed. A candidate's inner reasons may be excellent, but if those reasons remain unexpressed, the application will fail.

Mediocre answers are well-written, use good, solid logic, ring true, and are, overall, legitimate. They are problematic, however, because they don't contain enough compelling information to cause the application reader to want to rally to your cause. Since mediocre answers are good, they won't actively hurt your application. Yet, if they don't cause an admissions committee member to want to enthusiastically support you, they are not very helpful, either.

Providing mediocre answers does create one unfortunate outcome: more performance pressure is placed on the rest of the application. In other words, if answers to the two main questions are *merely* good, other elements of the application must be great, if not exceptional, in order for the candidate to succeed.

Remember: selective schools have far more qualified candidates than spaces to offer. This means schools will see many good candidates, but only great candidates will get offers. Crafting great answers to the two core questions is one of the easiest, and most important, ways to boost your application into greatness.

THE BENEFIT OF GREAT ANSWERS

Your ability to supply credible, compelling answers to the two basic questions will give you these important advantages in the admissions process:

* **Credibility.** Great answers to the two basic questions prove that you know who you are, you know what you want, and you know what to do to get there. They also begin to make a case for why a particular school plays a critical role in helping you reach your goals. This clarity of intention and purpose indicate a maturity and sophistication that create credibility. Credibility is an enormous asset to any competitive school application, especially given the high volume of applicants who simply don't follow through.

* **Articulation.** The two questions, at their core, are asking you to make a logical, persuasive argument to legitimize a major step in your life. A great answer creates comprehension (and, it is hoped, agreement), leaving the reader with the sense that you are reasonable, well-spoken, and articulate. Your answers give clues to how you think and reveal some qualities of logic.

- **Connection.** To the extent that great answers are personal, they take applicants far by building a critical emotional connection. There is no higher compliment (and no better bellwether for your chance of being admitted) than to meet a member of an admissions committee for the first time, who says to a candidate, "I feel like I already know you." *Good* answers don't make meaningful connections, but *great* answers do. Tone, candor, vulnerability, and dozens of other personal qualities that cause us to warm up to new people in person also come through on applications. Great answers successfully integrate some of these less tangible qualities.

- **A Foundation of Reason.** Just as every school's most significant decision criteria relate back to their big picture incentives, so should the various elements of your application relate back to your answers to the two core questions. A virtuous cycle will be created when echoes of these answers are in evidence elsewhere in your application.

WHAT IF YOU CAN'T COME UP WITH GOOD REASONS?

If you've sat down with a pen and a piece of paper for a good long while and still can't come up with reasons that both sound good to you and pass the "individuality test," consider the following next steps:

Step Up Your Brainstorming Game

Brainstorming is only effective if you truly commit to the process—this means allowing yourself to write or say things aloud that might not ultimately be reasonable, viable, tactful, ethical, or advisable to ever write on a school application. Often, we don't get great results from brainstorming exercises because we feel inhibited.

Good brainstorming requires a bit of deprogramming. We are conditioned from an early age to only offer up ideas when we are certain they will be of value. In school, we only raise our hands if we know the answer. In conversation, we are careful to screen what we say so that we may sound intelligent. We are conditioned to think before speaking.

This programming is not useful when it comes to brainstorming exercises. The objective of brainstorming is to express thoughts as they come to you, without first straining them through a mental filter (usually, your inner critic). Only by letting go will you reach deeper insights that set the stage for your ability to understand—and communicate to others—your desires and motives. Many wonderful books have been written about brainstorming. if you are still coming up short after informal research and a bit of trial and error, consider investing in one.

Seriously Reconsider

If you aren't finding compelling reasons to justify a particular application, it may be time to ask yourself whether what you have set out to do truly aligns with your goals. It is not uncommon for people to explore different paths based on fleeting inspiration, secondary objectives, or someone else's wishes.

The more honest we are with ourselves, the clearer it will become as to whether our reasons for pursuing a certain path are good, bad, or questionable. Though disappointing in the short-term, this honest self-reflection is to be commended. Just ask the thousands of individuals who are still paying off student loans for degrees that, as it turned out, they didn't really want, to schools they didn't really like.

If you don't have at least two or three unique reasons *that you can be proud* of to answer both questions, you are probably on the wrong track.

REAL LIFE EXAMPLE: WHY COLLEGE? WHY CERTAIN SCHOOLS?

If you had asked me at sixteen, when I was writing my college applications, why I planned to apply to college, my answer would have been "Because I am expected to." Yet even at that age, that's not an answer I gave on my applications or said out loud in interviews. This is why introspection is important: sometimes, in order to find an answer we're willing to say out loud, we have to look a bit deeper. The good news is that behind the "big" reasons that we think are driving us are often other application-appropriate reasons that are just as true and that also make perfect sense.

So, what else motivated me, at sixteen, to want to go to college? I wanted to move out of my parents' house and live on my own. I was interested in languages (Spanish was my favorite subject and at the time I was also learning German) and I wanted the opportunity to keep studying those. I had always been interested in diplomacy and international relations, which was not something I could study in high school. I knew that college would strengthen my job prospects, and when the time came, I wanted to be able to get a good job. However true it was that my parents would force me to go to college, I still had good, authentic reasons of my own.

In terms of the particular schools I applied to, I will admit that I had less compelling reasons to apply to some of them than others. There were schools that my mother loved, but that I didn't. I had "safety" schools that I thought I had a good chance of getting into. I also had "stretch" schools that appealed to me for name recognition alone. Yet, for each school I applied to, even if it was not my personal first choice, it became necessary to understand and focus on at least a few elements that attracted me to each school.

For example, I applied to two schools in New York City. My authentic answer for why I was interested in those schools was because I love New York. In my interviews, I talked about the few times I had visited—at the age of ten, my uncle took me to see "The Nutcracker" and I was amazed by the city's tall buildings and the throngs of people and the wonderful energy. I was consumed by the same feeling as a teenager when I paid a weekend visit to a summer camp friend who lived in Manhattan. My own father had attended school in New York City and I grew up hearing stories about parties in Brooklyn and chess in Washington Square Park. These answers were authentic, and unique to me. They were memorable to my interviewers, and because they were true, they hit the mark.

Another school I applied to had an open curriculum—one that allowed students to take whatever classes they wanted instead of requiring all students to take the same core set. I remember being impressed by a student I met when I visited, who was taking three dance classes and an English class as her only sections that semester. I brought that up during my interview. Again, the experience that I spoke about was authentic, and unique to me. Telling a story about a personal encounter was more effective than simply citing an interest in the open curriculum. Subtle differences such as these are important.

REAL LIFE EXAMPLE: WHY AN MBA? WHY NOW? WHY CERTAIN SCHOOLS?

If you're applying to a program that does not represent an expected transition (for example, the natural migration from middle school to high school or high school to college), be prepared to answer "Why now?" Particularly for graduate school and off-cycle transfers, such as switching elementary schools in the second grade or high schools in the 10th grade, admissions officers will want to know "Why now?"

Let's start with why I wanted an MBA. The truth was, I applied in 2002 when the U.S. economy was in a recession. At the time, my small online marketing agency had lost some clients as a result of the recession and I had to moonlight as a temp to supplement my main income. I had also decided, after living in New York during September 11th, that I was paranoid about remaining in the city. They were uncertain times, and I sought to park myself in school, in a different city, until the recession abated. Also, having lived in a city where I paid $1,700 monthly to rent a 450 square foot apartment with a mini-fridge, a tiny sink, and a hot plate instead of a kitchen, I wanted to earn more money. Certainly, the recession and the prospect of better earning potential drove tens of thousands of business school applications that year.

So how did I (and others) address motives authentically? For one, I struck a balance between being candid and being tactful. I focused on my view that it is wise to go back to school during a recession—it takes pressure off of the labor markets, and students who time their graduations with economic rebounds find themselves very much in demand. By answering in that manner, I revealed (albeit indirectly) that I had been negatively impacted by the recession. However, my answer also showed good strategic thinking, an understanding of the macroeconomy, and a positive attitude. Had I been too blunt in my response, it may have conveyed that I merely wanted a dry place to weather the storm. By being truthful, I was authentic. By being thoughtful in my response, I was able to highlight positive attributes and show tact.

But let's go deeper. As I said earlier, the first few answers to these "why" questions rarely tell the full story. Also true in my case was my feeling of wanting to return to a path of working in international relations (indeed,

I had become sidetracked since college and found myself in the world of online marketing completely by mistake). I also found myself as the owner of my own business but without any formal business training, as my undergraduate degree had been in foreign language and globalization.

Ultimately, all of these motivations made it into essays and conversations about why I chose to apply to business school. They are all true and the last two are uniquely relevant to me. They are both logical and memorable. They are good answers that became great whenever I had the opportunity to tell some personal stories around them.

In terms of the "Why this school?" question, I only considered programs that aligned with my aspirations and desires. For me, this made schools with international business programs attractive. Because this was consistent with interests shown during my undergraduate career, the expression of this motivation rang true. I chose schools with strong finance programs because I felt that my undergraduate degree was too "soft" and I felt that I needed to study more quantitative topics to balance the right-brained skills I already had. Finally, I was most attracted to schools with a flexible curriculum because it was a program feature that worked well for me in my undergraduate years.

The more connections that you can draw between choices you've made in the past and what the school has to offer, the better you will be positioned for a good result. Great answers lay out your key values, goals, and events that influenced you, and connect the dots among them. There is an enormous advantage to spending as much time as is needed to crafting answers to these two questions. There are no shortcuts to thoroughly considering your fit with individual schools.

> *All greatness of character is dependent on individuality. The man who has no other existence than that which he partakes in common with all around him, will never have anything other than an existence of mediocrity.*
>
> - James Fenimore Cooper

CHAPTER IV
THE ONE PLACE YOU DON'T WANT TO BE

Put yourself in the shoes of an admissions committee member: you're in the thick of admissions season and you'll read fifteen applications today. Three of them will be definite yeses, three of them will be definite nos, and the other nine will be somewhere in the middle. Applicants' grades, test scores, and prerequisites are all very good but very similar, and no other mitigating factor (such as legacy, siblings, target mix or any other strong influencer) is nudging you towards a decision to admit.

So you dig into the short answers or essays, hoping that even though every applicant was asked the same questions, you'll see some refreshingly thoughtful answers. Not because the typical answers are bad, *per se*, but because reading the same answer over and over only makes your job harder.

Let's say that again:

Reading the same answer over and over only makes your job harder.

That's because, if the nine duly excellent and very similar applications don't start to distinguish themselves pretty soon, you'll have to start making cuts based on some very minor, and very arbitrary, factors. Like who has an even ratio of vowels to consonants in his name and who mentioned the target school by name the most number of times.

Does my example seem extreme? Believe me—it's not. I'm only barely joking. If admissions officers could be candid about this fact, they would tell you the same thing. In some sense it is natural for students of similar interests, motivations, and goals to gravitate toward the same schools. Yet, homogeneity makes for difficult evaluation.

> *You must anticipate what others are likely to say, and avoid overstating those same things.*

That's why there's one thing you must learn for the purposes of your application, and that is: how to be different. I don't mean that you must cease being yourself or resort to outlandish attention-getting tactics. Rather, you must anticipate what others are likely to say, and avoid overstating those same things.

In order to fully express why it's important to be different, we should also discuss the broad dynamics of competition. This chapter will help you understand what typically constitutes a definite *no*, what earns a definite *yes*, and deconstructs why the vast majority of applicants are *maybes* until and unless they can distinguish themselves. Finally, you'll learn what must be done to either turn your application into a definite yes, or, if that's not possible, how to claw your way out of the middle.

DEFINITE NOS

Applications are definite nos for at least one of two reasons: in most cases, they simply don't meet the baseline requirements; in a smaller number of cases, the application raises some bright red flag. Students who don't seem like they can keep up with the work make up the majority of the definite *nos*. In many cases, these are students who know they haven't shown strong enough academics to be highly competitive, but are applying to the target school as a stretch. These *nos* are not students whose qualifications are borderline—they are outside of the ballpark.

For example, if the average GPA of admitted students is 3.5 and average test scores fall in the 93rd percentile, an applicant with a GPA of 2.5 and test scores in the 80th percentile would usually be a definite no, given serious doubts about whether the applicant could perform at the same level as other students. Bear in mind again that, in this market, most schools receive more qualified applicants than they have space for. Given no shortage of other applicants with GPAs closer to 3.5 and test scores closer to the 93rd percentile, it's easy to disqualify the applicant with low scores. Maybe this student *could* succeed at the target school, but why make exceptions when many other candidates can prove without a doubt that they can do well academically?

The second reason that can make for an immediate rejection is some kind of red flag. In some cases, applications go instantaneously from a *yes* or *maybe* to a *no* when some highly undesirable quality reveals itself. For example, if it becomes clear that the candidate has lied about something on the application or made some major *faux pas* (like using the name of the wrong school repeatedly) in essays, or if the applicant receives a scathing letter of recommendation, or says or does something highly inappropriate on paper or in the interview, it can become a definite *no*.

A child who hits or bites someone during a preschool or kindergarten group interview may be an example of a behavioral definite *no*. Parents or potential students who make an off-color comment in an interview is another. A colleague once told of an interviewee who stared at her cleavage for most of the interview and barely looked her in the eye. It's not common, but it inevitably happens every year that some small number of candidates uses bad judgment and say or do something that costs them a spot. In these cases, highly qualified (even superstar) candidates may find themselves rejected. Schools simply have enough great candidates that they don't need to take chances on loose cannons or wild cards.

DEFINITE YESES

Definite *yeses* are people who easily meet the baseline requirement and, above that, have demonstrated some extraordinary quality that shows extremely high potential or personal character. I mentioned a few in the introduction. Remember the four-year old who can count by tens to a million in three languages? The thirteen-year-old whose science project is too advanced and complex for most educated adults to understand? The

Marine who risked his life to save other men during combat? Applicants who perform well beyond what is expected are favored over others. These über-impressive candidates are also desirable because they are viewed as having the potential to become alumni who do well later in life, inviting good press—and potentially some good financial support—for the school.

This is also true for personal interactions. Some candidates have so much charisma and charm that they become definite *yeses* by virtue of being instantaneously and universally liked. Definite *yeses* can be decided as quickly as definite *nos*. A qualified candidate who does, says, or writes something that makes a clear, powerful, and highly positive impression can easily become a definite *yes*.

Again, most definite *yeses* solidly pass baseline requirements. They immediately distinguish themselves by showing something that makes admissions officers say *Wow*. They show talents or qualities that garner the admiration of committee members. They are people who the admissions committee doesn't merely want to offer a space to—definite yeses are candidates who committee members truly want to have become part of the school.

MAYBES (A.K.A. "THE MIDDLE")
Candidates in the middle have a chance at admissions that's theirs to win or lose. They don't have the top grades, perfect test scores, unbeatable resume candy or other obvious qualities that nudge them, early on, toward being a definite *yes*. They are in the middle because their stats—even if they are quite good—are very similar to most others in the applicant pool. In the absence of any early elements that show superstar qualities, these applications will succeed or fail based on the sum of what distinguishes them. For this reason, the middle is the most difficult place to be.

Most applicants won't fully appreciate the sheer average-ness of their applications, yet, a failure to realize this can be a fatal mistake. Even if you are far above average compared to your day-to-day peers, the applicant pool for your target schools will be as high-caliber as you. It is very common for parents in particular to be confused about the competitiveness of their children's applications.

In today's environment, those who think they will get into a school because they know their qualifications are "good enough" will be sorely disappointed. That's because good enough isn't good enough anymore. At the risk of sounding like a broken record I'll say it again: schools read the applications of more qualified candidates than they are able to admit. Getting in becomes a matter of distinguishing yourself from other qualified candidates. For applicants in the middle, it really is as simple as that.

EXCEPTIONS TO THE MIDDLE

While some find the offering of preferential treatment to be elitist, if not unfair, there is often good logic that underlies these decisions. Some applicants who would otherwise find themselves in the middle may find the scales tipped in their favor by reason of affiliation. None of the exceptions listed below can guarantee admission, but they typically help.

Siblings

For preschool, primary school, and (less commonly) secondary school, having an older sibling enrolled typically helps or guarantees admission. Though younger siblings usually have to complete an application, meeting the baseline requirements typically paves the way to a yes.

This is logical. Schools want families who can fully support their children's educational goals, and ferrying kids to and from multiple schools and dealing with conflicting academic calendars is recognized by admissions committees as impractical. At the younger grade levels, it is not only the children's fit, but the family's fit, that has to pass the test. By the time a second child is ready for enrollment, the family has already established itself within the community and demonstrated commitment to its culture and approach. Parents also understand, after having sent a first child through, the level of rigor involved in the program and overall expectations. In this sense, the applications of subsequent children are more credible because families can convincingly make a case for their child's fit (in contrast to brand new families who must make assumptions based on expectations rather than experience).

Priority treatment for siblings is one reason why primary and secondary school seats can be so competitive. Classes may be small to begin with, and it is not uncommon for a great kindergarten that admits forty students per year to have twenty or more of those seats go to siblings. This may seem like a disadvantage for brand new families, but often comes full circle as an advantage to the same families years later.

Most commonly, when siblings do not receive an offer, it is due to a large gap between the candidate's aptitude and the school's standard. Schools certainly want to make things easier on families of multiple children by providing a single school experience, but an increasing number of schools are not willing to do so if a candidate's capabilities would significantly compromise the overall strength of the incoming class. To the extent that parents of enrolled children know the standard, they often address known learning gaps well in advance, taking measures to get the delayed child up to speed by the time of application.

Feeder Schools

Some schools source large portions of starting classes with graduates of "reliable" feeder schools. These schools may have a formal or informal relationship with the target school, but regardless, they share an important connection: their curriculum meets the academic standards of the target school and the target school has experienced a track record of success with graduates of feeder programs.

An elite private K-8 school near my home acknowledges that 70 percent of the students it accepts into its thirty-six-student kindergarten program were students at its own preschool. This means that only eleven or so spots per year will be filled with brand new students, as twenty-five members of the incoming class will have been "grandfathered" into the program after showing promise in preschool. Another preschool in the area that is not formally affiliated with the same K-8 program also typically sends a handful of students per year to the target school's kindergarten, again because of its track record of producing children who are ready for a challenging program. This means that only five or six students not affiliated with these two programs typically enroll in this kindergarten each year.

The feeder school issue can be comparable at higher education levels, though generally at a smaller order of magnitude. Instead of 70 percent of the incoming class of a top university coming from a single feeder, the target school might be in the habit of giving several spots per year to candidates from the same handful of strong prep schools. At the high school to college level, for top universities, this typically dwindles to no more than 2 percent of an incoming class coming from a single school. In most cases, particularly for primary and secondary grade levels, target schools will tell you what their feeder schools are, if you tactfully ask. Something like "What preschools/elementary schools/middle schools do the students you admit typically attend?" can be a polite way to inquire.

Legacy

It's commonly believed that legacy, a family history of school attendance, improves a candidate's chances of admission. In truth, how much legacy matters differs from school to school. You are unlikely to be 100 percent sure of what this means for you and target schools because admissions committees will not be candid in revealing how much this factors in.

If you put credence in rumored practices, you may believe that the more family members who attended your target school, in the most linear formation possible, the better your chances of getting in, particularly if said related alumni donated large sums of money. In other words, candidates with a parent and grandparent who attended the school and who donated a million dollars apiece are generally thought to have better chances than candidates preceded only by a third cousin, twice removed, who never gave a dime. In truth, it's useless to speculate on whether, and to what extent, practices like this impact outcomes—if favoritism based on these elements is a factor, the people involved will never, ever (at least, not in any official capacity) tell you the truth; and since buying seats and practicing discrimination of any kind is illegal, and since the mere suggestion of such activity is risky, insiders will be loath to discuss the topic.

That said, there are legitimate and perfectly honorable reasons for schools and candidates to want to keep things in the family. Schools want students who will be evangelists for the brand, and who will be dedicated to upholding the school's standards and reputation. Candidates with a lifelong connection to the school and an existing admiration for the institution can speak convincingly on this topic and can also say with greater confidence that they understand what would be expected of them at a given school and what the experience might be like. Conversely, a candidate who is brand new to the school community may not be able to speak with as much credibility about whether he thinks he will thrive and whether he will be a good fit.

In many cases, legacy candidates can make authentic, credible cases for how a family connection was a catalyst for their attraction to the school. My own father graduated from New York University nearly forty years before I did—he recalled those years as some of the best of his life, and part of my authentic experience growing up was hearing about his love for New York City, memorable professors, and other colorful characters he met at school. He even had a large watercolor painting of the Washington Arch proudly displayed behind the desk in his office, and he often regaled me with stories of the legendary chess games he watched in Washington Square Park. By the time I applied to NYU, I had a genuine affection for the school that had been germinating my whole life. If you have a family connection to a school, don't be afraid to share personal stories that characterize that connection. It will not be perceived as a device, as long as it is heartfelt.

Race, Ethnicity , Gender and Cultural Diversity

Many independent schools have become tangibly committed to racial, ethnic and cultural diversity. This means that the admissions committee might actively work to admit classes in which a target mix is met. Some schools are more transparent than others in discussing their diversity goals. At the absolute least, you will probably find some statement in the school's literature about a commitment to diversity. At best, you will find schools that proudly publish detailed statistics about the racial, ethnic, and cultural distribution of the student body. How much information schools share about diversity programs and enrolled student demographics is usually a good indicator of the school's commitment in this area. However, commitment to diversity is still relatively new in the grand scheme of education, and most schools' programs continue to evolve.

Many applicants think that it helps to be a minority when applying to schools—in some cases, this could not be farther from the truth. Internal diversity targets and the number of people who fit your demographic in the year you apply will combine to determine your individual prospects and decide what role race, ethnicity and culture play. If there are few qualified candidates who fit your profile, you may have an advantage, but if many qualified candidates do, it could actually hurt your chances. This is explained further in the section about overrepresented demographics.

HOW TO KNOW IF YOU ARE IN THE MIDDLE

The first rule of the middle is: always assume that you are in the middle. Even if you have perfect test scores, a glowing recommendation from your boss (even if she happens to be the President of the United States), and you spend half your free time volunteering to save endangered baby snow owls, it's dangerous to assume you're a definite yes, even if all signs point to the idea that you should be. The same goes even for candidates with Nelson Mandela-esque charisma who can tell extraordinary tales of heroism and virtue. And it especially goes for proud parents whose adulation of their children is—frankly—blinding. There are simply no guarantees.

> " *The first rule of the middle is: always assume that you are in the middle.* "

For those who may believe they are in the middle because their known factor statistics (e.g., grades, test scores, prerequisites) are at or slightly below average, comprehension of the fact that you are in the middle and a plan to do something about it places you in a much stronger position than the majority of applicants, who won't fully appreciate the importance of distinguishing themselves, and therefore, won't be able to pull themselves out.

Yet, there's another way to view the middle that's more abstract than (but just as relevant as) its concept as a place inhabited by those who aren't definite yeses. In some ways, awareness of your "middle-ness" translates to awareness of how much effort it will take to get into a school, given your personal situation. Throughout the book, you will read about legacies, siblings, class mix targets, and other factors that increase or decrease candidates' chances of getting into a given school. In order to cultivate an understanding of whether, and how deeply, you are in the middle, you need to understand what separates you from the top.

Overrepresented Demographics

If you are aware that many other applicants fall into your ethnic, racial, and gender background and have similar credentials, such as education, feeder school, extracurricular activities and/or resume experience, you may be part of an overrepresented demographic. This is not uncommon, and may tie back to cultural or professional values that may be shared among many people in a certain group.

Suppose that an American MBA program that admits 400 students a year receives 4,000 qualified applications, and the top 500 are from well-qualified Indian nationals with degrees from top engineering programs. The American school will not accept all of those applicants, even though they are the most highly-qualified, because doing so would create classroom imbalance as well as other undesired consequences. Most schools want thought diversity so that students can learn from and challenge one another, and homogeneity may decrease the possibility of innovation.

In cases like this, schools are inclined to engineer the offer pool to fit prescribed diversity targets. Consequently, students in overrepresented demographics must not only be strong candidates, they must also stand out compared to others in their group. Because the merit-driven elements of school admissions do not carry perfectly throughout the process, it is rarely safe for candidates in common demographics to assume they are a definite yes.

If you think that's an extreme example, think again. Cuts like those are common in the admissions process, and are repeated when any question of creating a balanced class arises. Suppose a top high school finds that 60 percent of qualified applicants hail from the same middle school. Chances are slim that the target school will let a single feeder school dominate the incoming class. In that case, some of the very best applicants will be rejected because of the target school's commitment to craft a class that has students from a broader set of schools. The possibility that you come from an overrepresented demographic is another reason there are no guarantees in the admissions process.

Very Small Schools

Candidates applying to very small schools may effectively consider themselves in the middle. The level of effort it takes to get into a very small mainstream school with moderate standards can be as great as the effort to get into a larger school with higher minimum requirements.

For one, scarcity amplifies competition—a small number of total spaces reduced by the number of applicants with priority consideration can often make for an extremely small number of spaces for new students. At preschool and primary schools, this takes the form of deliberately small classrooms narrowed significantly by priority sibling enrollees. In higher education, small schools may have fewer priority applicants, but since each admitted applicant represents a larger percentage of the class, even a few priority admits can change the game.

There's another issue: at a small school, bad admissions decisions have noticeable implications. A college that only places fifteen students in a small room at a given time to learn a subject is seismically different than one that places 115 students into an amphitheater-style room. At smaller schools, the nature and expected level of engagement is often so different that when student fit is poor, it is often obvious and detrimental to the dynamic for all parties involved. For this reason, very small schools may look even harder at fit and class balance than larger counterparts.

HOW TO GET OUT OF THE MIDDLE

There is only one way to get out of the middle: to distinguish yourself from others sharing your space. This ubiquitous (to the point of frustration) advice to "stand out" is imparted again and again for good reason. For the process to not be arbitrary for students with similar qualifications, application readers are looking for logical, defensible grounds to admit students who are not definite yeses.

> *Advice to "stand out" doesn't mean you should become somebody you're not, nor does it mean you should to focus on things about yourself that you believe other people will find impressive.*

Fortunately for you, this advice to "stand out" doesn't mean you should become somebody you're not, nor does it mean you should to focus on things about yourself that you believe other people will find impressive. The best path out of the middle is to be as authentic as possible by sharing compelling stories about yourself. Much of this book is dedicated to helping you think about what's right for you, and how to communicate it in a way that will be effective in your pursuit of admission to the schools of your choice.

> *There is no greater impediment to the advancement of knowledge than the ambiguity of words.*
>
> -Thomas Reid

CHAPTER V

DECIPHERING UNHELPFUL ADMISSIONS COMMITTEE JARGON

It's alright. You can say it out loud. Direct advice from school admissions committees can be confusing as heck. They're not trying to confuse you (in fact, their feedback on how to be successful in the admissions process is typically quite honest). But it's not always stated in terms that are helpful to the untrained ear.

There are logical reasons why "official" guidance may seem cloaked in mystery. For one, admissions committee members must be diplomatic and conservative in what they say. Inside advice can't be dispensed to some applicants and not others; there can be no implications of hard-and-fast rules; there can be no insinuation of guarantees.

This chapter is dedicated to admissions committee jargon, to those phrases that make us cringe and want to pull our hair out when we hear them. We will highlight, and deconstruct, common answers to questions like "What are you looking for?" and "What are your admissions requirements?". By the end of this chapter, you will have a better sense for what admissions committee members are trying to convey when they respond.

"START EARLY"

If an admissions committee staffer tells you that it's important to start the process early, he or she may be getting at one of two things. First, particularly for a child, you may be hearing advice to submit an application well in advance of an enrollment date. Certain preschools and primary schools open the process a whole season or more in advance, and planning to apply the winter before enrollment may be too late to be seriously considered. Certain schools are candid about this fact and publish early application as a requirement of their process. Yet, in other cases, in which applying early is suggested but not required, you may not be told bluntly by an admissions committee member that it will seriously help your application to apply early. This may be because the committee member is reticent to imply that anything outside of the published application process is required to be considered for admission.

For schools with a recommendation (but not requirement) to apply early, a few superstars who swoop in at the eleventh hour might get a spot close to the end of the enrollment season, but if you are organized in your preparations, there's no reason to take that chance. That said, if you learn that a school accepts applications for enrollment years in advance of the current season, this is a clear sign that you might want to get a head start, particularly if skill levels and aptitude that are necessary to be perceived as a great candidate are already demonstrable. For extremely competitive schools, it's worth asking directly how early applications are accepted for your planned enrollment year.

Secondly, in being advised to start early (perhaps even within a single season), you may be getting a signal that the school takes the longevity and consistency of the candidate's interest into account. The message here may be that seizing opportunities to participate in admissions and other school community events matters. "Start early" may also imply that some candidates who are not successful fail to show adequate understanding of or familiarity with the school. A staffer who supplies this advice may be subtly advising you to become knowledgeable about the school and prepared to engage with the admissions committee at a sophisticated level.

While I do believe that schools seriously consider all applicants who submit on time, advice like this tends to highlight one action that may give one candidate an edge over another, when all other things are equal. In that respect, schools really aren't using unfair or arbitrary criteria to evaluate students at a basic level—rather, they resort to finer measures when they are required to choose between numerous qualified candidates.

"STAND OUT"

Particularly frustrating to candidates is the frequently uttered proclamation that the most successful applicants simply "stand out." This unleashes insecurities about whether one's most outstanding qualities are good enough, and creates unanswerable questions about what separates the ordinary from the extraordinary.

> *If you're funny, be funny. If you're something else, be that. Stand out by bringing more of you to the table.*

Admissions committee members who say they want candidates who stand out are directly addressing the dilemma of "the middle," as described in the previous chapter. They are admitting that they, as individuals, find themselves standing behind applicants who are memorable, while also making a general statement about the sameness of some portion of the applicant pool.

Contrary to the beliefs of many candidates, standing out does not only have to be about showcasing extraordinary qualities or stunning accomplishments. It does not only have to be about being smarter, more talented, or "better" in any way. Standing out in a way that helps your application can simply be about distinguishing yourself (positively, of course). Just as a grad school applicant who summited Mt. Everest would be memorable to an admissions committee member, so would one who shared a moving personal story or wrote a funny essay. I still remember most of the funniest application responses I have ever read. So, if you're funny, be funny. If you're something else, be that. Stand out by bringing more of you to the table.

"BE YOURSELF"

When an admissions committee member tells you to "be yourself," you are being cautioned against saying what you think the committee wants to hear. This is a tacit acknowledgement of the fact that many applicants adjust their approach or mute their natural personalities to pander to the committee. Remember, any advice that admissions committee members give is a reaction to behavior that they routinely see. "Be yourself" is frequently dispensed advice, largely because of how often it is ignored.

If you are being given "be yourself" advice in a one-on-one setting, the committee member may sense from your line of questioning that you are overly-focused on what *they* want, and not enough on what *you* want. Candidates who spend an inordinate amount of time grilling admissions committee members on how to get in to a given school run the risk of being viewed as someone so bent on showing the committee only what they think it wants to see, that they may not be fully committed to painting accurate pictures of themselves.

If anything, it behooves you not to write too many answers that could possibly sound like pandering, even if they are truthful to you. For this reason, I repeatedly suggest in this book to be simultaneously authentic and unique, as much as possible.

"WE HAVE NO MINIMUM REQUIREMENTS"

Candidates frequently ask what the minimum requirements are to be seriously considered for admission. Schools, of course, must say that apart from any published prerequisites, no such minimum requirements exist.

This is usually true. All admissions committee members can recall candidates with below average scores who wowed the committee and were admitted, just as some candidates who had stellar scores but bland personalities were not extended offers.

There's another reason why admissions committee members are loath to name minimum requirements. They don't want to appear to be promising you that you will get in (if you meet those requirements). They don't want hate mail or lawsuits from candidates who claim they were misinformed.

When you're told that there are "no minimums," the admissions officer is not just giving you lip service. Admissions committees truly evaluate each candidate on an individual basis. Though many schools publish statistics pertaining to former incoming classes, admission is not determined according to any unwavering formula. It's important that you demonstrate aptitude within the ballpark of what the school is looking for, but beyond that, it's simply not useful to overfocus on requirements and stats.

BUZZ PHRASES

If you hear a certain school use the same terminology over and over again to sum up what it is looking for—especially if it's terminology few or no other schools are using—you've just heard an internal buzz phrase. Such phrases are the product of school leaders summing up what the school is looking for into a single blended concept. In all likelihood, this central concept took hours of discussion—maybe even a corporate offsite or staff retreat—to hone. The problem for candidates is that, since you were not privy to said discussions, buzz phrases often seem to obscure underlying meaning.

When I was applying to the University of Chicago, admissions officers were focused on "intellectual curiosity." It may be easy to comprehend the surface meaning (which indicates a natural attraction to learning), but as I later learned while on the admissions committee, it encompassed several concepts that were rarely articulated. Buzz phrases are troublesome because, even if you understand them, they encompass so many underlying ideas that they may be difficult to demonstrate cohesively. If you continue to hear the same buzz phrase that you just don't understand very well, politely ask a committee member who seems as specific and articulate as possible for a deeper explanation.

PART III:

FINDING THE BAR
(AND KNOWING HOW YOU
STACK UP)

> *If you don't know where you're going,*
> *you might wind up someplace else.*
> -Yogi Berra

CHAPTER VI
BUILDING YOUR LIST OF TARGET SCHOOLS

Up until this point, I've spoken of the admissions process as wholly controlled by the schools, one in which you are but a hopeful minion looking to earn a much-coveted spot in a small incoming class. While it's true that final decision power resides with each school, you, the applicant, have the most important role to play. The more accurately you can assess your own academic readiness, a school's ability to help you reach your goals, and personal fit, the closer you'll be to applying to schools for which you can write strong applications and, therefore, schools you'll be able to get into.

Admittedly, school targeting is an imprecise science, and one that has been oversimplified at the expense of candidates and their families. Common counsel recommends choosing "solid" targets (schools to which the applicant believes he has a reasonable, but not assured, chance of getting in), "safety" schools (schools to which the applicant believes he has a very good chance of getting in), and "stretch" schools (schools to which the applicant believes getting in is a long shot). This method perpetuates a rather counterproductive mentality, one that suggests a goal of attending the most prestigious program that will grant the candidate entrance, rather than the school that is the very best holistic fit.

Because this solid/safety/stretch method is misguided, it often fails to yield logical results. In theory, candidates should get into all safety schools, many solid schools, and some small number of stretch schools. In reality, this rarely happens—primarily because most people anchor solid/safety/stretch schools to prerequisites and scores instead of holistic fit). More serious flaws arise from the idea of aiming for "the best" school you can get into: the school that most improves your pedigree may not be a tolerable match, and two years or more is a long time to spend in a place where you cannot thrive or even be happy. Though goals of attending prestigious schools are logical, the benefits of attending a school that is *perfect* for you should not be understated.

So, let's reframe the issue. Targeting should be about finding the group of schools that:

- challenge you to learn and grow at a pace that will energize you (rather than exhaust or bore you as "stretch" or "safety" schools might)
- feature specific programs and curricula that are aligned with your current interests and future goals
- are made up of students, faculty, and administrators you will connect with intellectually, academically, and emotionally, and could see yourself or your family building meaningful relationships with
- share missions and philosophies of learning that align well with your own

Not only will you or your family be happier in a program that includes the aforementioned criteria—you will be far more likely to get in to such a program, given your ability to write an application that genuinely and convincingly conveys multi-dimensional fit.

FIGURING OUT WHAT YOU'RE LOOKING FOR

It's time to begin mapping out the specifics of what you're looking for in a program; several methods of thinking through this build upon one another. We'll start with a method that asks you to think organically about what feels right to you. From there, some light exploration of the types of programs you are considering will bring more possibilities to your attention. The goal is to document whatever likes and dislikes arise as part of this introspection to anchor you to your true desires and preferences. Later in the process, these insights will help serve as a safeguard against unintentionally meandering toward schools that may not be right for you. Before beginning these exercises, let's clarify the concept of "fit."

What is "Fit"?

"Fit" may be the weightiest, yet least understood, term in the school admissions lexicon. It is thrown around freely by administrators and admissions officials, but applicants aren't always sure exactly what being "a good fit" means.

There are typically two dimensions of "good fit": the first involves parallels that you, the candidate can bring to the table. It is your job to let a school know which of your own personal interests, values, goals, and strengths align with or complement what is offered by that school. These "fit" elements must be actively injected into your application and articulated very clearly. These correlate directly to the "Why this school?" question and to all targeting efforts.

> *"Fit" may be the weightiest, yet least understood, term in the school admissions lexicon. It is thrown around freely by administrators and admissions officials, but applicants aren't always sure exactly what being "a good fit" means.*

For example, an elementary school that, as part of the mandatory curriculum, offers violin lessons to all children and features computer time at every grade level might be particularly appealing to a family in which one parent plays classical string instruments and in which both parents believe that comfort with technology will be vital to their child's future success. In this case, the applicants clearly recognize ways in which the school is a good fit for them and must mention these fit elements explicitly. In order to do this effectively, the family must go beyond saying that they merely like the violin and computer curricula offered by the school. They must "connect the dots" for the admissions committee and show why, and how much, they care about these things.

The second dimension of "good fit" is some set of intangible qualities that candidates cannot anticipate or try to demonstrate—this typically has more to do with a feeling or sense that an admissions committee member may have about the candidate based on numerous impressions. It may answer the question: "After meeting and speaking with this person, and based on reading her application, could I see her being content and productive among others in the school?"

Why is Fit Important?

It's not enough simply to screen students based on academic aptitude and admit the top achievers to a given class. Schools each have their own values, cultures, and internal goals, and finding students who are in sync with such elements creates a more cohesive, more productive student body, with better outcomes.

Students also get better results when they attend schools that are a good fit. It's easy to make friends, be motivated, find things to do that you love, and perform well where the level of academic work is challenging but doable, and where you can find things in common with other members of the community.

Schools know this. That is why effectively demonstrating fit, both academic and cultural, makes for the strongest applications. Students who target schools for the wrong reasons will have a difficult time demonstrating fit, and, therefore, a difficult time earning the desired spot. For this reason, choosing the right targets is the most important determinant of how good your chances of getting into a given school are, and how happy you will be once you get there.

The Consequences of Bad Fit

Most candidates learn a bit too late when they have targeted the wrong schools. In some cases, this manifests at decision time when it is revealed that a candidate has not earned a spot at any desired school. Also common is the realization, once a student is enrolled in a school, that he is not happy, or he's struggling to keep up. Many students are at first thrilled to learn that they've been offered a spot in an elite program—only to find themselves alienated by a culture of fierce competition and crushed under the pressure of a massive workload. Other students may be good at targeting desirable schools, but careless about choosing backup options, and end up at schools that are both academically and culturally wrong.

You don't have to take my word for it. In a 2010 survey of 1,303 four-year colleges and universities, *U.S. News* cited a freshman retention rate of roughly 75 percent. That means that some 25 percent of college freshmen during the survey years (fall 2005 to fall 2008) did not return to the same school for sophomore year, and may not have returned to school at all. From the same study, only 137 schools (just over 10 percent of those surveyed) had a freshman retention rate of more than 90 percent. This means that a large number of students abandoned schools they only recently chose.

However tempting it is to try to get into the "best" school that you can, remember this: the admissions process is short, but time at school is long. No matter what type of school you are applying to, you are signing up for between two and thirteen years (if you consider K-12 schools) at a place that you (or your child) must attend every day. In order to be a stepping stone for something better, the student must truly be positioned to thrive.

Examples of Thinking Through Fit

The following examples discuss the potential thought processes of two hypothetical candidates, demonstrating why it's critical to consciously and proactively consider fit. Candidates may not be familiar with differences among programs near the beginning of the process, but a little self-reflection and program comparison often clarifies significant differences.

Example #1: MFA Hopeful

A college graduate wishes to pursue a Master in Fine Arts that focuses on writing. All programs are not the same, however. Some are particularly strong in poetry, while others focus on fiction writing, and others offer less common areas of focus. Some require total residency while others only require on-campus class attendance for a few weeks each semester. Therefore, it would not be useful for any student to simply research the "best" MFA programs and attend the top-ranked program he can get into. Rather, before researching programs, he must determine what he is *really* looking for.

Suppose our candidate determines that he would like to focus on fiction, would like a program in a warm weather location, and prefers not to be required to write a book-length thesis. He also wants to find a program with a soft, non-aggressive workshopping method, because he is far more comfortable with supportive feedback environments. This degree of self-reflection will help the candidate immeasurably in his search. Before searching for the "best" schools, candidates must ground themselves in their own deal breaking criteria. It then becomes easy to do Internet searches, tap personal networks, and speak to counselors about schools.

Example #2: Preschool

Parents of young children may assume that all families investing in private education at such a young age have similar goals for their children, yet this is simply not true. Even if you think your target list of preschools should be a no-brainer given the seemingly universal goal of kindergarten readiness, you stand to significantly increase your chances of a good fit by ensuring that your own values and your child's personality and interests factor into your decision.

For example, Montessori education focuses (among other things) on helping children build confidence through independence. If your family values independence, you may consider a preschool that emphasizes the Montessori method. In this case, the search recommendation would be reversed. If you aren't sure exactly what program features you are looking for, search for resources that profile early childhood learning methods.

How to Figure Out What Fits You

The following exercises are meant to help you create or validate a set of criteria for evaluating schools. They are appropriate for those still at the starting line as well as those already immersed in the process. For the purposes of targeting the right schools, as well as deciding on the right program once you've received acceptances, it's critical to be anchored to what you really want and where you really stand.

Make a List/Brainstorm

So that you won't become overwhelmed by what you discover in the course of active research, take an hour to consider a few questions. If you are in the thick of it already, choose the time of day at which you are the most clearheaded, well-rested, and least stressed. From there, consider the following:

+ What subjects or majors do you care most about studying?

+ What teaching methods do you prefer?

+ How important is experiential or participatory learning?

+ How rigid or flexible should the curriculum be?

+ How important are extracurriculars (and which extracurriculars, specifically)?

+ What balance should there be between social life and academics? Between work and play?

+ How much emphasis should be placed on teaching or discussing values and ethics?

+ Is a faith-based institution strongly preferred (or to be strongly avoided)?

+ What personal qualities do you expect of the people you see every day?

This can be a group exercise. Parents should sit down with children (even young children) to talk about interests and preferences. This exercise may even teach them a few things about what truly energizes their child, though the younger the child, the more conversations the parents should have to weed out flights of fancy vs. true preferences. Even students old enough to think about this on their own may benefit from turning the exercise into a conversation with a friend or partner who can mirror ideas and ask more probing questions without biasing the candidate with their own views.

Remember, brainstorming isn't about being judgmental, critical, or narrowing down your list just yet. It's about discovering what might be important to you. You can pare down your list later. At the beginning, you are simply bringing forth possibilities and trying different ideas on for size.

Read a Good Book on the Topic

Though the focus of *From Preschool to Grad School* is to highlight the fundamentals of admissions and the commonalities among all competitive admissions processes, a number of excellent books dedicated to specific learning levels do an excellent job of describing program options. Particularly if you are unfamiliar (or your understanding is less than up-to-date) regarding the type of school you are targeting, it will help to read a more in-depth book that goes further into program specifics and current options. For example, parents helping a child apply to a private high school may themselves be twenty to thirty years (or more) beyond their own high school experience. In cases like this, it's worth gaining fresh perspective on life at competitive high schools now.

Casually Check Out a Few Programs

Maybe you already had a couple of target programs in mind before you picked up this book. Take an hour or two to browse the web sites of those programs and some others that you turn up through a simple Internet search. Observe your reactions to the various features that you see.

Notice every reaction (I mean it—*every* reaction) from how pictures of the campus make you feel to what you think of specific data related to the curriculum that is offered. Document your reactions, and think about how strongly you feel about the new things you've seen. Get in the habit of noticing and recording these reactions later on in your research and during campus visits.

To help illustrate the intention of this exercise, I did this myself, in reference to my long-time unfulfilled dream to attend film school. For the very first time, I did an Internet search on "continuing education film schools" in order to find programs for people who want to study film without having to obtain a four-year degree. I also browsed the web site of a program that I've known about for ten years and always held in high regard. Here's what I observed about my reactions:

◆ One program I saw seemed focused on the business side of film production, and didn't have screenwriting programs or a strong emphasis on film history or appreciation. My (negative) reaction to this observation helped me realize that I would prefer a program that values screenwriting and offers courses that teach and discuss it.

- ◆ The same program seemed to have a lot of celebrity lecturers—actors, directors, and producers who are very well-known in the film world. This seemed like a great perk, but I wasn't sure I cared enough about it to make it a hard requirement.

- ◆ A different program offered 4-week, 8-week, and 12-week intensives focusing on various areas of filmmaking. I liked the fact that there were opportunities to learn at a fast pace, instead of meandering through a slower, lengthier program.

Notice that I didn't search "top film schools" or "best film schools." The idea wasn't to anchor myself to what the "best" programs offer. Rather, it was to give myself a chance to get a glimpse of, and react to, different program structures and offerings in order to get myself closer to my desires and what would truly excite me. This type of exercise—one that anchors you to what truly lines up with your preferences and has the potential to energize you—will be invaluable in getting you closer to targeting schools that fit you best.

Read Opinion Pieces and User-Driven Practical Advice

Your target program or desired level of education has been written about dozens (if not hundreds) of times; even if your search is very limited in scope and geography, there's a good chance that you can find someone who has expressed a thoughtful opinion online. While no article you find on the Internet will offer a comprehensive method for finding, evaluating, or getting into school, they might expand your thinking. Your task now is first to find articles on the Internet that address what you're looking for, and, second, to take what you read with a grain of salt.

Suppose you're in the market for a preschool and want to learn more about Waldorf education. Search for "pros and cons of Waldorf schools," and dozens of relevant articles will pop up. Alternatively, you can search criteria that you know are important to you. For me, that might be something like "film schools with screenwriting programs" or "how to choose a good screenwriting program." Undoubtedly, some person who shares your values or goals has put some thought into the matter and hopefully, will have done some good research to support their thinking. Now it's your turn to reap the benefits of what they have learned. After all, they've written it for you.

Just make sure not to take everything you read at face value. The Internet is an unregulated place where anybody, whether credentialed or not, qualified or not, can say anything about any topic. In that sense, you'll want to use good judgment as you interpret what you find. Your goal is to extract whatever value you can to help your own thought process.

What to Do If You Don't Know What You Want

If you've spent several hours pursuing all of the aforementioned exercises and you still don't know what you want, one of two things is happening. First, it's possible that your inner voice is being suppressed by self-judgment, external considerations, or general feelings of being overwhelmed—in which case you need to work on quieting the noise that is competing with your ability to hear what you really want. The second possibility is that you don't find yourself moved by any early thought or research because you are on the wrong path altogether. If you can't develop a strong sense for what you want and why, you won't be able to show admissions committees why an individual school is right for you.

RESEARCHING THE UNIVERSE OF SCHOOLS

Before choosing the list of programs to which you will ultimately apply, you'll want to get a sense for the universe of schools that fit your goals and capabilities. After compiling a long list of potential targets, you can narrow the list by choosing a subset that fits the most criteria, and is holistically sound. I won't pretend this process is easy, or quick. But knowing schools intimately at the targeting stage will pay dividends when it's time to begin writing your applications. Speaking with confidence about what you're looking for, and why, will only improve your chances of admission.

> *Knowing schools intimately at the targeting stage will pay dividends when it's time to begin writing your applications.*

Periodicals with Rankings

For most students with their sights set on top schools, periodicals that issue rankings are a key source of information. The most prominent American magazine ranking national and international schools issuing popular degrees is *U.S. News & World Report*, which covers prep schools, colleges, universities, and highly enrolled graduate programs. *U.S. News & World Report* also issues dozens of rankings on a broad spectrum of niche sub-topics such as the best online education programs, top party schools, the schools with the most international students, and the top schools for B students. Even if you aren't preoccupied with rankings, *U.S. News & World Report* can be a good starting point, to the extent that it lets you search by criteria or by school, and offers well-crafted and helpful school profiles.

Other large players, like test-prep outfit The Princeton Review, have entered the ranking business, often splitting their focus between overall "top school" rankings and other special interest rankings like most politically active schools, best college towns, biggest frat and sorority scenes, and a list I particularly like called "dorms like palaces."

Lots of popular periodicals, including *Forbes*, issue their own rankings. And in this age of Internet news services and rampant reprinting, hundreds of other periodicals from *the New York Times* to *the Huffington Post* adapt content from all of these and other original sources.

If you're looking at a specific type of program, chances are that a more focused publication has ranked it. For example, the *Wall Street Journal*, the *Financial Times*, and *Business Week* (now *Bloomberg BusinessWeek*) have traditionally issued undergraduate business and/or MBA program rankings.

If you're researching foundational education levels—specifically preschool to 12th grade, in addition to the occasional profile article about individual schools, many local papers and magazines rank them and tackle topics related to college prep.

Guide Books with Indexes

They are a bit of a dying breed, but once upon a time, guide books that indexed and scored groupings of schools were prevalent. Many of these books are well-written, witty, and offer unique points of view. But, since rankings and school stats naturally change and since so many reliable sources make their rankings available on the Internet, publication of guide books has dwindled significantly in recent years. Among those still publishing nationally targeted guide books are The Fiske Guide, The College Board, and The Princeton Review, all of which are targeted toward candidates headed to undergraduate and/or graduate programs.

If colleges and universities aren't your focus, niche books developed for specific geographies about lower grade levels may be available. For example, the *Manhattan Family Guide* to Private Schools and Selective Public Schools by Victoria Goldman published its sixth edition in 2010. *Private High Schools of the San Francisco Bay Area* by Betsy Little and Paula Molligan published its fourth edition in 2008.

Niche books for specific degree pursuits are also available. *Medical School Admission Requirements (MSAR): The Most Authoritative Guide to U.S. and Canadian Medical Schools* is updated and published each year by the Association of American Medical Colleges. *A Guide to College Choices for the Performing and Visual Arts* by Ed Schoenberg and Kavin Buck was published in 2008. Take the time to hunt down the latest guides pertinent to your specific focus; choose based on those with the best endorsements and reviews.

Generally speaking, the niche market books are likely to have more substance than whatever you can find about a specific market online. Yet, comparable ratings, scoring analysis on the most popular programs (e.g., undergraduate, law, and business programs) will be widely available online for free.

Official School Materials

Schools' marketing materials run the gamut from glossy print packets received at admissions events to web sites featuring academic programs and admissions guidance. In truth, school web sites have increased in importance as sources of information for prospective students. Low distribution costs for online information, along with heightened competition and a shift toward communicating short lead-time information, have compelled schools to make more information than ever available online. This means that a lower percentage of what you see will be marketing jargon, and information that you may not have seen made available five or ten years ago is easily accessible now.

Instant access to information and tools is the first advantage of leveraging school web sites for information. Program descriptions, admissions criteria, successful applicant statistics and other matriculated class demographics are commonly available at the college and graduate levels, and increasingly so at the K-12 levels. The dates of open houses, application deadlines, and other recommended events are also readily available, and often RSVPs for such events can be filed online.

Bonus features that are relatively new may be FAQ pages, blog postings from current students or admissions committee members, and a social media presence on sites like Facebook and Twitter. Such features allow for unprecedented engagement among candidates, school community members and decision makers.

But, remember—however impressed you feel by a school based on the information it supplies, these are marketing materials designed by professionals who know exactly how to cast the school in the best possible light. After all, the school wants all of its own top picks to accept their offers for attendance, and errs toward making itself seem as attractive as possible at all times. Always remember to temper what you hear from schools with your personal reactions as well as balancing opinions from students and alumni.

Associations and Accreditation Organizations

Associations focusing on independent education may also provide school listings and other information of interest to prospective students. These associations have different reasons for existing: some of them provide accreditation and networking opportunities to schools, while others are geared toward serving as a resource for the prospective student community. Increasingly, many do both.

The National Association of Independent Schools and the National Association for the Education of Young Children are two examples of such organizations. Local and regional organizations with similar focus, such as the Association of Independent Schools in New England, the Arizona Private School Association, and the California Association of Independent Schools, also exist. Even the U.S. Department of Education maintains an open Database of Accredited Post-Secondary Schools and Programs.

Research through organizations like these can save you a lot of footwork if the web sites are robust and make information clear and accessible.

Using the Internet

Beyond school web sites and online rankings, the Internet holds millions of articles, blogs, and other forums for opinion about searching for and choosing schools. Try to stick to respected, timely information sources. This means looking at the publication dates of things you read and thinking about the integrity of information that might come from a given source. For example, an article written in *the New York Times* may be considered more reliable than a blog posting written by a private citizen with unverified credentials, given fact-checking standards and the inclination of the *Times* to provide journalistic balance. Similarly, for-profit companies who undertake commenting about school admissions (even the ubiquitous *U.S. News and World Report* and the Princeton Review fall into this category) have a business model tied to the information they provide, a fact that should be taken into consideration.

So, while reading opinions from all of these sources is advised, be cautious about what to accept as fact or take seriously. Ultimately, these sources and tools are meant to help you establish your target list. Beyond early identification, it will be up to you to get to know individual schools in a more tangible way.

The People in Your Life

Many people in your life may have thoughts about what school you should choose, yet the relationships and personal dynamics that drive these opinions should be noted. When receiving advice about schools from personal connections, ask yourself: what is the advisor's connection to the school? What is the advisor's connection to me? How will the advisor feel about where I (or my child) go to school, and whether I take the recommendation?

Advice from people you know can be tricky because many people who supply advice will be drawing too heavily on their own experiences. In some cases, they will be reliving their own time spent looking at schools for themselves or their children and projecting those views onto you. Even when this advice comes with the noblest of intentions, it can be a problem because you're not them—you're you. It's important to distinguish those whose advice is a reflection on them from those whose counsel has truly been considered with you in mind.

People from whom you might hear imbalanced feedback include those who are evangelists for their own alma maters, other parents with children the same age as yours, or close friends and family members who seem to have a very strong opinion on where you "should" go to school. Advice from these people must be regarded very differently from that received after speaking with a guidance counselor, admissions consultant, or mentor. It is the role of the latter group to be impartial and keep your best interests in mind.

A Note on Finding Local Schools

To the extent that you have a basic understanding of competitive schools in your area, many local school searches are halfway over before they begin. Yet if you live in a large metropolitan area or if you're looking for a special interest school (e.g., religious, performing arts, multilingual), there may be more options than you are aware of, even if you've lived in the area for a very long time.

If you're looking for schools on behalf of your children, getting the lay of the land via colleagues at work, neighbors, or friends with older children who have attended independent schools is a good idea. Chances are they will be aware of a universe of schools via their experience with their own children, and also through accumulated knowledge of many other parents and of their children's friends. Parents of older children will also have more feedback and observations about various schools than your own peer group, who may be—just like you—looking at certain schools for the first time.

Particularly if you're looking for preschools and kindergartens, contacting or joining a local parents' group may gain you access to shared knowledge and personal reviews. Other people who spend a lot of time with kids, such as seasoned babysitters or nannies in your network, may have exposure to families who sent their children to potential schools. As always, consulting anybody in your personal network is a judgment call—don't take to heart the advice of anybody whose values you already know you're not aligned with, or who seems unqualified to render an opinion. But do take advantage of the potential of personal networks for basic facts about schools and insights and opinions from people you trust.

An efficient local school search should also leverage the internet to query terms that will get you the most complete list of viable programs in the smallest amount of time. Suppose you are in search of a competitive high school in Chicago. Searching "Chicago private high schools" would yield good results, but so would a search on "Chicago independent high schools," "Chicago prep schools," "Cook County private high schools," "DuPage County competitive schools," "Chicagoland preparatory schools," etc. The point is this: expand the search for results in your own town, surrounding towns, relevant counties, using relevant nicknames for your geographic area (e.g., "Chicagoland" in Chicago, the "Bay Area" in San Francisco, etc.), and alternative or casual names for the types of school you are looking for. Beyond search engine results, it makes sense to go to the official web sites of the county in which you live and the cities or towns in which you would consider schools. Often, these resources list all schools—both public and private—under their domains.

Beyond Internet searches, it is also possible that somebody has written a book about relevant schools in your area. Many major metropolitan areas have had books published that index specific private schools, which would be well worth exploring. Even if the author's approach doesn't perfectly match what you're looking for, it's likely to save you some time and footwork.

Finally, comb local periodicals not only for rankings or listings but also for articles about individual schools. If this information does not seem easy to find via the publication's web site, take some time to call someone at the paper—perhaps an editor with a memory for relevant articles—to see what else you can discover.

RESEARCHING INDIVIDUAL SCHOOLS

While certain schools are highly transparent about the admissions process, some simply aren't. A glance at the University of Chicago undergraduate admissions web site, for example, reveals full statistics on the most recently admitted class. Very precisely, it states that the class of

2015 saw 21,762 applications; offers were made to 3,539 candidates and 1,411 candidates accepted. Beyond basic benchmarks, the school shares detailed information about gender distribution, public vs. private vs. international admit rates, standardized test score ranges, ethnic diversity, high school activities undertaken by applicants, and U.S. geographic distribution. Schools that present this level of detail are a huge asset to applicants because closely reading this will reveal a school's values. Understanding what a school values is critical to determining whether it is a place you truly want to be. If you decide that a certain school is a place you want to be, understanding what the school values and how it chooses applicants is key to getting in.

Unfortunately, most schools do not make this degree of detail so readily available. In fact, some schools are loath to supply any hard admissions data at all. This hoarding of admissions data may be motivated by several factors including:

- **The Competition.** Schools may not want to publish their own admissions statistics and standards if they fear that it will expose them to speculation about their standings vis-à-vis a competitor school. Suppose that one competitive high school publishes average admissions test scores in the 90th percentile, only to find that a competitor has published average scores in the 95th percentile. Some applicants and observers will conclude that the latter has a more rigorous program because a key application element has a more difficult requirement. In order to avoid unwanted comparisons to competitors, schools may opt out of saying too much.

- **The Culture of the School.** Schools with exacting cultures may be more inclined to publish quantitative admissions data. The appearance of detailed statistics on the University of Chicago web site is consistent with the university's data-driven culture. Schools with less of a cultural emphasis on precision and metrics may be less likely to publish this kind of information. Schools aptly recognize their willingness to participate in the game of stats and scorekeeping as reflective of their personalities.

- **Signaling Values.** Schools or programs that focus more on intangible factors such as artistic (vs. quantified academic) talent or overall fit may choose not to publish admissions statistics in order to signal to applicants that focusing on fit (and not numbers) is the wisest approach to the admissions process. Scores, grades, and demographics are important to every admissions committee, but candidates are not chosen by the numbers. Admissions committees wishing to signal a shift in focus away from the numbers may deliberately steer candidates away from this paradigm.

- **Testing the Tenacity of the Applicant.** Some schools will deliberately omit important data from the admissions process in order to be able to screen for truly engaged students vs. those who may have crafted their applications with virtually no interaction with the school. Schools must not only admit qualified applicants—they must admit applicants who are likely to attend if made an offer. Therefore, it becomes important to separate qualified students trying to get into as many schools as possible from qualified students who show a genuine interest in the school. Whether a student has truly gotten to know a school, done her homework, and come to understand a school shines through on an application. Sometimes a dearth of information comes from schools that want you to find things out on your own.

Sussing Out Standards

Research about an individual school's standards should always begin with a thorough read of the school's official admissions materials. Many secondary publications presumably copy and aggregate individual school stats, but it's easy for aggregator sites to become outdated, and sometimes even use some strange formulas that calculate general requirements according to averages of older data. If inspection of the school's web site and independently distributed admissions materials doesn't get you close to what you're looking for, don't be pushy about it, but do ask. For reasons cited above, some admissions committees are willing to say more in personal interactions than they are willing to put in print.

Some of the information that you will want to know about any school:

- What does the academic profile of a successful applicant look like?

- What is a typical GPA, test score range (or, for young children, skill proficiency level) for the students you admit?

- How many people do you admit to each incoming class?
- How does your commitment to diversity manifest in the admissions process? (Note: make clear that you are referring to class balance and target mix—not only ethnic/racial/gender diversity)

Beyond the stats are a set of other questions that are often overlooked, but are genuinely more important:

- What qualities do students who thrive at your school demonstrate?
- What does it take to be successful in your program?
- How high are your graduation/retention/transfer rates?
- What types of professions are pursued (or what schools are attended) by alumni of your school?

As always, when interacting with admissions committees, be polite and use a tone indicating curiosity and inquisitiveness, and not interrogation.

Social Media and Blogs

Many admissions committees have carved out a presence on popular social networking sites like Facebook, Twitter, and YouTube, for the express purpose of communicating to and interacting with prospective students. Sites like these offer unprecedented access not only to the independent commentary of a school's admissions committee, but also to the committee's interactions with other prospective students. By following the social media sites of the admissions departments of the schools to which you plan to apply, you will learn a tremendous amount about the process, as well as the culture of the school.

When used productively, these sites give an opportunity to have questions answered, receive real-time information about new developments in the admissions cycle, and to simply observe the type of content the committee is generating outside of answering inquiries and communicating about the nuts and bolts of the process.

But, be careful. Lack of etiquette, polish, and self-awareness still haunt the social media space. Don't fall into the same application-damaging mistakes that an astonishing number of prospective students do. Read your posts carefully before sending them. Check your spelling and punctuation. Do a gut check on whether your question or comment is tactful. Simply put, don't use language that portrays you as anything other than a mature individual who has done her research and has something valuable to add to the conversation.

> *Don't just pay attention to what the admissions organization has to say—if you really want to get a sense for a school, investigate other online places where members of the school community are speaking out.*

As well as highly interactive social media there are admissions blogs, which some schools host on the admissions area of their web sites. Though readers may typically comment on posts, the level of interaction tends to be lower and less direct than that seen on true networking-based social media sites, and much less conversational in nature. Still, well-written blogs can offer rich insights about a school's values, admissions process, and student life.

But don't just pay attention to what the admissions organization has to say—if you really want to get a sense for a school, investigate other online places where members of the school community are speaking out (student YouTube videos may be particularly interesting). These may also be found on general interest online media outlets (e.g., the Facebook or Twitter page belonging to a university as a whole, rather than the one belonging to that university's admissions department).

Graduation Rates

One way to anticipate the relative happiness and success of students at a school is to compare graduation rates. The way this is measured may vary widely and is hotly debated at the undergraduate level. Certain schools (particularly at the preschool and primary school levels) might not formally track this statistic, but should still be able to ballpark how many students in recent years have started, but not finished, the program. If you can get past a bit of data variance, this is always a telling statistic.

In addition to measuring retention (which can equate to the ability of schools to make students want to stay) and achievement potential (the ability of admitted students to succeed in the program), graduation rates often lead to secondary conclusions about the quality and potential fit of the school. Getting to the bottom of graduation rates can reveal things about the internal dynamics of a school. Whereas high turnover rates at one school may indicate a culture of motivated students using it as a stepping stone to trade up to something better, it may indicate dissatisfaction and gaps in the school's ability to help students succeed at another.

According to a study from the National Student Clearinghouse Research Center, approximately one third of students transfer away from the college in which they started. Statistics such as these highlight the complexity of the educational environment, and good intentions notwithstanding, prove how far removed getting into a school is from being able to be successful once there.

Workload and Stress

It's commonly speculated that only the "best" schools with the most achievement-oriented cultures carry a heavy workload for students who attend. Make no mistake: even when we're not talking about the top programs, it is still possible for students to get in over their heads if they choose schools with workloads beyond their comfort zones.

Choosing a program in which you will be overworked and overstressed completely misses the point of finding a good fit. Beyond strengthening knowledge through academics, students stand to benefit from building relationships with other students, faculty, and staff. They learn and grow by participating in clubs and student groups, and engaging in other areas of the community. They stay healthy by maintaining balance in their lives. The importance of choosing a program in which you will be positioned to participate holistically, and still get eight hours of sleep a night, cannot be overstated.

In some cases, a bad fit in terms of workload and stress extends beyond simple discomfort and can carry serious, if not tragic, consequences. Severe depression among young people is becoming more prevalent as parents (intentionally or unintentionally) place more performance pressure on their children. The stakes are simply higher than they used to be, and even young children begin to feel very early that parents have anxiety about their performance in school, and, frequently, stress about paying for school as well.

In 2010, *the Daily Beast*, a division of Newsweek, ranked the top 50 most stressful colleges by weighting tuition (35 percent), academic rigor as recorded by U.S. News (35 percent), acceptance rates(10 percent), the presence of graduate engineering programs(10 percent), and crime rates(10 percent) at top universities. The study found that suicide rates at top universities broadly correlated with the criteria of the study. Some colleges may even be known for their suicide rates. Cornell University, for one, had 15 students commit suicide via jumping off of area bridges and into gorges between 1990 and 2010, according to an August 2012 article in the Ithaca Journal.

AVOIDING COMMON TARGETING MISTAKES
Applying to school can feel like an endlessly long, confusing and emotional process. It's easy to become fatigued and disoriented as it goes on. As you go through the process, from time to time (not just when you're creating your initial list), check in to ensure you're not making one of several targeting mistakes.

Common Targeting Mistake #1:
Choosing Schools Based on Statistics and Rankings
Many students have their sights set on going to the "best" schools they can get into, as defined by national publications like *U.S. News and World Report*, or by locally-respected publications if searching for preschools, primary, secondary schools, or regional colleges and universities. The problem with choosing your own target schools solely based on external rankings is that, even if you do get into a top school, your own personal experience of attending that school, and the results you think you will see, will be below-average—if it is not a good fit.

Certainly, rankings are relevant, and the results cultivated by students and alumni are important to consider, but rankings should be one of many considerations. A look at retention rates proves that not all students do well at great schools, and that many choose not to stay.

> *You will not know your actual out-of-pocket cost for any school until you apply, get in, and receive a financial aid package.*

Consider Harvard University's freshman retention rate, which, according to a 2006 to 2009 U.S. News study, stands at only 97 percent. Based on an average incoming class size of about 1,650 students, this means that roughly fifty students each year decide, within a series of months, to leave. Given Harvard's stature, it is unlikely that most students who leave after freshman year are "trading up" for a more favorably regarded school. So, it is plausible to think that many of the fifty freshmen who leave Harvard each year simply aren't happy, so much so that they are willing to leave one of the most respected institutions in the world.

Common Targeting Mistake #2:
Weeding out Expensive Schools Too Early

Many students and parents don't bother applying to schools with hefty price tags, knowing the tuition is more than they can afford. While I do not recommend attending a school that you can't manage financially, the fact is you will not know your actual out-of-pocket cost for any school until you apply, get in, and receive a financial aid package.

Don't dismiss this advice. I mentioned in the introduction that I was not a 4.0 student. In fact, I applied to (and got into) three of the top ten business schools, with a 3.16 GPA. I was certainly not the most promising student to be considered for any of the programs I applied to. Yet, two of the three aforementioned programs offered me full tuition fellowships (one of them even included a $20,000 annual living stipend); the third awarded me a $20,000 grant. The offer I took added up to $160,000 in free money that I would have never received had I not bothered to apply to this school.

What you see listed as published tuition and estimated living and incidental costs shows what will be paid by students and families who don't apply for or who are deemed ineligible for aid. Yet nearly all competitive schools offer financial aid programs, and a large percentage of students typically receive some aid. Also, scholarships offered by the schools aren't the only source of funds. Private scholarships, grants, and fellowships may also be pursued. These are not guaranteed, and you certainly can't count on free money, but you also should not rule it out. (The one exception to this rule pertains to international students. Often, U.S. schools place full cost responsibility on non-citizens.)

The best advice is to apply to some schools that are a good fit and that are affordable, but also to some schools that are a great fit that you don't think you can afford. Give yourself the space to make a final decision when you know your final costs and have all of the facts.

Common Targeting Mistake #3: Distraction

It is easy to become distracted by shiny new facilities, star faculty, flashy statistics, and all manner of other impressive morsels that may make a school seem attractive. Ultimately, what may impress you on a campus tour or in a profile piece may actually be tangential to your desired experience. This isn't to say that impressive data points are to be ignored—only that they shouldn't hold sway over your decision if they're not critical to what you're really looking for.

I recently toured a boarding school that was in the home stretch of a multi-million dollar gymnasium and sporting facility remodel. Seeing the truly spectacular sports complex was among the most memorable highlights of the tour, but if strong athletics were not close to my hypothetical list of wants, amazing athletic facilities should not be a compelling reason for me to attend a school. Similarly, I attended a school which, in its marketing materials, boasted that more Nobel Laureates in economics were affiliated with it (as either graduates or faculty) than any other school on the planet. Again, very impressive, but that was irrelevant to my decision process given my lack of interest in studying economics.

The antidote to becoming distracted is to have a good sense of what you're looking for—and better yet, to have documented it so that you can scrutinize early contenders in concrete terms. For example, if you care very much about music as part of your general school experience, any school with weak music programs should be removed from consideration, no matter how impressive the school is across other dimensions.

Common Targeting Mistake #4:
Following Your Friends and/or the Crowd

It's popular for both students and parents to be lured by the idea of attending programs that friends or close acquaintances are planning to attend. Reasons for wanting to follow others can be complicated. Parents may be motivated by not wanting their child to feel lost or alone in a new place, or by "keeping up" with other families. Children (particularly high school children) with a close-knit group of friends or a girlfriend or boyfriend headed to the next level of schooling may want to preserve the relationship by attending the experience.

This can be a mistake, of course, because what is right for your or your child's friends may not be right for you or your child. If you are having trouble convincing yourself or your child that separation for the sake of educational choices is natural, remember what was said about fit. If you take the time to find a school that is a good holistic fit, finding people you connect with and making new friends won't be a problem.

> *If you take the time to find a school that is a good holistic fit, finding people you connect with and making new friends won't be a problem.*

Common Targeting Mistake #5:
The Blind Leading the Blind

The tech-savvy crowd will find plenty of online communities to meet like-minded applicants looking to share empathy and information. Some of my own fondest memories of applying to business school recall the *Business Week* message boards (now Bloomberg BusinessWeek message boards) on which MBA hopefuls from all over the world collectively lamented the obscure admissions practices of top schools. (As you might imagine, for the quantitatively-oriented engineering types who typically apply to business school, not knowing the formula for admission was particularly painful.) Forums like these can be valuable places to find support during uncertain times, and, occasionally, can be good sources of information. But before listening to the advice of anyone in such a community, remember this: most of them are in the same boat as you.

> *If you take the time to find a school that is a good holistic fit, finding people you connect with and making new friends won't be a problem.*

Given this fact, learn to regard much of what you read on forums like this as highly speculative. Did the person who just spewed out a two-paragraph diatribe about what Columbia is really looking for actually go to Columbia, or is he applying this year, just like you? Chances are, if he's on an admissions forum, his situation is similar to yours. Always take that into account. It's fine to pay attention to and engage in what's written on these boards, but carefully think through what you decide to believe. By maintaining clarity and perspective throughout the process, you will optimize your position.

> *An ounce of performance is worth pounds of promises.*
>
> -Mae West

CHAPTER VII
GRADES AND TEACHER EVALUATIONS

Most people know that grades (or, for younger children, skill proficiency reports) are very important, but few understand how much weight they will actually carry on active applications. This is because most applicants cannot anticipate the way in which the reputation of the grade-awarding school is taken into consideration. Many parents mistakenly believe that if their child simply gets straight As, they will be able to get into a great college, but this is just not the case. Grades and proficiency reports are very important, but they are a fundamentally imperfect measure of performance. Applicants can get a better sense for the extent to which their grades will truly help or hurt their applications by tempering the quality of the grades themselves with the quality of the school that issued them.

WHY GRADES MATTER
Admissions committees care about grades for two reasons: first, they help to measure your performance vis-à-vis others in your class; secondly, depending on the caliber of the school in which you earned the grades, they may begin to tell a story of your overall academic aptitude.

For example, a mediocre student at a school with a track record of turning out high-performers may be more desirable to an admissions committee than the best student at a school with a low bar for academic achievement. For this reason alone, target GPAs (if admissions committees even publish them) may be the least useful benchmark to try to match.

Grades are also important because they serve as the best indicators of subject-specific aptitude. Contrasted with standardized tests, grades tell a more complex story. For primary and secondary school children, grades show aptitude in the arts, language, science, and other areas that don't easily reveal themselves through standardized tests. For college and post-graduate work, grades also allow a student's interests to shine through, bringing one's chosen electives to light and telling a more complex story of interests and aptitude.

For certain schools, particularly those with a specialized focus, grades are extremely important when performance in specific subjects clearly indicate the applicant's abilities vis-à-vis a specific program. For example, a school like Juilliard cares very much about the rigor and performance related to prior musical training. Similarly, a school like MIT, with a majority of programs in the scientific and engineering fields, may hold particular value for the breadth of exposure to, and performance in, courses requiring quantitative skills.

Specialized program focus is yet another reason to put less credence in target GPA as the almighty indicator of your individual standing. Depending on what you and the school are focused on, certain grades may be favored over others when considering your application.

YOUNGER CHILDREN AND TEACHER EVALUATIONS

While younger children may not be issued grades, developmentally- and academically-oriented early childhood education centers may issue detailed skill and behavior assessments. It is not uncommon for the parents of one- or two-year olds enrolled in learning-based child care centers to receive skill evaluations for children whose age is still being commonly referred to in months!

When applying children to preschools, it is routine for target schools to ask for teacher evaluations in a format provided by target schools.

Questionnaires typically focus as much or more on developmental milestones as on personality and temperament. Schools without traditional A through F grading systems tend to rate age-appropriate skills on a three-tiered scale—something akin to Developmental/Average/Proficient, to indicate whether a child is behind, on par with, or ahead of the curve.

> ## *It's important not to fall into a common trap: overestimating your school's standings based on too shallow a pool of feeder schools.*

If your toddler has been cared for at home, or attends a child care center that does not routinely issue report cards, the lack of visibility into your child's development may be frustrating for parents given the preschool admissions process. Unless you are trained in early childhood education, you may have no structured insight into how to understand or self-report your child's development, nor may you understand how your child's teacher views his or her holistic development. For the purposes of applying to preschool, sitting down with your child's caregivers (who may have formal training in early childhood education) should yield good insights and give you a preview of what will be said on the application. If you have raised your child from home and feel that lack of a professional opinion will weaken your application to a very competitive preschool, you may want to consider getting an independent assessment and seeing whether the preschool will consider it.

HOW DO YOUR CURRENT AND PRIOR SCHOOLS STACK UP?

Even if you believe you know your current and prior schools' reputations, it won't hurt to update your knowledge. Public school average test scores and graduation rates are often available through state and local web site archives. Compare your school's scores with state averages to understand how your school has performed vis-à-vis others in the state. If you have attended private schools, there is a good chance that local media or an independent school association in your area has issued awards for excellence or created lists of rankings.

It's important not to fall into a common trap: overestimating your school's standings based on too shallow a pool of feeder schools. Your school district or local private schools may be the best in your immediate area, but this only matters if most other applicants to your target school are applying only to schools in your area.

For example, if you're the parent of a child applying to a private high school, chances are that the local reputations of feeder schools will be extremely important. Yet when your child applies to college, the local reputation of the high school will matter a lot less than the school's state or national standings. This is because college applicants will hail from a much wider pool of schools; the relative ranking of your child's school will be different than what is known locally.

If you come from a poorly performing school, don't panic. This does not mean that admissions committees will automatically assume that you are lagging behind. This is where standardized tests play an important role. For top students from poorly performing schools, admissions committees will rely on standardized test scores to assess whether candidates are also top achievers with respect to the wider population.

HOW FAR GOOD GRADES GET YOU

Good grades prove that you are a high achiever within your own environment. They prove that you understand what is expected of you, and that you possess the ability to work to the standards set forth by your current school. The higher you rank in your class, the greater the indication that you have a personal commitment to excellence. Good grades across multiple subjects show a well-rounded intellect and a versatile mind that can be successful in excelling at many different subjects.

Depending on the rigor or focus of the school, they may signal other qualities. A high GPA at a very competitive school signals superior commitment and abilities, while outstanding grades in related domains (e.g., music and foreign language) might signal predilection to a particular talent. Perhaps most importantly, good grades signal that you are a driven, disciplined individual, who takes academics seriously and whose work ethic, when applied to talent, produces good results.

WHAT TO DO IF YOUR GRADES ARE BELOW YOUR TARGET

Grades and teacher assessments are the single element of your application that can't be changed or improved. You can prepare well for interviews, craft wonderful essays and short answers, and even retake standardized tests. But how prior programs have scored you is something you cannot change.

You can, however, explain your performance. If you believe your grades are a problem, it's a good idea to do so if there are mitigating circumstances the admissions committee should be cognizant of. I faced this very issue when explaining my 3.1 GPA to MBA admissions committees. For my first two years of college, I had maintained around a 3.7 GPA, which dropped dramatically in my junior year when I studied abroad in Paris. But there was a good explanation: I had squeezed four semesters of French into the summer between sophomore and junior years so that, once in Paris, I could take all of my classes in French.

Explaining this achieved a number of things. For one, it proved that I didn't get lazy, or simply discard my commitment to academics in order to gallivant around Paris for a year. I believe that it actually worked in my favor, showing that I was willing to undertake the difficult task of trying to become fluent in French in a single summer. It showed that I was willing to sacrifice my GPA for the sake of the ultimate goal: enriched learning. By the second half of my year in Paris, I had become so good at French that I was one of eight students selected to attend a class at l'Institut des Sciences Politiques, a prestigious college in the Paris university system. Though my grades suffered, I remained committed and I succeeded. It made for a great story on my application.

Most people have other, more common, reasons for dips in academic performance. Did some event (such as a personal or family tragedy, a health issue, or some other personal struggle) impact the candidate's performance at a specific time? If so, it's important to mention this in a way that doesn't make excuses for poor performance, but acknowledges that there were real life circumstances that led to the performance lags. In cases of adversity, candidates will ideally be able to show that grades were pulled back up at a later time.

Also, if you have below-target grades at a difficult school, don't worry: admissions committees will factor in the rigor of your program. Test scores will also sweep in to show your overall potential.

If you simply have below-target grades, without any mitigating factors, be ready to make other aspects of your application shine. Be prepared to advocate that much harder for why you deserve a space in the incoming class of your target school. Admissions committees may wonder whether students with below-target grades have the personal commitment and aptitude necessary to do well in their programs. Any other area of your application in which you can demonstrate these will become doubly important.

CHAPTER VIII
THE ROLE OF STANDARDIZED TESTS

The role of standardized tests is frequently misunderstood, though not in the same way as grades. Admitted class test scores published by schools are commonly regarded as minimum requirements for admission rather than what they truly are—averages that encompass a range of accepted scores. They show that some percentage of applicants scored below what was listed and still got an offer from the school. Admitted class scores are different from prerequisites, which a relatively small number of schools use to formally name a minimum test score requirement for admission. When self-assessing the strength of your test scores, it's appropriate to apply to schools if your scores are reasonably within their range. If your scores are at the lower end of the range, you can work to successfully demonstrate other strengths and holistic fit.

WHY THEY MATTER
Standardized tests are one of the few mechanisms in the admissions process that truly level the playing field. Whereas grades are relative to the rigor of an individual school and interviews are subjective, test scores go further than any other evaluation tool to place candidates on common ground.

Of course, test scores aren't everything, and a look back at the fundamentals makes it easy to understand why. Test scores measure only those dimensions of a candidate's qualifications that speak to skill, aptitude, and knowledge. Yet the best schools routinely pass over applicants who seem to have pure intellectual horsepower and not much else. The myth that the most competitive schools simply choose the "smartest" students with the best test scores is simply not true.

So, why do test scores matter? Because schools want to know whether candidates have aptitude in the specific type of intelligence needed to excel in their programs. For example, the Law School Admission Test (LSAT) tests logic, reading comprehension, and verbal reasoning—three skills that are critical to understanding the material to be taught and keeping up well in law school programs; they are also the skills necessary for doing well in typical post-graduate career paths such as attorney, law maker, politician, and judge.

In addition to wanting to know whether aptitude is present at all, schools use scoring tiers to understand the degree of aptitude. Broadly speaking, higher scores indicate that students will be able to start at a higher level and move at a faster pace once enrolled in school. The best schools want high test scores because they want to move through the material the fastest, helping their students reach an extraordinary level of knowledge and capability by the time of graduation. Low test scores are a hindrance (but not always a deal breaker) to those aiming for top schools, because admissions officers aren't sure whether candidates with scores outside of the target range will be able to keep up.

WHEN TO TAKE THE TESTS

It's always a good idea to take tests early enough in the process to allow you to retake them if you are dissatisfied with your score. Even if you feel confident that you can deliver a great score on only one pass, remember that illness, fatigue, or unexpected stress on test day could throw off your performance.

It won't hurt for parents to think in the same terms when planning testing for their children. Everyone has bad days, and children can be particularly sensitive to external factors, depending on their ages. Timing testing to allow for retakes is a wise hedge against less than ideal circumstances.

There is no downside to testing early—if you achieve your target score, some degree of mental pressure will be alleviated and you can move on to other things. Better yet, it will leave you ample time to make an excellent effort in other areas of the process. If you don't do as well as planned, the gap between your actual and target scores will give you valuable feedback around what end result you can realistically expect. They let you know whether you're close to hitting your goal or if you are even in the same ballpark. They let you regroup, rethink, and check your expectations. Either way, it will help you realize where you stand, sooner.

To determine when to take your test, first understand the delay in delivering official scores and the deadlines of your target schools. Though most tests taken on a computer will tell you your score immediately, there is often a delay in having official scores issued. Some tests taken on paper take weeks to score, let alone have scores issued to target schools. The first test should be taken far enough in advance to receive the scores, study for a second test if necessary, take the second test, and have the official scores available in time for application deadlines.

It's also a good idea to factor in other priorities that may compete with your ability to study for the standardized test(s). Particularly for graduate school applicants, who theoretically can set their own study schedules, it's easy for good planning to lead to good timing. Younger students may still be learning the skills necessary to do well on tests, in which case, operating on a tighter schedule may be warranted to enable children to build necessary skills. In cases where children are too young to pursue that kind of rigor, it is more acceptable to allow children to simply take the test at their current level of development, without significant study. Alternatively, some wonderful books have been written on play-based skill building for very young children. Also, if you want to prepare your toddler for preschool and kindergarten evaluations, some good books have been written on the topic.

WHETHER TO TAKE A PREP CLASS

Preparation courses such as Kaplan or the Princeton Review help students across two dimensions: classes are structured to help students build and expand upon critical skills through instruction and practice, as well as to employ pacing and problem-solving strategies that will help them manage the time constraints of the actual test.

While prep classes can't hurt, they offer no guarantee that they will make students do better on a test, or that they will yield better results than a student would find through independent study. They do, however, add structure to the study process, and instill students with test-taking skills and confidence. They can be of particular help to procrastinators, students with poor study skills, and personalities who work well under deadlines imposed by other people.

> *If the student is a naturally self-motivated and self-disciplined type, she will do fine on her own without the assistance of a prep course.*

Taking a prep class (if you can afford one), will teach you problem-solving and time-management tricks that you may not come up with on your own. However, much of what is offered through prep classes is simple practice—running drills on as many questions as possible, taking many timed practice tests, identifying areas of weakness, and developing a strategy to tackle troublesome questions.

If you or your child lacks self-motivation, internal discipline, or good study skills, and a prep class is not in the budget, create a study timeline similar to those of the big testing companies in order to stay on track. Also, if the test-taker responds better to external motivation than to self-motivation, designate a person or create a system that can hold him or her accountable. In this case, make sure the person or system chosen to keep the student on track is somebody or something the student will actually respond to. (In other words, a parent might not be the right person to keep a teenager positively motivated to study for the SAT unless the natural tone of the relationship can withstand it.) If the student is a naturally self-motivated and self-disciplined type, she will do fine on her own without the assistance of a prep course.

WHETHER TO HIRE A TUTOR FOR AN OLDER CHILD OR ADULT

If a prep class won't fit into your schedule or isn't financially feasible, it's easy to hire a tutor who is familiar with the test. This comes at a fraction of the cost of an entire test prep course and allows you to focus on your weaknesses. Typically, the most desirable tutors are those who are proficient not only in the skills tested, but with the test itself, and who know how to teach the material. Current and former instructors from test prep outfits such as Kaplan and the Princeton Review frequently hire themselves out for the purposes of supplying individual help. Increasingly, the test prep services themselves are offering a tutoring option, though this may be less flexible and more expensive than finding somebody on your own.

When approaching a tutor, you'll get the most for your time and money by coming to sessions prepared with questions you've gotten wrong as well as a general understanding of which categories or areas are your weakest. Standardized tests are fairly formulaic, so if there is a type of problem you're having trouble with, learning how to do better at answering that type of problem can pay dividends. Ask your tutor to explain the rationale behind right and wrong answers and to give you tips on solving problems that you find difficult—and then, tips on doing it quickly. This option is also worthwhile for students already taking test prep courses who still need extra help.

TEST PREP AND YOUNG CHILDREN

Test prep/tutoring for children in preschool and primary school is a taboo subject, and rightfully so. Barring any defensible learning deficiency on the part of the child, such acts are most often symptoms of anxiety on the part of parents. It's clear why parents want their children to get into good schools—ultimately, the deepest hope is that children are positioned for security and success in life. Yet engaging relatively young children in formal test preparation carries as many risks as it does rewards.

The largest risk to enrolling younger children in test prep relates to signaling. It tells children that something hugely important is on the line and that it will matter very much—particularly to you, whose approval they deeply value—how well they perform on this task. Beyond preparing for the test itself, they will pick up on any other anxiety you may be feeling about the application process. Even if you save most of your conversations about their school search for times when they're not around, they will have already gleaned from other clues that what is happening is critically important. Add to that the admissions events they'll suddenly spend their weekends attending, having to dress in their finest clothes, and needing to be on their best behavior during interviews and other strange situations.

Do you see what I'm getting at? The more that elements of the process infiltrate their lives, the sooner they will come to understand, and become impacted by, the intensity of the admissions cycle. Though parents may be emotionally prepared for this, younger (and even older) children may not yet have the psychological tools to survive the pressure unscathed.

Before deciding whether to enroll a younger child in test prep, think about the potential payoffs. Is your child already well-prepared and you're just looking for an extra edge? Or does your child truly have some skill deficiencies which, if addressed, could help your child not just on the test but in other areas of development and education?

HOW FAR GOOD SCORES GET YOU

If you've taken the test and scored within your target range, congratulations! Now is the time to move on to other things. But don't be fooled—scoring well is a mark in your favor, but good scores alone are not enough to get you into the school of your choice. Great scores will get you so far as proving to the admissions committee that you have the intellectual skills to survive the program. But bear in mind that many other applicants will have achieved high scores, and it is incumbent upon you to use other areas of the application to show that you would be a good fit for individual schools and an asset to the school community as a whole.

WHAT TO DO IF YOUR SCORES ARE BELOW YOUR TARGET

If your first score falls below the target, assess what might have caused you to score lower than you wanted. The first time I took the GMAT, I ran out of time on the final section and left seven questions unanswered when the clock stopped. I knew that when I retook the test, better time management would be essential. If other easy-to-interpret events occurred—such as you being ill or tired on the first test day, your task is to do enough problems each week to keep your skills fresh until you can take a second test.

Suppose you felt fine, finished the test, maybe you were even confident in your answers, but found that you scored below expectations. In that case, it's time to do more practice questions to see in what areas you need help. If you are scoring well on practice tests, but you did not score well on the exam, you may need a harder set of practice questions. Find a resource that drills using sample questions that are noticeably more difficult than the ones you've been practicing with.

What if you've been through the process twice, your scores remain below target, and it's time to submit your applications? Your next steps will depend on how far out of range your scores are with respect to benchmarks named by your target schools. If your target schools ask for scores in the 90th percentile, and you are in the 75th or 80th percentile, it's time to rebalance your list to include a majority of schools in your tested aptitude range. Scores aren't everything, but schools will not admit you if they doubt whether you can keep up with the curriculum—your target list should find at least half of the schools you apply to within your target testing range. If your scores are in the 85th percentile and you're aiming for a large group of schools with 90th percentile targets, do an assessment of all other areas of your application to figure out whether, realistically, you have enough other attractive qualities that would cause the committee to care less about your score.

Now it's time to focus on the rest of your application. If your scores are not where you feel they need to be, look at your profile for other evidence of qualities that prove you can keep up with the work. Find ways to make a case for how you might thrive in a challenging academic environment. It is always possible to take weaknesses in your application and neutralize them, or even turn them into strengths, by finding creative ways to balance or address them. If you believe there is compelling evidence that you can keep up with the work, despite what the test scores say, work it into an essay answer, something you say in the interview, or how you answer any catch-all questions.

HOW MANY TIMES TO TAKE THEM

Some people who don't get the test scores they want after two tries may be tempted to continue until they achieve their target scores. Yet, multiple retakes (even if the target score is eventually achieved) rarely have the desired result. In the applicant's mind, scoring inside the target range convinces the admissions committee that he is qualified to attend. However, an applicant who needs three or more tries to qualify may rouse suspicion that he needs extra time or special study in order to perform similarly to candidates who scored well the first time.

The assertion that admissions committees only look at the highest score and/or only take into account the final score you submit is, in my opinion, dubious; and the fact that not every school is willing to look at only your best score serves as evidence that some schools think the number of times you have taken a test matters. Even if the official policy of a school is to only consider a single score, a reader privy to complete test-taking history may read into this knowledge. Multiple retakes, if transparent to the application reader, are difficult to ignore.

The least desirable scenarios would find a candidate taking a test multiple times, yet seeing only marginal change. This signals to the committee that significant improvement, despite additional study, isn't possible. The worst case scenario would find a candidate regressing (scoring worse on tests subsequent to the first), calling into question the viability of the first (and, by then, the best) score. Barring extenuating circumstances, I don't recommend taking any test more than twice.

A final note: persistence to the point of obsession reflects badly upon applicants. It's one thing to show drive and perseverance and another entirely to spend months on a single test. The central lesson is clear: take the test very seriously and give it your best shot from the very beginning. Chances are that if you study the material well and take full practice tests early on, you will be adequately prepared to get the very best score you can the first time.

> *When you're looking [at] math and languages, if you fail to master one (basic) class, you'll fail the other one above it. We do need prerequisites to show the kids what bar they need to reach. Otherwise we're giving kids whatever they want.*
>
> -Jeff Conklin

CHAPTER IX
INDIVIDUAL SCHOOL PREREQUISITES

Prerequisites vary by school, so they may very well cover a broad range. In some cases, schools set forth minimum guidelines that all students must meet prior to the first day of school; in other cases, schools want to know how a candidate performs on additional standard measures to help them assess his readiness for their programs. Typically, prerequisites are designed to test for one core necessity common to every school: students who can keep up with the curriculum. Schools demand certain prerequisites to screen out students who they believe might fall behind, and to set the baseline for skills that are needed to succeed in their program.

PREREQUISITES FOR YOUNG CHILDREN
Since toddlers, at preschool age, are still learning basic life skills, it's common for schools to look for benchmarks of self-sufficiency. Schools dealing with toddler age groups often name successful toilet training as a non-negotiable prerequisite; most competitive schools are looking for this and other evidence of independence at all ages in the preschool to kindergarten range. Capabilities like feeding and dressing oneself, managing one's own belongings and other self-care skills may be on the table, and may be specifically required by the school. By explicitly

naming them as prerequisites, schools are signaling that it is the parent's responsibility to teach their children these skills and that children may be expected to demonstrate them during the application process.

Birth dates can make a big difference in terms of the readiness of young children to enter school; consider the child whose fifth birthday makes a published cutoff date vs. the child who is eleven months older, about to turn six, and therefore missed the previous year's published cutoff date by one month. Therefore, it's common for private kindergartens to set benchmarks for incoming-student skills. It's a challenging task to get children with varied backgrounds on track to begin learning within a common range, and for the most selective schools, to have children ready to learn at the high benchmark set forth. Consequently, kindergartens set guidelines that let them establish a baseline of capabilities they expect for all admitted children; this also serves as a signal to parents whether their children are ready for the rigors of the school's curriculum.

Often, children who don't exhibit the emotional or academic readiness to enter kindergarten at the parents' desired age are encouraged to attend a pre-kindergarten program to build necessary competencies. Behaviors that have to do with separating from parents, following directions, responding to authority, and being open to discipline all have an impact on a child's readiness to learn. *Behaviors* are distinct from *skills*; the former are typically observed in interview settings and the latter may be specifically named as requirements. Candidates whose children simply require further development, but who may otherwise be a great fit for the school, often apply successfully to the kindergarten in a subsequent year.

Prerequisites for private kindergartens vary greatly, depending on the school's rigor. Increasingly, pre-kindergarten programs also have prerequisites. Unlike higher grade levels, which typically have prerequisites that can be evidenced on a paper application, most prerequisites for young children need to be witnessed—consequently, most prerequisites at this age are addressed in the interview setting. Skills like counting, recognizing numbers and colors, reading or writing short words, sorting by shape, using short patterns, demonstrating an understanding of opposites, and showing an understanding of the concept of time may be observed. These are discussed at greater length in Chapter 15, which discusses interviews.

Most schools are candid about the skills they want children to have, and children are expected to demonstrate these skills at the time of interview and application—not the time of admission. Though some parents may be tempted to prepare their children by drilling them based on prerequisite lists, it is important to remember that the requirements exist for a reason beyond simply being admitted. It would be unwise to place your child in a position in which she can pass the test, but does not know skills well enough to keep pace in the target environment.

ADVANCED PLACEMENT AND HONORS COURSES

Even if Advanced Placement (AP) or honors courses are not officially required, their successful completion sends a strong signal that a student can manage additional academic rigor. In the case of AP courses, which are designed to mimic college-level courses, schools surmise that high-schoolers who succeed in AP courses can be successful in standard courses at college. Similarly, honors courses at the middle school level may signal readiness for AP courses in high school.

According to the College Board, "Many colleges recalculate applicants' GPAs, giving extra points for honors or AP courses," and they go on to say that the National Association for College Admission Counseling's (NACAC) annual State of College Admissions survey "consistently finds that student performance in college preparatory classes is the most important factor in the admission decision." Though I believe the last statement must be taken with a grain of salt (increasingly, more than enough students are able to prove readiness, making admissions increasingly about factors beyond basic aptitude), I do agree with the overall sentiment. Doing well in AP and honors courses sends very strong supporting signals.

COURSE-BASED PREREQUISITES

As early as middle school or high school, and continuing into college and graduate programs, some schools want to see that specific courses have been pursued. At the middle and high school levels, some competitive schools operate on a track that may be one or two years ahead of typical grade level curriculum. Prerequisites offer schools the opportunity to screen out candidates who may not be ready for their advanced curricula. For example, if your child is applying to a high school that finishes with algebra by grade ten and is on to trigonometry and calculus by eleventh and twelfth grades, the school may want to be sure that your child is ready to hit the ground running with Algebra II in ninth grade. In cases like these, criteria may be explicitly named as prerequisites, and not preferences, because the school sees no feasible way to work around the absence of a necessary skill.

At the graduate level, a school may also require specific courses that align with its core curriculum. These prerequisites are also driven by practicality: if you don't have good foundational knowledge in an important topic area, schools can't see how you will comprehend, participate, grow, and learn.

CONCENTRATION/MAJOR-BASED PREREQUISITES

Some graduate schools require, or strongly suggest, that you hold a previous degree in a relevant field. As with all prerequisites, they want to know that you have an aptitude for and a proficiency in certain kinds of work. Unless you have a very compelling case and hard evidence of proficiency in areas in which you did not major, you probably won't be successful in applying to a school for which you don't meet the prerequisite. Even if you do have that hard evidence, you will still need a compelling story to tell about your goals and what may seem (to some) like a counterintuitive choice.

Suppose you do hold a major, but the grades you received in the major were poor. This can also impede you tremendously from achieving your goal. For schools with a specific area of study or specialization, your track record of performance in that specific area is disproportionately important. A track record of interest and commitment are important, but proficiency is king.

UNOFFICIAL PREREQUISITES

Some programs, particularly those at the graduate school level, may not officially require applicants to have completed a certain undergraduate major—yet, in practice, they admit a majority of students with very similar backgrounds. The pre-med "track" rarely requires a specific major, yet students majoring in biology, organic chemistry, and physics often knock out many med school course prerequisites through the requirements of those majors. Something similar is true for law school: there is no such thing as earning a pre-law major at most schools, but the American Bar

Association readily acknowledges that many law students major in "history, English, philosophy, political science, economics or business."

> *If the majority of people applying to your program have a very specific background that is different from yours, it makes sense to start thinking of yourself as having an "alternative" background.*

If you don't have (or don't plan to pursue) coursework through the unofficial prerequisite path, don't worry. Unless particular courses are listed as official prerequisites by your target program, you are not required to have taken them. That said, if the majority of people applying to your program have a very specific background that is different from yours, it makes sense to start thinking of yourself as having an "alternative" background. Anticipate what an admissions committee member may view as a gap in your application by understanding the courses that many of your competitors have taken, which you have not. Be prepared to show evidence of relevant proficiency that parallels any classes you may have missed.

TEST OF ENGLISH AS A FOREIGN LANGUAGE (TOEFL), THE INTERNATIONAL ENGLISH LANGUAGE TESTING SYSTEM (IELTS), AND OTHER LANGUAGE REQUIREMENTS

Schools want to be certain that you are proficient in the language in which classes will be taught and that will be spoken in most official settings. If you are an international student applying to U.S. schools at the collegiate or graduate level, chances are you will have to take the TOEFL or IELTS to prove English language aptitude. Remember: schools want students who can thrive in the academic environment. No matter how smart or talented you are, you cannot be successful in a program through sheer intellectual horsepower alone. Inability to prove that you can speak the language can be a deal breaker, even for candidates who are ideal in every other respect.

Since it's not enough to simply comprehend a language aurally, most proficiency tests contain elements of speaking, reading, and writing—this also tests practical comprehension via the conversational portion of the test. It is not sufficient for a student to merely understand a lecturer or to be able to read a text; to fully engage in the community, students must be comfortable and capable to speak up in class, express themselves clearly on assignments and tests, and interact effectively with classmates. In the absence of these capabilities, students simply cannot thrive.

As with all prerequisites, cramming to pass the test in the absence of true proficiency defeats the purpose and misses the point. Foreign students who struggle with language proficiency should invest substantial time in building English language skills well before it's time to take the test. If you arrive at a school with inadequate English language skills, you run a serious risk of being asked to leave—I've seen it happen. Work hard at building those skills before you take the test—retaking it too many times may be a signal to a school that you will never get up to speed.

CONDITIONAL ADMITS

Some schools will admit students who still need development in certain areas on the condition that the student attains those skills before the first day of school. For example, certain MBA programs require all incoming students to take college-level calculus and statistics. Many applicants will have already taken those courses, but for applicants who have not, equivalent courses are recommended, if not required. Some schools also recommend refresher courses in core topics for incoming students who have not had recent exposure to the subject matter. This may be especially true of graduate schools willing to admit students with real-world track records of success, but who may be removed from academic connection to the subject.

WHAT TO DO IF YOU FALL SHORT

If there is a prerequisite that you lack simply because you haven't pursued it, move forward and get it done. Sometimes prerequisites are easy to fulfill for people who are confident in their aptitude, and simply need to take the time to prove what they are capable of.

In other cases, the ship has sailed and little or nothing can be done in the near-term about the lack of evidence of a certain aptitude (e.g., you didn't major in your target graduate school field in college); or, perhaps aptitude is forthcoming but not quite where you want it to be (e.g., your child doesn't hit all the readiness marks for your target kindergarten). If this is the case, you can still apply and make a case for yourself, but be cautious and honest in thinking it through: given the circumstances, do you (or does your child) really have the skills to thrive in the program without the cultivation of additional proficiencies?

If you have missed the mark in some other, more permanent, way (e.g., you scored below target three times on the TOEFL), it may be time to rethink your path. Though falling short of prerequisites can feel disappointing, it can actually be a blessing in disguise. Most private schools are designed to be challenging even for the most qualified students, and those who are not truly ready for the workload may face serious practical consequences and emotional challenges as they scramble to get up to standard.

> *I'm not telling you it is going to be easy–*
> *I'm telling you it's going to be worth it.*
>
> -Art Williams

CHAPTER X
FILLING IN THE GAPS

Any fact, opinion, or logic that would raise a red flag for the reader or trigger an unspoken fear creates a gap, or an area of weakness, in your application. Before submitting your application, take the time to think about whether you have any gaps. For some applicants, gaps will be obvious (e.g., below-average grades or scores); for others, the gaps may be harder to find (e.g., a lukewarm recommendation from a person who was designated as a recommender but who may not like you). Either way, it behooves you to be honest with yourself about what questions or concerns an admissions committee might have about you while reading your application.

STEP #1: FIGURE OUT WHAT'S PROBLEMATIC

Obvious gaps are elements that you are proactively worried about. These are things which, if you received a rejection, you would immediately suspect detracted from your application. You may be a foreign student with low TOEFL scores. Perhaps something in your past left a stain on the overall picture of your academic performance, like being held back a grade or taking six years to graduate from college. Maybe you were suspended or expelled for reasons that portray you in a very bad light. Maybe you're sure that one of your required references will give you a terrible recommendation. Obvious gaps have the potential to cast serious doubts about whether you are ready for a given program; they usually involve aptitude questions, performance weaknesses or reveal facts about you that carry some sort of stigma.

> *The gaps you identify should provide a roadmap for choices you will make when crafting the messages in your application.*

Less obvious gaps expose major contradictions to common logic, like applying to a program that emphasizes math and science despite showing no previous interest in either of those disciplines, or to a bilingual school when you have little to no knowledge of the second language. A subtler example of this is applying to a school for which you simply don't fit the typical applicant profile. To the extent that may raise questions on the part of committee members, it must be treated as a gap. These types of fissures may cast serious doubts about whether you are right for a given program, or at least create a big question mark about why you are pursuing a given path. Any element of your goals that may be counterintuitive, or any factors that may not be easily understood, can be considered gaps to the extent that they require additional explanation.

STEP #2: DECIDE HOW TO ADDRESS IT

At this point, you already have a wealth of information about how to address certain gaps. This book has been deliberately written in such a way to help you infuse your application with information and context that constantly validates your potential to excel on your chosen path. For example, effectively answering the two central questions discussed earlier (*Why this path? Why this school?*) should have allowed you room to figure out how to address gaps like major contradictions in logic. Guidance on how to answer essay questions that open the door for you to humbly address growth areas and frame weaknesses is forthcoming.

Essentially, the gaps you identify should provide a roadmap for choices you will make when crafting the messages in your application. You can't reverse doubts the admissions committee might have about you unless you are positioned to address them.

So, if you are applying to a highly quantitative program, yet you have very little advanced math on your transcript, you should pre-identify that as a gap and look for opportunities to address it in a short answer or essay question. If you have low grades or test scores, when answering application or interview questions you should plan to mention other evidence that proves your academic aptitude. Similarly, if your prior education doesn't match your target school, but your work experience does, it is essential to crystallize these qualifications within the framework of your applications. Admissions committee members read a lot of applications and may be tired and overworked during admissions season. It's necessary for you to make important points very clear, anticipate even small questions, and proactively address potential doubts.

For example, my own undergraduate degree was in Foreign Language and Globalization, yet I made the decision to apply to two of the most quantitatively rigorous MBA programs in the world—the University of Chicago and the Wharton School of Business. I had only worked in online marketing since graduating from college, so it was not obvious from my work experience that I had any quantitative aptitude. I knew that many others applying to MBA programs had engineering or finance backgrounds and that, by contrast, I would be viewed as weak in these areas. The onus was on me to proactively show that I could handle all of the statistics and math.

Here's how I did it: I showed the admissions committee that online marketing is not about soft skills. I talked about how I did statistical analysis on web traffic for my early employers and their partners, and later for my own clients; I explained how I had to draw business conclusions that synthesized large and often ambiguous data sets describing user data such as country of origin, browser of origin, click and conversion paths, bounce rates, site visit times, and many other factors. Finally, I showed my commitment to further educating myself in quantitative topics by mentioning that I was taking two courses—one in statistics and one in calculus—through the continuing education program at New York University. I was successful in getting in to both of these schools, and after graduation, I went on to work in finance.

The bottom line is this: if you believe you are qualified to attend a program but you see how the admissions committee might not draw the same conclusion, you have to connect the dots for them. Doing this effectively not only improves your chances of admissions—it gives you the opportunity to demonstrate good communications skills, good logic, and the critical thinking skills that enable influence and persuasion.

"IS THERE ANYTHING ELSE YOU'D LIKE TO TELL US?"

Many school applications provide space for additional information that you feel would help the committee make their decision. This space should be used if there is some relevant piece of information that had no natural place elsewhere in the application. Generally speaking, this is not a place to put "closing arguments" (that is, it should not be used as a place to make some general, final appeal to the admissions committee about your candidacy). This space is truly for those for whom some special situation, mitigating circumstance, or other pertinent fact needs to be communicated. If the assessment above has led you to the conclusion that you do have a mention-worthy item to share with the committee, take some time to think about the facts, and also the message you want to convey. If you do choose to utilize this bonus question, be humble, be tactful, and—above all else—be authentic.

Explaining Why You Didn't Follow an Instruction

Some applicants may need to provide an explanation for why something that was specifically requested is missing from their application, or why something that was not requested has been added to the packet. For example, at the time I applied to business school, I was running a company that was completely owned and managed by me. Therefore, instead of including recommendations from supervisors (which I could not do because I had no supervisor), I included references from clients. I briefly explained this when presented with this bonus question on my applications.

Acknowledging and explaining why you didn't follow an instruction shows that you had a reason for disregarding certain guidelines. Failure to explain your reasoning (even if you think it should be self-evident) may cause the admissions committee to view you as rogue, or inattentive to detail. Admissions officers may be tired, time-crunched, and inundated with other applications while they are reading yours. Make it as easy as possible for them to keep track of what's going on, by taking a moment to show them.

Explaining Negative Performance

If negative performance can be traced back to a decision or circumstance, your discussion of the situation should make clear that you are giving an explanation and not making an excuse — particularly if you are explaining negative performance. Show the admissions committee that when faced with adversity (self-imposed or not), you found a way to persevere. In many cases, bad decisions or outcomes ultimately create better decisions and good qualities. Make sure to give these qualities a chance to shine through.

For example, if you are the parent of a young child whose behavior suffered at some point (suppose your child was hitting or biting at school), you can be sure that this fact will come to light through previous teacher assessments. Answering the bonus question (or even attaching an explanatory letter to your application if no such question is asked) gives you an opportunity to show what the current status of the behavior is and what steps your family took to remediate it. If a target school hears from a previous school that your child had behavioral problems, the target will be looking for evidence that the family is committed to doing whatever it takes to address them. Answering this question gives you the opportunity to address the school's unspoken fear — that the burden of disciplining your child for the sake of the other children's safety might fall on their shoulders if you are not sufficiently engaged.

Poor performance may also have been caused by some sort of trauma, tragedy, or life change. What if a death in the family, a serious illness (on the part of the student or a family member), a move to a location, a divorce, remarriage, new baby, or any other major change created some temporary difficulty in focusing on school work? If this was a real factor in your (or your child's) performance, it's fine to give facts about the circumstances and, again, to show what was done to get performance back on track. The goal here is to help the admissions committee view your application through the correct lens. If the reason for a performance drop-off was something other than the work being too challenging or because you were lazy, it makes sense explain.

Finally, suppose that you are applying to graduate school and your GPA is lower than target because you performed poorly freshman year. Perhaps the real reason is that you went out with your friends every night and didn't take going to class and doing your work seriously. Maybe your performance was so bad that you came close to failing out of school, and even much better performance during sophomore, junior, and senior years never fully repaired your GPA. Maybe your cumulative GPA is 2.8 but would have been 3.8 without your disaster of a freshman year. In a case like this, answering this bonus question will help your application. Telling your authentic story will show that you are willing to admit (and correct) your mistakes; it will show that you learned and grew as a person, became more mature and responsible. It will make you more human. Admitting mistakes always makes you seem more honest, which will lend credibility to other areas of your application.

> *Admitting mistakes always makes you seem more honest, which will lend credibility to other areas of your application.*

Explaining a Problematic Relationship

You may have a complex or problematic relationship with a person who was required to contribute to your application. This is most common among applicants who are being asked for the recommendation or reference of one specific person who cannot be chosen from a group of several possibilities. Your child's only teacher (if there is only one in his or her classroom) or advisor may dislike you or your child; or, if you need a professional reference from your direct supervisor, it may be the case that you have a troubled relationship with this person. Since there is only one of him or her, you may be stuck with asking this person for a reference.

If this is the case, and you suspect that a person who had to contribute to your application will not portray you or your child in a favorable light, you may want to acknowledge to the admissions committee that the relationship is strained. But be cautious. It's important not to seem petty, not to point fingers, and to be tactful and discreet. Your goal in mentioning the strained relationship is to signal that you and the person in question don't see eye to eye; it's your job to do so without getting into the details of the soured relationship. Sending this signal is important, because without it, the committee will assume that the reference is somebody you trust to assess your capabilities. If the relationship has a checkered past, you must let them know, tactfully.

One way to address this is to include a recommendation or reference from an alternative person in addition to the requested person. Then, in reference to the bonus question, you could say something like: "I am including an additional recommendation from a former supervisor/teacher who I feel is in the best position to comment on my/my child's strengths and weaknesses. Though I honored the committee's request for a current supervisor/teacher reference, I do not believe that I/my child have/has formed a meaningful relationship with this supervisor/teacher. I would like to give the committee the opportunity to hear from another person who has formed a deeper relationship with me/my child. I hope you will take this additional reference into consideration."

Ultimately, the committee will decide whether or not to use the second recommendation, and will draw its own conclusions about whether it thinks the original reference's opinion is valid. Your only job is to give the committee context you think is relevant to help understand your application. Be careful of your tone, but don't be nervous about explaining real mitigating factors like these. The price of silence might be rejection. After all, you don't want to become a question mark if the committee can't understand why your application looks stellar with the exception of a single bad recommendation. In this case, a simple explanation could go a long way in framing the dynamic.

Explaining Anything Else that Might Look Bad
Rule #1 for how to handle anything that might look bad is this: under no circumstances should you pretend that it doesn't exist. You can be sure that if you've been expelled or suspended, have a large gap in your work history, or lack some core prerequisite or qualification, the committee is wise to this gap and has taken notice. By not addressing this, you'd be doing two things: 1) leaving the story to take on a life of its own in the application reader's imagination, and 2) subtly signaling that something might really be wrong because you don't seem to want to talk about the big pink elephant in the room.

Your best bet in this situation is to observe a basic rule of public relations: own the story. If you want the admissions committee to see things your way, you have to be willing to communicate your point of view. By not addressing this, you are missing the opportunity to explain why a certain path and a certain school still make sense, despite something that has happened in the past. In some cases, it is *because* something bad has happened that we are motivated to do, and be, better. As always, don't be dishonest and don't pander to what you think the committee wants to hear. But if you made a mistake, admit it, and show how you have grown.

Let's consider the example of a person with a gap in her work history. There may be an explanation that exposes an extraordinary quality or character trait. For example, suppose she took two years off of work to care for her ailing grandmother, or undertook some other honorable task that would not be listed on a resume as a job. These are important facts that should be mentioned, and would answer any questions or suspicion around the work history gap. This shows, again, where a little bit of explanation can go a long way.

Suppose, on the other hand, the work-history gap was due to a layoff or some other factor beyond her control. Layoffs have a stigma attached to them because of the belief that low performers are let go while high performers are allowed to stay. Though I don't believe most admissions committee members hold this old-fashioned view of layoffs (particularly in a recession economy), it will still help to state the reason for the gap instead of letting it remain a question. Additional context may also help your case. For example, if you were part of a 10,000-employee layoff, say so. Such a detail makes it clear that a general downsizing—not your individual performance—was the cause losing your job. Similarly, if your entire department or line of business was cut, relay that information. Being a victim of circumstance is very different from being fired from your job for non-performance.

Again, make sure your tone is humble, and neutral. You are not making excuses or placing blame. You are making sure the committee has all the facts before making its decision.

HIGHLIGHTING AN EXTRAORDINARY ACCOMPLISHMENT

Generally speaking, you should try to highlight your extraordinary accomplishments somewhere other than on the bonus question. Most applications are designed to allow you to showcase strengths and weaknesses. If you have done something extraordinary, if you've won an award or competition, committed some act of kindness or charity, or performed some amazing athletic or physical feat, look back at the main essay or short answer questions and see whether you can frame the answers to those through the spectacle of your amazing accomplishment. In other words, I am cautioning against using this space to continue tooting your own horn unless there really was no other place in the application to include information about your extraordinary accomplishment.

PART IV:
CRAFTING YOUR STORY

> *Actually ideas are everywhere. It's the paperwork, that is, sitting down and thinking them into a coherent story, trying to find just the right words, that can and usually does get to be labor.*
>
> -Fred Saberhagen

CHAPTER XI
COMPLETING THE APPLICATION FORM

Application forms used to be paper things that came in packets you ordered directly from target schools, filled out by hand, and (if you were thorough) sent in via certified mail. By now, many paper application packets have been replaced by downloadable forms, if not application systems, that ask the applicant to submit all information online. If both options are available to you, you may want to deliberate about whether you prefer one format over the other. This brief chapter will review some considerations that apply to paper vs. online application forms, and to filling out application data in general.

PAPER APPLICATIONS

Paper applications have their advantages. For one, they let you preview the entire application before you have to start filling it out. Requests for standard information about you will be the same across all applications, but it can be nice to learn of any out-of-the-ordinary requirements and read essay and short answer questions ahead of time.

They also allow for you to add a bit of personalization. Reading a typewritten form feels pretty dry and impersonal compared to a handwritten one. If you have supremely legible handwriting and can appreciate the value of a little personalization, handwritten applications are for you.

A final advantage involves avoiding some shortcomings of how online applications may appear to admissions officers. A paper copy of your resume that you have formatted attractively will win out against the version of your resume admissions officers will see as it displays on a computer screen, or from a system printout. Aesthetics matter, and the better-looking and easier-to-read your materials, the more appealing they will be, however subliminally. By submitting a paper application, you will maintain a great deal of certainty about how it will look to a committee member.

Yet, there can be disadvantages to paper applications: poorly constructed ones may fail to leave enough line space to answer certain questions, and can be generally out of proportion vis-à-vis the requested information and the room provided. Something as simple as having a long name that doesn't fit neatly on a line in a paper application can make you look sloppy, even if the application itself is the culprit.

That said, if you have a choice, and you like the idea of paper application forms, only use them if you can fill them out neatly. You can feel free to use typewritten documents for any enclosures (e.g., essays, letters, resumes).

ONLINE APPLICATIONS

Online applications have accelerated in use because they allow schools to manage the process better. Paper applications require manual verification on the front end (e.g., *Is the application complete? Do we have essays, recommendations, and all other supporting materials?*) and data entry on the back end (e.g., *Who is getting offers? Who is waitlisted?*). They can also create high printing costs, a need for physical storage and hard document archiving, and force admissions committee members to come up with complex logistics for managing multiple reads of a single hard copy. It's no surprise that paper applications are becoming a thing of the past.

With online application systems, schools can maintain a constant, real-time understanding of the number of applications have been started vs. completed (by students), whether supporting materials have been submitted, whether reviews are complete, and what the decision of reviews was. Online applications also give greater confidence that certain materials (such as recommendations) are secure (rather than forged or otherwise manipulated), and they make it very easy to communicate admit or deny decisions to applicants. Finally, online applications make analysis of the applicant pool very easy—for example, if all students enter their test scores into an online system as part of the application, it's very easy for admissions committees to run reports in any configuration they'd like about elements like average test score. Online applications relieve an administrative burden.

Yet, despite being easier for admissions committees, and easy enough for web-savvy students and their families, online applications leave more than a little to be desired. As with paper applications, they are only as good as the person who designed them and some are more user-friendly than others.

Completing an online application typically requires users to create an account that can be logged in to multiple times in order to complete the application piecemeal. Schools with online applications won't expect you to sit down and complete the application in a single sitting—naturally, you will have to gather supporting materials and think through the answers to certain questions. There is usually an opportunity to review a long-form version of the entire application at the end. It's a good idea to proofread this version for quality, and to print out a copy for your records.

While some schools maintain a neutral position about which application they would like you to use, it is increasingly the case that schools express a strong preference—if not a hard requirement—that candidates apply online. Smaller schools and schools at the preschool, primary, and secondary school level are currently less likely to utilize online application systems. Over time, as such systems become affordable for smaller schools, this may change.

COMMON VS. INDIVIDUAL SCHOOL APPLICATIONS

At some education levels, a common application is offered at the discretion of individual schools. If nothing else, the mere existence and increasing adoption of common applications is a testament to the idea that schools are fundamentally looking for the same things. At the undergraduate study level, many major colleges and universities have pledged to use a common application as the school's only application—as of the writing of this book, that number stands at 152 and includes colleges such as Amherst, Oberlin, and Swarthmore and universities such as Tufts, Stanford, and Yale. In addition to allowing students to use the common application, some schools offer the option (or maintain a requirement) to supplement with elements of its own application, which may ask different or additional questions.

In other cases, common applications may be required to gain some special opportunity or advantage. The Consortium for Graduate Study in Management is a high-profile competitive fellowship program that offers full tuition and fees to MBA hopefuls who may be targeting any of the eighteen member schools that participate in the program. Schools in the current member group include the University of California at Berkeley's Haas School, Dartmouth's Tuck School and the NYU Stern School of Business, and candidates may apply to up to six member schools with a common application. The advantage to candidates is hundreds of dollars of savings in application fees and a guarantee that at least one offer of admission will come with a fellowship that fully covers tuition and fees. The disadvantage is that, even if a student receives admission offers from multiple schools, she will be offered a maximum of one fellowship from one school. Consequently, the student benefits from an easier application process but will miss out on the possibility of receiving individual financial packages from each accepting school. There can be no way of knowing under which circumstances the student may have been better off.

Views are changing about common applications, as is their ease of use. Traditionalists who believe in historical norms insist that it is necessary to fill out individual school applications as a signal of extreme interest (which, admittedly, remains important in getting an offer from a school). Increasingly, some admissions experts are backing away from that view, and schools are making it easier to allow a common application to comprise 90 percent of the requirement with an option (or mandate) to supplement the common application with materials that apply directly to the target school. In my interviews with current admissions officers, opinions were split: pragmatic types appreciated the efficiency of a streamlined process and felt that standard applications still offered more than enough information to make good decisions about candidates, while others felt that only their individual school applications allowed candidates to paint the picture of themselves that would be most useful to the committee.

I'll be honest. If I were applying to school, and multiple application fees were within my budget, I would use individual applications wherever possible. Whether individual applications are valued over common ones is likely to depend on the culture of the individual school, and unless you have total visibility into how much one is valued over the other (which you probably do not, unless the school explicitly names a preference), I think it's better to play it safe.

If numerous individual application fees are unaffordable, go through individual target school applications and figure out which ones seem to ask questions that are a bit different. From there, choose the schools with the most unique applications, and complete those individually, while economizing with the others by using the common application. Beyond that, find other ways to communicate your interest in schools for which you have submitted a common application—for these schools, underscoring interest will be doubly important.

WHAT SCHOOLS WANT TO KNOW ABOUT PARENTS

If you are applying on behalf of your child, you may notice that a great deal of information about the entire family is requested on the application. This isn't merely administrative (that is, schools don't just want the parents' names and mailing addresses in order to know where to send the bill). In some cases, schools request a statement from parents (generally short essays or short answers) as well as from children. Schools want to fully understand what kind of home a child comes from in order to gauge how much support the candidate is likely to receive from his family, and whether any personal issues will be brought into the classroom.

If you are a parent, be prepared to be asked about your profession, your marital status (and if you are divorced, in whose home the child lives), what languages you speak with your child at home, and what schools you have attended (though this question has become less common). If a parent is deceased, there is typically a space to indicate that as well. Discussing siblings (how many there are and their ages) also gives schools context regarding the family situation. These elements combine to paint a picture of the child's life at home.

For example, the only child of two married parents, both of whom are post-graduate level professionals, is likely to have a very different support structure than a child in a family of four other children who are all younger than the applicant and parents who are divorced and never completed college. It's logical to conclude that the first child will benefit from the undivided attention of parents who themselves have strong study skills and years of experience completing academic programs. The second child is unlikely to get as much parental attention, may have more responsibility at home (in terms of helping with the other children), and the quality of the help the parents provide may not be as robust given the parents' own education level.

But let's go a bit deeper: only children come with their own set of challenges and developmental quirks as a result of limited feedback from and co-existence with sibling-peers, just as children from large families learn certain social adjustment and co-habitation skills (not to mention maturity) inherently. I don't believe that most schools have a single family ideal they are looking for. Though they do want evidence of sufficient support at home, they are simply looking for information that can help teachers and administrators understand circumstances that will help the future student to be more successful.

Schools also want to understand—if parents are separated or divorced—how strong the partnership between the estranged parents is. In order for children to be successful in challenging programs, parents need to form a united front. Schools don't have the resources (or the inclination) to step in and provide excessive academic and emotional support when the family unit falls short. Schools need and expect a certain level of engagement from parents, and these questions help schools anticipate various outcomes.

If you are applying on behalf of your child to a K-12 school, you may see some version of the following two questions designed specifically to screen for current or potential challenges your child might be experiencing:

- Please describe any circumstances which have affected or may affect your child's academic performance, participation in school events, or attendance in school (e.g., frequent moves, changes in schools, separation of a significant person in the family, disciplinary actions, serious illnesses or learning disabilities).

◆ Has your child had any history of a physical or emotional condition which has required professional attention or which might require special attention?

Questions like these, though delicate, are actually a great gift to applicants. This is because they designate a space for you to talk through difficult issues, rather than forcing you to feel awkward or uncomfortable bringing them up in another context.

Finally, if you are applying to a boarding school for your child, you are likely to be asked questions designed to gauge whether your child is ready to live away from home. Can your child independently maintain his living space? Does he have the emotional maturity to separate? All of these are critical indicators of your child's readiness.

LEGACY INFORMATION

The legacy question may take several forms, if it appears at all. Some schools (even very old ones) don't directly ask whether anybody in the candidate's family has attended the school in question. In the case of schools that do ask about family ties, schools for younger children are often asking for practical purposes (e.g., Does the candidate have any siblings currently enrolled in the school? Does the candidate have younger siblings?); in these cases, the school wants to understand the extent to which the candidate's enrollment in the school may follow in the footsteps of, or blaze the trail for, brothers and sisters.

Other schools ask about specific family members who have attended the school. In these cases they are trying to ascertain whether any close relatives tie in. It is not uncommon to be asked whether parents or grandparents have attended the school—this guards against applicants pulling in distant relations that schools care a lot less about (e.g., a great-step-uncle, or fifteenth cousin thrice removed). Finally, some schools leave it open-ended and simply ask whether any family member has ever attended. In these cases, admissions committees will decide whether the specific relationship creates a relevant tie.

For the purposes of the application, I advise naming any logically relevant familial ties to the school. This includes people who have a legitimate close relationship to the applicant (include stepparents—particularly ones who raised or are raising the applicant), and does not include people with a tangential relationship to the applicant (such as in-laws, for adult students). It won't reflect well upon applicants who lay claim to legacies if there are no meaningful ones.

So, why is one relationship more meaningful than another, and why are legacies relevant? In a broad sense, legacies may indicate a tradition of commitment to education within a family. If a parent and a grandparent attended the target school, it signals that the candidate probably understands and embraces the school's academic standards; it also indicates a better-than-average chance that the candidate knows the school's values and culture. Finally, legacy from close relatives shows that the candidate has probably been raised in an environment that will help her meet expectations. For this reason, legacies who are distant relatives are weaker connections because there is no logical reason why somebody outside of a close family unit would instill the candidate with a deep understanding of, and appreciation for, a school.

If you have a legacy relationship to a school and you are not directly asked about legacy, but you feel a strong tie to the school because of that relationship, it is appropriate to bring that up in the application (perhaps in an optional essay or as part of an interview). It is not recommended to use a legacy as a name-drop alone (which would not reflect well upon the candidate if presented without context or connection), but rather to mention it only if it is truly relevant to the candidate's motivations for attending the school. For example, throughout my childhood my father talked endlessly about his experience at NYU, and it truly influenced my interest in the school, my familiarity with the culture, and my desire to apply. To the extent that I could tell substantive stories about it, I mentioned it during the application process.

A FINAL NOTE ON APPLICATION FORMS

Application forms may feel mundane and tedious to fill out, but they are still important, and taking the time to complete them thoughtfully and with attention to detail will make a difference. Even if it feels as if you can fill out facts about yourself or your child in your sleep, take the time to proofread and, for short answers, take the time to construct well-written sentences. Thoughtfully-completed application forms are critical to cultivating an application for which whole adds up to greater than the sum of its parts.

> *Letters have to pass two tests before they can be classed as good: they must express the personality both of the writer and of the recipient.*
>
> -E. M. Forster

CHAPTER XII
GATHERING RECOMMENDATIONS

Candidates commonly underestimate the critical role they play in helping chosen individuals craft effective recommendations. In most cases, they simply hand off pre-formatted instructions to willing supporters, leaving them completely on their own. Yet providing just a bit more up-front guidance to their benefactors will yield dividends for the applicant while also giving recommenders the focus needed to help them best carry out the task.

Whether a recommender is teacher who does this for many students each year, or someone else from your network who writes such letters only once in a blue moon, a few good practices will ensure better results. The trick to approaching those who will write many recommendations in a single season becomes one of helping them to remember your most redeeming qualities. This type of recommender may be overwhelmed by the task of supporting many applicants inside of a short time frame—your task is to make their job easier by being as organized and helpful as possible.

The problem with leaving the infrequent recommender on his own is that even if he wishes to say glowing, fantastic things about you, since writing such letters is rare, he may not have the best idea of what the committee is looking for. Even if your recommender once walked the same path as you (e.g., is an alumna of the target school or graduate from the same kind of program to which you are applying), he may be years removed from the process, and therefore disconnected from what approach can help you the most.

Here's where you come in. Your job is not to coach your recommender on what to say, but rather to provide a framework that goes further than the brief (and frankly, inadequate) instructions appearing on most school admissions forms. Your recommenders want to help you. This chapter is dedicated to choosing the right advocates and setting them (and you) up for success.

WHY RECOMMENDATIONS MATTER

I could list ten reasons why recommendations matter, but a single one trumps them all. Recommendations are critical because of their potential to make you stand out next to many other applicants who seem similar to you on paper. Admissions officers will read hundreds (if not thousands) of applications every season and may read a dozen or more in a single day. It is difficult to get into a competitive school if your recommendations fail to add color and personality to important indicators of your performance.

> *Recommendations are critical because of their potential to make you stand out next to many other applicants who seem similar to you on paper.*

This is an important distinction for those who think that a simple positive recommendation is enough. A letter in which your advocate gushes about your finest qualities, vouching for you in strong, certain, language but lacking any stories or examples to make his claims come alive can, at best, be considered only "good." Recommendations don't cross into the realm of "great" until and unless they show the reader something that the more quantitative elements of your application could never, ever show.

HOW TO CHOOSE PEOPLE YOU WILL ASK TO VOUCH FOR YOU

The first step in securing recommendations that make your application more competitive is to identify the people who can tip the scales in your favor. This is rarely straightforward, as most schools already have in mind the type of person they want to write the reference. In order to be successful, you must choose somebody who fits the requested profile, but who also has the skills and motivation to execute the request in such a way that will yield above average results. Some rules of thumb for choosing the best recommender follow.

Include the School's Choice Recommender. If a school asks for recommendations from a specific person, such as current or former teachers, professors, direct supervisors, etc., by all means, narrow your search to the requested pool. Believe it or not, some people ignore this request, and when they do so without explanation, it is always a red flag. It signals that the candidate may have ignored the request because no person the target school considers important could be trusted to say something favorable about the candidate. It also sends a message of arrogance, conveying that the candidate believes himself to be above following the rules.

Schools ask for specific references because they want to hear what somebody who has observed you in a specific capacity has to say. For example, kindergarten candidates are almost always asked for recommendations from a preschool teacher, MBA candidates from a current or former supervisor, etc. Requests for specific kinds of references typically align with a school's desire to know targeted information about how you have performed in a proxy environment.

Sometimes there are good reasons not to address a target school's request, but if you take that route you must explain why. For example, if your child's teacher who observed him for most of the year just went on maternity leave, you may decide that the brand new substitute teacher who barely knows your child at all may not be the best person to give a recommendation. In this case, ask the admissions committee whether they would accept a recommendation from a teacher who has known your child for longer, or at least who has witnessed your child's progress over time and understands some competencies better than the new teacher.

Similarly, if current colleagues or supervisors are not aware that you are applying to school (and you don't want to tell them) ask whether there is a substitute recommendation that you can provide. Or, if the person who was requested has since left his or her position for some other reason and cannot be reached, explain your situation. What is not acceptable is to seemingly ignore the admissions committee's request by supplying an alternative recommendation without explanation. If you go off script, ask permission and explain why.

Choose People Who Will Say Favorable Things About You. It also sounds intuitive to choose people who will say favorable things about you, yet I have read dozens of applications that took subtle, or even blatant, jabs at the candidate in question. Beware the recommender who may acquiesce to the job out of a sense of duty, but who may not be a true believer or supporter. If the recommender is lukewarm about you, or even hostile, believe me—it will shine through.

Ask yourself: *Would this person feel obligated to write a recommendation for anyone in my position, or is it clear that this person has taken a special interest in me? Is it part of this person's job description or a professional expectation that he/she supply recommendations? How many other letters of recommendation do I suspect that this person has written or will write this year?* Again, if you are being asked for a recommendation from a person in a specific role, it may be difficult to freely choose your strongest advocates. In this case, do the best you can. But don't be afraid to use whatever wiggle room you have to choose those who will have the very best things to say about you.

For example, suppose your child had two preschool teachers, a head teacher and an assistant teacher, and the assistant teacher really loved and connected with your child. Even though the head teacher may be more senior and seem like the more natural choice to write the teacher review, go with the assistant teacher.

Or, if you are being asked for a current or former employer and your relationship with your former boss is better than the one with your current boss, go with the former, even if feedback about you from your present boss would be more current. Such maneuvers allow you to follow the rule while allowing you to be portrayed in the most favorable light.

The intention here isn't to mislead the admissions committee in any way, or to be dishonest. The goal is to be thoughtful about making sure the person you ask really knows and cares about you, rather than defaulting to somebody who might not take the process seriously or have your best interests at heart.

Choose People Who Really Know You. How well somebody really knows you will be evident in the recommendation. Letters from someone who really knows you will better be able to tell pertinent or even poignant stories, and display a more heartfelt and genuine tone. One common mistake is to choose as a recommender a person who has a great deal of influence or cachet but who may not be able to speak convincingly about your merits. For example, receiving the recommendation from the head of an academic department at a high school or university will be an excellent addition to an application only if the recommender has something compelling and personal to say about the candidate. If the recommender barely knows the candidate and cannot share stories that demonstrate the candidate's merit, somebody with a more genuine connection to the candidate would have been a better choice.

> *A recommendation claiming that a candidate is a good citizen is weaker than one that cites an example of a candidate organizing a community service event.*

Choose Good Storytellers Who Have Stories to Tell About You. When choosing recommenders, look first for people who know you enough to have some good stories to tell, or illustrative examples to back up their claims. A recommendation claiming that a candidate is a good citizen is weaker than one that cites an example of a candidate organizing a community service event. Similarly, a recommendation claiming that a candidate is a capable public speaker is weaker than one who describes a speech the candidate gave that received a standing ovation. Choosing people who can go *beyond simply telling* admissions committees how wonderful you are, but instead *showing* what an asset you would be to their school will make an invaluable contribution to your application.

While you should screen recommenders for their storytelling abilities, after you have made your choice, gently make your recommender aware of the "show, don't tell" strategy. This can be conveyed during a conversation that takes place after he or she has agreed to help you but before the recommendation has been written. Invite the person to tell any memorable stories about you that show qualities that are relevant to the program to which you are applying, and let them know that specific examples will go the furthest in supporting your application.

Choose Good Writers. Choosing recommenders who are good writers may not always be an option, but if all else is equal and you have a great writer and a mediocre writer to choose from, go with the former. Even those who are tremendously supportive of you may not be the best choices if they have trouble communicating effectively in writing.

Bad writing is a problem for several reasons: primarily, thoughts that are unclear or poorly crafted will not accurately convey what the recommender intends. Bad writing also makes the writer sound less intelligent, and less intelligent people are regarded as less credible. Good writing, of course, has the opposite effect. When ideas are presented clearly and with good logic, they are more likely to be taken at their word. Consciously or not, we all react more favorably to better writing.

Look for evidence that potential recommenders are effective written communicators. If you can track down papers, articles, or presentations they have written, wonderful! (This may apply in academia.) If not, go for something even simpler: how well-written are their e-mails? If you are looking at a teacher or supervisor, how well-written is commentary on report cards or performance reviews? All of these will be good proxies to determine whether writing is a strength or weakness.

If you have identified somebody who is overarchingly qualified to give your recommendation but who is not a great writer, help the recommender by providing extra guidance in terms of how to structure and organize the letters of recommendation. You can do this without being offensive by handing them an article about how to write effective letters of recommendation (a good one is available on my blog), under the auspices of giving them a time-saving tool that nudges them in the right direction in case they have not done something like this before. If you are inclined to give this nudge, exercise good judgment, extreme respect, and tact.

Choose Somebody Who is Qualified to Judge Your Readiness and Aptitude for Your Target Schools. Whenever possible, it helps to choose a recommender who can credibly assess your readiness for the next step in your education or for a particular school. For example, if you are applying to a creative writing program and are invited to supply a personal reference, it is fitting to choose somebody who has pursued the same degree, understands your target program, and can supply an opinion as to how well he or she thinks you will do. Similarly, if you are applying to a specific school and an alumnus of that school knows you well enough to write your recommendation, it will strengthen your application for your advocate to say that he or she believes you will excel in the program.

If you have chosen a recommender partially or fully based on this quality, be sure to ask the person to mention his or her own background in the letter. Sometimes recommenders will be so focused on saying nice things about you that they forget to supply valuable (and helpful) background information that legitimizes their qualifications for rendering an opinion about you.

HOW TO ASK

Giving some thought to how you will approach a recommender is the first step to cultivating a positive experience. Asking somebody for a recommendation is a signal that you respect their opinion and is also a gesture of trust. Often, the very act of asking for a recommendation can strengthen a relationship.

Showing that you have prepared and that you're treating the interaction with a bit of formality will signal that you are taking the act of applying to school seriously. By setting such a tone, you can hope your supporter will take the process seriously as well.

The following are some simple guidelines to help you ask potential targets for a recommendation. They are written with elements of courtesy, good organization, and a commitment to authenticity in mind:

Schedule a Short Meeting. However easy it might be to ask—and get agreement—in passing, it is far better to spend at least a few minutes chatting about your plans. A recommender can write a letter that aligns best with your own thoughts on the matter only if he knows what those thoughts are. The best letter of recommendation will give you not only a glowing review, but harmonize with the story that you, yourself, have told. A short meeting with your recommender will get you both on the same page and yield a better letter.

Prepare an Elevator Speech. Let the person know, briefly, why you are pursuing this next step in your education, how this fits into your long-term goals, and why you think you are qualified to pursue this step. This will help your recommender understand your motives and queue up a reaction that reveals how he feels about your plan. If you ultimately ask him, and he ultimately agrees, this exercise will have started him thinking about insights and observations that might support you.

Ask Questions That Start a Two-Way Conversation. Asking questions about your recommender's thoughts on your pursuit of this path can be a rich experience, particularly because your supporter may give you insights you haven't considered. The feedback and commentary your recommender gives you with respect to his reaction to your plans may also give you a view into what the recommender is inclined to say in the letter he writes to the admissions committee. However, don't treat the conversation like a recon mission—it's not about fishing to get a précis of the letter. Show a genuine interest in knowing how a person who can speak to your strengths and weaknesses views your plans and you are likely to learn something that will help you grow. And, don't forget, you can always...

Abandon Ship if Necessary. If, through your conversation, it becomes clear to you that your recommender is lukewarm about you or your choice to apply to your target programs, don't be afraid to abandon your plans to ask for a recommendation. Your goal in asking for recommendations is to find people who will understand and support your plans, and who can speak independently about their support. If the person you thought would be willing and/or wholly supportive turns out not to be, step back and don't ask for a recommendation.

If you get the sense that somebody you've already asked has agreed grudgingly, and may not write you a favorable recommendation, find a way to ask somebody else and remove the original person from the rotation. If it is your responsibility to collect sealed recommendations, simply discard those from the original person without sending them in. If it is incumbent upon the original person to submit electronically, find a graceful way to withdraw your request before the person has a chance to write it.

Ask Only if It Feels Right. If the conversation has gone well and you believe your recommender supports you and has something to add to the conversation, conclude the meeting by asking for the recommendation. If you receive consent, move on to the next steps.

HOW TO HELP YOUR CHOSEN REFERENCES ONCE THERE IS AGREEMENT

Once you have received agreement that your supporter is willing to write you a recommendation, take a bit of time to make sure she has all the guidance she needs. This advice will be less relevant if your supporter is a teacher, professor or manager of many employees—people in these roles are frequently asked for recommendations, and if you have followed earlier advice about choosing a good target, your supporter is likely to be fine on her own. But if you get the sense that your reference is competent, but inexperienced or rusty at writing recommendations, observe the following practices to get the best result.

Start Early. Make sure you are giving your recommender the courtesy of more than enough time to complete the task. This means asking several weeks in advance of the deadline, and specifically mentioning the time frame to your recommender during your meeting. Ask whether he'd mind if you check in in a few weeks to see whether he has any questions. This means that both of you can feel that when you follow up you won't be nagging.

Provide Guidelines and Best Practices. Acknowledge to your recommender that the recommendation letter instructions issued by the schools can be somewhat open-ended and vague. Then invite your recommender to share evidence and examples of your contributions, letting him know that he does not need to completely sum you up in a single letter, but rather to give the admissions committee a glimpse of who you really are. This may come as a relief to your recommender, who may now be able to simply recall one great story about you and write that, rather than to wordsmith an all-encompassing document that distills you into to broad, descriptive text. The goal is to free your recommender from old notions of what a great recommendations should contain.

Guide Recommenders in a Direction that Helps Fill In Your Application's Gaps. If there is some area in which you believe that your application is lacking, gathering recommendations from people who can address those gaps is a good idea. Share with your recommender the types of insights that you believe could strengthen your application. For example, if you believe that certain parts of your application clearly show that you have great writing talent, it's perfectly fine to say so to your recommender. A comment like, "I think that my grades and transcripts already go far in showing my aptitude for writing; if you have other strengths that you think you can speak to, those would be very helpful."

RISKY CHOICES AND STICKY SITUATIONS

Sometimes, the benefits of using a certain recommender may not be straightforward. Should your mother vouch for you? How about the CEO of your company? The President of the United States? What if you must get a recommendation from your boss who hates you? This section explores the tradeoffs of choosing recommenders whose position or content will garner a lot of attention.

Famous and Notable People. Suppose that you are in a position to have the President, or a Nobel Prize winner, or a celebrity everybody has heard of, write you a letter of recommendation. Will this improve your chances of getting in? Not much, unfortunately, unless the notable person truly knows you and is among one of the most qualified people to vouch for your readiness for your target program.

I have read letters of recommendation from state senators, Army generals, movie stars, and all other manner of notable people—in every case, it was easy to see which ones reflected real relationships and true grounds to comment honestly on the candidate's qualifications. Recommendations from people with stature but not knowledge of the candidate usually hurt an application. If a notable person knows you only tangentially, no matter how much name cachet they carry, heed this simple rule: do not use them as a reference.

I'll give you two more reasons not to use a tangentially relevant celebrity recommender. Since there is usually a limit to how many recommendation letters can be submitted, using a "weak" celebrity reference also squanders your opportunity to be supported by a person who really does know and can strongly vouch for you. Finally, more cynical admissions officers will view it as a signal that reflects poorly upon your character, one saying that you believe just because you know the President, the Queen, or the Pope, that your connections to this person should help get you into the school.

All that said, if you have a genuine, relevant relationship to the celebrity in question, certainly, use it. For example, if you are applying to a writing program and you have done a workshop with a famous author who knows your work, it would be appropriate to have her write a reference. Similarly, if you are applying to an MBA program and you were in the reporting line of a notable business mogul, it is appropriate to receive a letter of reference from that person (so long as said person actually witnessed your work).

But, if Congressman So-and-So or Celebrity X is your uncle's business associate, and is barely (if at all) an acquaintance of yours, steer clear of placing your application in this virtual stranger's hands — you'll be wasting a valuable opportunity to have your story told.

Excessive Recommendations. Some applicants operate under the mistaken impression that more recommendations are better. Generally speaking, miscellaneous recommendations are not well-received by schools. For one, you can be sure that schools explicitly request what they feel they need to evaluate your candidacy; barring any special circumstances, schools are unlikely to feel that they need to see more. (In any case, requirements related to special situations should be discussed with the admissions committee directly.) Secondly, admissions committees are busy — reading hundreds or thousands of applications within a very narrow decision window requires efficiency. Bluntly, supplying them with excessive recommendations creates more work for them.

There's more: submitting excessive recommendations subtly signals that you don't trust their process and that you don't respect their time. A more cynical lens would view the act as one of presumption, and you don't want to be perceived as someone who thinks you deserve special treatment or that you don't need to follow the rules. "Multiple letters are strongly discouraged," reads the web site of New York's Trinity School quite plainly. If you feel compelled to take this route, take the possible consequences into consideration. Also, understand that there is a real possibility that the extra recommendations simply won't be read.

Family Members and Others Who Will Be Viewed as Biased. Family members (or others who are as good as family, such as godparents and in-laws) are largely thought to be unreliable references. Family references are rarely regarded equivalently to those supplied by non-family members.

In some cases, there are reasons to include them as part of an application, but when doing so, it's best to treat the family recommendation as extra or optional.

It may be appropriate to use a family-member reference if the role played by the family member is specifically requested as part of the application. If you are homeschooled and are asked for teacher references, supply them, but ask the admissions committee whether there are any additional references they would like to see, given the circumstances. The same goes for a reference from a parent who is also the requested work supervisor or professional colleague: provide what is asked for but make sure the admissions committee knows your situation and can request a reference from another person if they deem it necessary.

WHAT TO DO IF YOU ASK AND THE PERSON REFUSES

If somebody you ask for a reference declines your request, consider it a blessing and an opportunity—a blessing, because it is possible that the person has declined due to an unwillingness to wholeheartedly support your plans. It may sting to hear that somebody whose help you need or whose opinion you respect is not aligned with what you view as your next step. Yet it's better to tend to your wounds and regroup in private, instead of having a lackluster recommendation make it all the way to an admissions committee and cost you an offer.

Hearing that your request has been declined is also an opportunity for you to ask yourself two important questions: first, why did that person decline? And, second, what signs did you miss when judging that person as a willing candidate? A straightforward person might give you feedback about why he declined—listen to any indication given at the time. Perhaps the person thinks that you are not ready for the program or that you lack certain necessary skills. Take any direct feedback you are given and amplify it as you reflect on it—most people will have understated the feedback to spare your feelings, so read between the lines.

Some people are less direct and will not give you feedback. A potential recommender may make an excuse as to why he is unwilling to provide a recommendation to avoid any type of awkward confrontation. If you are given a simple "no" or "I don't have time" or "my plate is already full with other things," please do some independent reflection about why you might have been refused.

If you find yourself completely surprised by the decline, ask for feedback from somebody who has a history of being candid with you, and who is as close to the situation as possible. Make sure you—not the admissions committee—are the first person who is aware of your strengths, weaknesses, and potential disadvantages.

> *Don't tell me the moon is shining;*
> *show me the glint of light on broken glass.*
> -Anton Chekhov

CHAPTER XIII

WRITING STRONG ESSAYS AND SHORT ANSWERS

Most candidates know that essays and short answers are important—but what does crafting strong answers mean? Is it about showcasing good writing and communication skills? Is it about revealing fit by demonstrating substantive, well-thought-out answers? If it's about both, what is the level at which these should combine to perform?

Beyond that, what are the fundamental questions that most admissions committees want the answers to, and why are they asked on every kind of application, from preschool to grad school? This chapter will tackle the commonalities among essay questions, and reveal what the admissions committee really wants to know, and why.

WHY ESSAYS AND SHORT ANSWERS MATTER

On many applications, essay and short answer questions offer candidates the only guaranteed opportunity to speak for themselves. Much of the rest of the application is facts and figures. Apart from recommendations (which, of course, the candidate doesn't get to write), and since interviews may be by invitation only, personal statements offer the only secure chance for candidates to bring themselves to life. This makes essay and short answer sections critical to making a case for why you belong at a school, while simultaneously familiarizing the committee with you as a person. Essays and short answers should strike a balance between persuasion and revelation. They should give logical reasons that support your candidacy but also be vibrant with color about who you are.

> *Essays and short answers should strike a balance between persuasion and revelation. They should give logical reasons that support your candidacy but also be vibrant with color about who you are.*

Schools want to know the answers to three fundamental questions after reading your short answers and essays:

- Can you express yourself clearly with skill and sophistication befitting your education level?

- After reading your essays, will we have a better sense of your personality and who you are?

- Do we understand, and find credible, your reasons for wanting to be here?

Your essay and short answer questions should combine to yield "yeses" to all three questions.

WHY COMPOSITION QUALITY MATTERS
Composition quality (e.g., "good" or "bad" writing) matters because, in addition to wanting students with skills that will enable them to thrive in academic programs, schools want alumni who meet an acceptable standard of written articulation. Writing reveals a candidate's level of organization, knowledge or authority about a subject, quality of logic, power of persuasion, personal voice, attention to detail, and general tone. Bad writing is a problem for several reasons (the same reasons cited in the section about recommendations): thoughts that are unclear or poorly crafted will not accurately convey what the recommender intends. Bad

writing also makes the writer sound less intelligent, and less intelligent people are regarded as less credible. We all react more favorably to better writing.

IF YOU'RE A GREAT WRITER...

If you're a great writer—and you know it—now is your time to shine. Feel free to break out of the standard essay format and craft a more masterful story if you are comfortable in doing so. Some of the best essays I've read were from candidates who took risks and found original ways to present their stories. It's not a good idea to go totally off-script or try too hard to be cute or original (e.g., to answer the "Why this school?" question in a three-act play, if an essay was what was requested). But if you can think of a better way to convey your story that still adheres to the basic requirements, and you've got the chops to back it up, by all means, go ahead. One goal here is memorability, and if you've got the skills to package yourself in a way that breaks the monotony of the basic essay format, nothing should stop you from taking that opportunity.

If I were applying to NYU today, I might write something like the following as the first paragraph in response to an essay question like "Why this school?"

> *It's certain that I knew how to spell "N-Y-U" before I learned to spell "K-i-m". My father graduated from what was then known as Washington Square College some sixteen years before I was born. He went there on the G.I. Bill after years spent living in Europe as a major in the Army. Living abroad had made him not only worldly, but curious, and history became his passion. Beyond the cosmopolitan backdrop of New York City, he talked of dynamic professors, eclectic students from everywhere on earth, and a general sense that at NYU he was among the smartest people he had ever met. Though I don't share his passion for history, I share his wanderlust and romance for all things international. I grew up knowing there was no better place to learn about the world than NYU.*

Something like this is effective because even though it doesn't quite follow a classic essay format, it still delivers affirmative answers to the three fundamental questions schools care about. After reading only a paragraph of this essay, we already see the desired answers emerging. Yes, the answer is expressed clearly with skill and sophistication. Yes, the committee definitely has a better sense of who I am. And yes, my reasons for wanting to go to that particular school are completely credible!

If you try something more creative, check to make sure that the three central questions are being answered. If they are, you are on a path to writing something memorable.

IF YOU'RE A GOOD WRITER...

If you have good writing skills (e.g., you can effectively organize ideas and you have an academic understanding of good sentence, paragraph, and essay structure) but you're not confident that you can pull of something artful, aim for a solid presentation that adheres to classic rules. For essays, this means having an opening paragraph that introduces the topic and states the hypothesis, supporting paragraphs with strong topic sentences, a conclusion that shows how ideas presented in the middle paragraph support the hypothesis, and a thread of credibility and good logic to tie it all together. If your task is to write short answer questions, bear in mind good sentence and paragraph structure (and review these topics if needed). The task of a good writer is to rely on the foundations of classic literary construction, letting the focus become the quality of the ideas presented within.

IF YOU'RE A WEAK WRITER...

If you know your writing skills are weak, or if you suspect they may be, and you (as opposed to your child) are the candidate who will attend target schools, now is a great time to take steps to improve your skills. Learning to be a better writer will help you during and after the admissions season by positioning you to write stronger essays now and to perform better on written deliverables once you arrive at your next school. If you can, take a writing class through a private organization or, if you are an adult, you can try out your town's continuing education program or community college. If there's no time for that, read a book (like *Writing Down the Bones* by Natalie Goldberg) that provides accessible, practical, advice for making your writing better.

At the absolute least, review the rules of good structure, and try to write according to common essay and paragraph frameworks. Don't try to "dress up" weak writing skills by attempting ambitious sentences that you can't successfully tie together as a whole. Keep it simple and write the best essay that you can at the highest level at which you can write effectively. Focus on clearly communicating simple ideas rather than introducing complexity that your writing aptitude may not be able to handle or stretching to try to create a masterpiece work. Also, see the common mistakes section near the end of this chapter, which discusses the ethics of hiring essay-writing help and using admissions consultants.

IF YOU'RE A FOREIGN STUDENT APPLYING TO A U.S. SCHOOL

Having has lived abroad, traveled extensively, and learned three languages that were foreign to me, I can truly appreciate the difficulty of crafting effective written answers, even if you are functionally fluent in a language. Reading comprehension and conversational fluency come easier to some people than academically viable writing. Even if the story you want to tell is clear in your mind and you have rich insights and fine points that beg communication, if you lack the prowess to replicate that story in the target language, it may be wise to default to the best story you can tell given your highest level of English writing skill.

For example, though I am functionally fluent in Spanish (I learned the language as a teenager and I now speak it every day at home) and could do a solid technical translation of my "great answer" example, I simply don't have a level of fluency that would allow me to convey the same sentiment and capture the same tone in Spanish that I'd convey easily in English. So if I were tasked with delivering an essay in Spanish, I would probably start from scratch and begin writing in Spanish, bearing the same communication goals in mind. By doing this, I would avoid a common pitfall routinely seen among foreign students: attempts at translation that, frankly, often fail.

So, why is translation—composing well-written statements or essays in one's mother language and converting them into English—usually a bad idea? For one thing, unless you have a very strong grasp of idioms (especially the ones that may be in your mother-tongue version), and can effectively infuse the translation with any sense of the irony, humor, or deliberate finesse that appeared in the original document, chances are your finished product will be rendered choppy and unpolished. Even worse, if your essay is too choppy, readers may wonder whether you relied too heavily upon a dictionary, or, worse yet, translation software).

Effective translation is a true skill (indeed, a certifiable profession) and most people simply don't know how to do it well. Even most professional translators only translate in to—not out of—their native languages. A better approach is to outline the points you want to convey and to write out the basic bones of the story in English. You may be reduced to simpler concepts with this approach, but well-written simplicity will still play better than poorly executed complexity.

COMMON ESSAY AND SHORT ANSWER QUESTIONS

The most common essay and short answer questions may come in different forms, but can be broken down into basic profiles that get at the heart of what is being asked. This section showcases real application questions taken from highly competitive preschool, kindergarten, middle school, high school, undergraduate, and graduate programs. It is useful to note that most questions that at first may appear distinct are often asking the very same question. When you are reading application questions, always read between the lines to try to discern whether something deeper is being asked, and whether what is being asked corresponds to any of the most frequent question types.

Why this path? Why this school?

To the extent that an entire chapter is dedicated to these questions, I won't repeat here why they are so important or provide advice on how to answer them. The examples shown are meant to demonstrate that, even if all schools don't overtly phrase these questions identically, fundamentally, the questions they're asking are indeed "Why this path?" and "Why this school?"

Examples of "Why this path?" questions include:

* Have you ever applied to an independent school? (Gateway to Prep Schools Application - Common Application for Member Schools - Pre-K-12)

* Why are you interested in private education? (The Dorris-Eaton School - Preschool Application)

- Has your family had any experience in attending independent schools and/or a French-speaking school? If so, please describe. (Ecole Bilingue de Berkeley - K-8 Application)

Examples of "Why this school?" questions include:
- Why would you like your child to attend Quarry Lane School? (Quarry Lane School - Preschool Application)

- How did you become interested in Porter's? (Miss Porter's School - 9th-12th Grade Application)

- What motivated you to apply to Rice University? (Rice University - Freshman Application Supplement)

- Why are you pursuing a career in medicine? What piqued your interest in this field? (American Medical College Application Service - Common Application for M.D. Programs)

- What do you hope to gain from attending the Conference? (Middlebury College - Bread Loaf Writers Conference)

The Success/Strength Question

Questions about your successes and strengths invite you to showcase your most impressive accomplishments or your most admirable character traits. I have chosen to lump them together because discussing the former typically accomplishes the latter, and both of these can be tackled in the same way. If you get a question asking you to write about a success or accomplishment, evaluate the character elements evident in the success. Conversely, if you are asked about your strengths, go beyond merely listing them—be prepared to share a success or accomplishment to substantiate your claim.

For example, if the candidate is a child whose proudest accomplishment is building a complex model airplane from several hundred individual parts, and the model took weeks or months to complete, telling this story will create the opportunity to show characteristics of ambition, patience, and dedication. If the child encountered obstacles during the project, such as making a mistake that created the need to go back and spend hours undoing or redoing certain tasks, or breaking a specific part and having to figure out how to make another, discussing these mistakes can go even farther in revealing the child's character—in this case, they show perseverance and problem-solving.

The key to answering questions in a way that is memorable is to write from a genuine, heartfelt place and use an example to tell a story. At some age levels, opportunities to accomplish extraordinary things may be limited, so where the magnitude of the accomplishment is comparatively small, creating an emotional connection to the personal victory is recommended. But even when it comes to hugely impressive accomplishments, a dose of humanity and emotional connection are recommended. Tone matters, and there is a difference between bragging about climbing Mt. Everest and weaving an honest tale of tough circumstances rewarded by the pride of accomplishment.

> *The key to answering questions in a way that is memorable is to write from a genuine, heartfelt place and use an example to tell a story.*

Another strategy that makes sense on the success/strength question is diversification. There's no need to name a success story or strength that is clear as a towering strength elsewhere on your application. For example, even if your proudest accomplishment is earning a 4.0 GPA every semester for four years straight, you might want to choose your second proudest accomplishment in answer to this question. Since the committee can see your transcripts, writing on that topic wouldn't tell them much about you that they don't already know.

Examples of success/strength questions include the following:
* Please describe any academic or personal achievements of which you are especially proud. Use this area to note any academic honors you have received. (Gateway to Prep Schools Application - Common Application for Member Schools with Pre-K-12 Classes)

* Evaluate a significant experience, achievement, risk you have taken, or ethical dilemma you have faced and its impact on you. (The Common Application for Undergraduate Admission)

The Failure/Weakness Question

The failure/weakness question is intended to gauge your candor in discussing your flaws, whether those flaws manifest as a general area of weakness or as flawed judgment that led to a bad decision. The committee wants to get a sense of your ability to reflect upon a past mistake and to know whether and what you learned from the situation. Part of the test here is to see whether you will allow yourself to be a bit vulnerable and 'fess up to a significant flaw or failure, one with a tangible impact on your life. If the failure you highlight is inconsequential, it may rouse unwanted suspicion—everybody makes mistakes and has weaknesses, and by avoiding discussion of a significant example, you are signaling either a distorted self-image (e.g., an "I don't make big mistakes" attitude) or some discomfort around exposing uncomfortable or unpleasant things about yourself. Neither quality plays well with schools, so it's best to come up with an example of a real failure and be ready to discuss it.

> *Our society rallies to the aid of flawed people and underdogs. Sharing a true failure will make you seem more human, and more real, and will make people sympathize with you and root for you.*

This isn't a bad thing. The discussion of real failures and personal weaknesses provides the opportunity to show personal growth and maturity. It gives you the opportunity to rise above an obstacle and become a hero in your own story by making some high-quality lemonade out of lemons. There's another advantage to telling a good failure or weakness story: our society rallies to the aid of flawed people and underdogs. Sharing a true failure will make you seem more human, and more real, and will make people sympathize with you and root for you as they read through your example. It's almost better to find one of your more egregious failures or weaknesses to sweeten the payoff related to your change. Hitting it out of the park on questions like this often means showing how you corrected for a blind spot or fixed a royal blunder with an act of redemption.

For example, if I'm reading applications of high school students applying to college, and the question is "Tell us about a mistake you made," I will remember, relate to, and find credible the essay of a candidate who tells the story of a time he had a party while his parents were out of town, got caught, and had to suffer the consequences of (and learn from) being punished for a long time. What I would find less memorable, and what I would suspect is a watered-down choice of a mistake is the essay of a candidate whose "mistake" was taking a cooking elective instead of a computer class. Some candidates think they're playing it safe by not revealing anything too scathing about themselves on the failure/weakness question, but, usually, this reluctance is foolish. Schools aren't asking the question so that they can judge your character by reading into the mistake or personal flaw itself—they are gauging your self-awareness and your perseverance in the face of adversity.

So, just how far should you go in revealing your weaknesses? Give the committee something meaty, but something that still falls short of self-incrimination. If you not only had a party while your parents were out of town but also got arrested and charged with underage drinking, drug possession, and contributing to the delinquency of minors, you may want to choose another failure—that one is too hefty to deal with in 500 words.

If you're wondering whether your failure or weakness is flawed enough, ask yourself about the stakes. Were they high? Did it involve a consequence that felt serious at the time? If what you have in mind has never caused you to lose any sleep, shed any tears, or, specifically in the case of a personal weakness, spend real time trying to remediate, you probably need to rethink your choice.

If you're being asked to provide insights about your child's weaknesses, the admissions committee is asking you to raise any red flags they should know about, and they are also seeing how candid you are willing to be about your child and the inevitable presence of flaws. School administrators don't want families who see their children as perfect angels who can do no wrong—this kind of parental thinking completely undermines the ability of schools and parents to be accountable partners in a child's success.

Examples of failure/weakness questions include the following:

- Please note any special concerns or questions [about your son] to which you would like to draw our attention. (The Haverford School - PreK-12 Application)

- Have you ever struggled with something and failed? How did you respond? What would you attempt to do if you knew you could not fail? (Noble and Greenough - Grades 7-12 Application)

- Tell us about something you learned on your own. (Phillips Exeter Academy)

The Hero/Inspiration/Influence Question

Any question that asks who your hero is, who or what has influenced you, or what inspires you is trying to elicit your values. Typically in questions like this, candidates provide clues as to what kind of person they want to be (or, in the case of discussing a negative influence, not to be). Suppose you say that your hero is Rosa Parks—chances are that, through the course of writing your rationale as to why she is your hero, you will mention qualities like courage, advocacy, and a strong sense of justice. Whether or not you explicitly say that you admire these things, admissions committees will get the message: the qualities of your hero are qualities that are valued by you. In the event that the person you name was an influence because of the many undesirable qualities he possessed, the message is reversed: the values demonstrated by the negative influencer are not ones you wish to emulate.

The Hero/Inspiration/Influence question can be tricky because admissions committees can get bored reading the same answer over and over. Many candidates name their mother or father as their hero, which may be a very heartfelt choice—however, given the sheer number of people using this as an answer it's very difficult to write essays about Mom or Dad that truly stand out. Religious and spiritual figures are common answers (again, it may be heartfelt that Gandhi or Mother Teresa deeply inspire you, but if you want your essay to stand out against the ten essays the committee member has already read about Gandhi, yours has to be new and different). Even people who try to be different and write about somebody a little less common might be surprised by how many other people attempt to do the same. We asked a version of this question when I was on the committee at the University of Chicago; nearly a dozen people said their hero was Yoda.

So, what should you do? Brainstorm a few of your heroes, and get to the heart of the matter by jotting down qualities you admire and values they demonstrate. From there, think about your target school and that school's own values, and figure out which of your hero's values most align with the target school's values and, therefore, the side of yourself that you want to show the school. By doing this values-matching exercise, you're creating an opportunity to show alignment between yourself and your target school.

Let's keep thinking about that list. Is there someone on your list who not only embodies the values of your target school but who is also a figure that a large number of other people may not choose? It's smarter to go with a lower-profile subject to pique the interest of the reader. Despite the best of intentions, admissions committee members may tend to tune out a bit when they feel like they're reading the exact same essay again and again. It's absolutely fine to use people who are obscure as long as they truly fit the values you are going to convey. If you go in this direction, take the time to give a solid explanation of who the person is.

A final note: take this question seriously. Some candidates are so hell-bent on standing out when answering this question that they choose a very memorable figure who lacks substance. Most commonly, candidates who have a shallow understanding of the advice that tells them to "stand out" try to write a cute, funny essay about an unlikely choice. At times this works (Harry Potter, for one, is a well-developed character who is fun to write about and who has defensibly admirable and virtuous qualities); but, other times it doesn't (we received two David Hasselhoff answers one year; cute, but Hasselhoff's reputation as a person of high character is questionable, at best).

Common iterations of the "Hero" question may be:

* Indicate a person who has had a significant influence on you, and describe that influence. (Common Application for Undergraduate Admission)

* Consider the books, essays, poems, or journal articles you have read over the last year or two, either for school or leisure. Please discuss the way in which one of them has changed your understanding of the

world, other people, or yourself. (Duke University - Undergraduate Application Supplement)

- ◆ Tell us about a person who you admire and look up to. Why do you respect this person? How is this person important to you? (The Bentley School - Middle School Application)

The Passion/Interests Question

Questions about interests and passion are seen universally, but may be seeking different kinds of responses at each level of education. For younger candidates, questions about interests and passion create the opportunity to reveal a child's personality in ways that might not come through in an interview setting. This may be necessary since young children can be unpredictable and shy when confronted with school visits and may not behave typically during brief interactions with admissions staff. If you are asked this on a preschool or kindergarten application, schools want you to show them things that are important to knowing your child, but that they might not have a chance to witness firsthand.

Older children and adults can represent themselves better and speak to their own interests in writing—for them, schools want to hear not only about a passion or interest, but also some rationale for why it is important. Doing so helps committees gauge a candidate's level of conviction, quality of logic, and, in some cases, reveals more personal information about the candidate.

Certain phrasings of this question ask what drives you to action or what compels you to want to succeed. This angle is typically reserved for undergraduate or graduate school candidates and its goal is to surpass the "why" and the "how" and learn more about your personal philosophy or sense of purpose. This slant can often get at themes of citizenship and community, subtly or overtly asking how something you are passionate about manifests through your participation in your own community, if not society as a whole. For example, a medical school candidate may be interested in epidemiology after watching a loved one fight HIV. At this education level, the passion question can (and often does) resemble the inspiration question.

Common "passion and interest" questions may include:

- We want to learn more about your son – his special interests, hobbies, character. Please use the space below or attach a separate sheet (The Haverford School - PreK-12 Application)

- Discuss your favorite hobbies and activities outside of school and why you enjoy them. (The Bentley School - Middle School Application)

- At Porter's, we challenge our students to become informed, bold, resourceful, and ethical global citizens. Elaborate on one of the activities you listed above and describe a moment when you found yourself to be informed, bold, resourceful, or ethical. (Miss Porter's School – 9th-12th)

- Johns Hopkins offers 50 majors across the schools of Arts & Sciences and Engineering. On this application, we ask you to identify one or two that you might like to pursue here. Why did you choose the way you did? If you are undecided, why didn't you choose? If any past courses or academic experiences influenced your decision, you may include them in your essay. (Johns Hopkins University - Undergraduate Application Supplement)

Multimedia Content

Though most schools don't request or require it, some offer you the option of including relevant multimedia content with your application. The following application questions encompass the types of additional materials the candidate might have the opportunity to include in his application:

- If you would like to provide a URL to an existing website with multimedia content, you may do so below. Examples of multimedia content that students have provided in the past are: links to newspaper articles, YouTube videos, music files, or a personal website they have created. Be sure to provide a description of the link in the space provided. (Gateway to Prep Schools Application - Common Application for Member Schools with Pre-K-12 Classes)

- You may provide your selected college(s) with a link to any online content you feel: 1. Tells the college more about yourself; 2. Demonstrates a particular talent you possess; 3. Highlights an activity in which you participated. Some ideas include linking to an online video you created, a portfolio (pictures or photographs), a musical composition, or a newspaper article. Please briefly describe the contents of the link you provided. (The Universal College Application)

This is something that a candidate with an existing piece or portfolio of work that is only available online (or that could be made available online) should jump to take advantage of. If you write a blog, have press clips, have a body of artwork or photography, perform music or step dance, perform a black belt routine in karate, make film or videos, or engage in any other work for which you have a tangible, digital, product, take the opportunity to showcase it via this question. Questions like these let talented candidates who would not have found a natural place to share their work on the applications of the past.

However, if you don't have an existing body of work, don't feel that you have to come up with something in this category to seem robust or be competitive. A hastily-assembled work product is unlikely to positively impact your application.

COMMON ESSAY MISTAKES

The most common essay mistake—that of failing to write answers that stand out—is addressed extensively elsewhere in the book. Before answering any essay or short answer question (or when proofreading answers you have already written), ask yourself: how many other people might have written an identical answer? Refer back to the "Great vs. Good vs. Bad" answer examples in Chapter 3 for specific advice about how to personalize your answers memorably, and how to choose unique alternatives and remain authentic.

Beyond this overarching advice, there are three other practices to avoid: using an overly formal tone, bad proofreading, and relying too heavily upon outside interference and advice.

An Overly Formal Tone

Many people, when on their best behavior or intending to convey professionalism and sophistication, may default to an overly formal tone. It is important to present yourself in a way that confirms that you take the process seriously, but going overboard with formality can be a big mistake. Being overly formal is problematic because it sanitizes your personality, allowing you to show mastery of proper language and decorum, but at the cost of making you sound impersonal and dry. Stripping your writing of personality robs the admissions committee of its chance (and, therefore, its desire) to get to know who you really are. Well-written essays that are overly formal may clear the writing bar, but not give you very much upward movement in terms of your standing. Avoid über-formality by writing with good attention to standard language use and grammar, but be willing to speak more colloquially in places where doing so will soften the tone and better reveal the real you.

PROOFREADING, QUALITY CONTROL, AND AVOIDABLE MISTAKES

When candidates fail to thoroughly proofread and spell-check responses, their careless mistakes make the job of the admissions committee easy: your ideas may be great, but your lack of commitment to quality might make you a "no." Not taking the time to review your responses shows habits that most admissions committees don't want—they signal that you may be lazy or disorganized, and that you don't take your candidacy to their school seriously enough to make an effort to do a thorough job of applying. If you want to be taken seriously, you have to treat the process seriously, taking the time to be thorough and proofread your answers.

> *Being overly formal is problematic because it sanitizes your personality, allowing you to show mastery of proper language and decorum, but at the cost of making you sound impersonal and dry.*

Of course, quality control is important beyond essays. Other written items, such as short answers, application form elements, and even e-mails and letters to the admissions committee should also be quality-reviewed. Poor writing has become so commonplace (even expected) on many of the most frequently used media, such as e-mail, texting, and social sites like Twitter and Facebook, that many young people aren't conscious of how far below standard their interactions have become. For the purposes of your application, at the absolute least, revert to using proper English. Accept that even mindless tasks like making sure your own name and the street on which you live are shown correctly is something you must take the time to do.

HAVING SOMEONE WRITE OR EDIT THEM FOR YOU

First things first: having somebody write or significantly edit your work is cheating. Just as you wouldn't hire somebody to take a test for you, you should not hire somebody to write your essays for you. Unfortunately it's easy to buy custom-written essays online, and to hire unethical admissions consultants who are willing to more or less rewrite your work, rather than provide an appropriate degree of feedback and send you back on your own way.

Many students wonder whether they "should" hire an essay consultant— it may feel as if "everybody" is doing it, and if you listen to the wrong people, it may feel as if you should want or need a professional essay review before submitting your application. But the truth is that admissions committees design applications that every applicant or family should be able to complete independently of help. The notion that you can't complete an application on your own and still be successful at getting into target schools is simply is not true. Beyond that, it's very difficult for people who are not you to emulate your voice; it is often very obvious to admissions committees when essays are not written by the candidate.

So, what constitutes appropriate help? The last candidate I provided feedback to (a high schooler applying to undergrad) found me giving him advice on how to improve his essays, rather than improving his essays for him. Here are excerpts from what I told him (verbatim):

> *Use paragraph breaks. The current essays read as one long paragraph. Break up ideas by separating them where there are natural pauses. Also, use MS Word spell-check and grammar check. There are a few technical errors.*

> *Show, don't tell. Try answering the essay questions in a way that tells a story. For example, in the "Who am I?" essay, instead of listing off things that you'd like us to know about you, tell us a story that tells us who you are. It doesn't have to be a story of heroism or extreme virtue. But it should be a*

story that's memorable and makes your personality and essential qualities come alive.

Consider using classic essay format. *Your essay has good ideas but they will make more sense if they are organized a bit differently. It opens with several statistics, but we don't find out until more than halfway through what you think and why you care about the statistics. If this were structured in a classic essay format, it would lead with your hypothesis that students don't take education seriously, you would place the supporting statistics in separate paragraphs in the middle (while adding your own language to explain why they are important), and you would integrate your conclusion into a final (separate) paragraph.*

Advice like this is very different from having somebody come in and "correct" your essay, and is certainly different from outsourcing the writing of the essay altogether. Here's what it comes down to: feedback that requires you to go back and make your own changes is help. Having anyone other than you become a creator or editor of content is cheating.

FINAL NOTE: DON'T OVERTHINK IT

Despite the many books dedicated to strategies for writing great application essays, being successful with this element truly does boil down to the basics. No matter how many examples of winning essays you may read, the best essay for your application will be the one that tells a personal, authentic story and rings true in your own voice.

> *Resume: a written exaggeration of only the good things a person has done in the past, as well as a wish list of the qualities a person would like to have.*
>
> -Bo Bennett

CHAPTER XIV
BUILDING YOUR RESUME

If you are applying on behalf of a younger person with no job history, you may be tempted to skip this chapter. Please don't. Most schools ask what I call "resume questions," even if they don't ask pointedly for a resume. Don't be fooled into thinking that just because you are applying on behalf of a young child or high-schooler, you aren't being asked for specific details designed to understand Junior better by learning how he spends his time. That's exactly what you are being asked! Though candidates for graduate schools are explicitly required to organize their activities into a formal resume, candidates at the high school, middle school, and even kindergarten and preschool levels are typically asked to provide similar information, in more subtle ways.

CHILDREN HAVE RESUMES, TOO
For children, resume elements manifest as questions about things like extracurricular activities, awards and honors won, special talents, and membership in student organizations. Notice how these categories parallel the types of things an adult would include on a resume. In this respect, resume elements requested of children and those listed by adults are very much the same.

Unlike adults, children are typically asked singular questions that probe for this information, rather than being required to create a central document showcasing the sum of what they do. The Gateway to Prep Schools common application for preparatory schools contains a section that allows students to list up to nine extracurricular, personal and volunteer activities and include details about the number of years, hours per week, level of involvement, honors, and plans for continuation the student can tie to that activity. A subsequent section asks about academic and personal achievement—again, categories that would appear on the professional resume of an adult.

> " *Some parents wonder how many and which activities children need in order to be competitive—but thinking in these terms is probably a waste of time.* "

To the extent that even preschool children may be enrolled in activities, some schools ask directly about such engagement. The preschool application of a top Chicago prep school asks: "Is your child involved in classes or organized programs? If so, please list and describe how often your child attends." For many two- and three-year-olds, life is already full of art, music and dance classes, foreign language courses, and structured play. The goal here is for schools is to learn what types of socially-, personally- and academically-enriching activities your child has been exposed to. Again, this parallels adult resumes, which speak to activities of personal, academic, and professional relevance.

Some parents wonder how many and which activities children need in order to be competitive—but thinking in these terms is probably a waste of time. Admissions committees are rarely looking for parents (or children) to check specific boxes, and it's rare that a school would render any yes or no decision based on resume elements alone. Elements like these simply create a clearer picture of the child and may serve to corroborate or contradict other assertions you have made. If you noted in a separate question that you were interested in the target school because of its strong music program and one of your child's activities is a music class or violin lessons, you've now made a connection that will strengthen your application. On the other hand, if you answered a previous question asking you to describe your family values by saying that your family values balance, yet you have your two-year-old booked in ten activities per week, this may weaken your application.

Remember, admissions committees are looking for consistency. They want to see claims you make echoed by evidence elsewhere on the application. View questions about resume elements as an opportunity to connect some dots.

CORE RESUME ELEMENTS

If your application requires a formal resume, many existing resources serve as worthy guides for its organization, story flow, and an overall strategy for presenting such a document. For the purposes of mastering the admissions process, we will deconstruct the core resume elements and discuss why they are important to admissions committees.

YOUR 9-TO-5

What you do with most of your time—your "9-to-5"—is a key element of your resume. If you are currently a student, you won't explicitly be asked to describe your daily activities or your performance in those activities because the transcripts you provide will serve that function. For candidates who are already working in the professional world, your "9-to-5" is your work experience. Unlike students who are evaluated externally on their performance, you will self-report much of your activity through the composition of a formal resume.

Fundamentally, grade transcripts and work experience are parallel resume elements. They both have the potential to enhance your application by showing alignment—does the way you've been spending your time make a logical connection with the path you're on, and with your target schools? Does the coursework you're taking in a current school align with what's offered at target schools? Does the job in which you've been working align to your target degree? In that job, have you had a chance to demonstrate the qualities necessary for success at the next level of education and in your target profession?

Beyond *alignment,* you want to show *proficiency* in the areas you care about most and the ones most related to your future goals. For example, if you have your sights set on a medical program, it will be important to show evidence of altruism and integrity. For those in the professional world, the work experience section should clearly provide evidence of proficiency; for current students, grade transcripts usually won't, and it will be important to affirm your qualifications by showing proficiency elsewhere on the application

EXTRACURRICULAR ACTIVITIES

If we take the Latin translation of "extracurricular" activities literally, we know that these refer specifically to activities outside of (extra) school work (curriculum). To the extent that, for our purposes, their meaning is identical, we'll discuss extracurriculars (for students) and personal interests (for non-students and adult candidates) together. Also included in "extracurriculars" are memberships (from student organizations to professional associations) and affiliations.

> *Hyper-focused automatons with invisible personalities and zero interests are the opposite of the good community members and ambassadors that most schools are interested in.*

The "extra" part is accurate. Target schools care about what you do "outside" of your nine-to-five job, whether it's attending school as a full-time student or going to work. Firstly, they want to know that you do something—anything—productive. (Pulling straight As by day and spending six hours a night playing "World of Warcraft," or, worse, spending all of your time studying, will not be well-regarded). That old axiom about being "well-rounded" comes to mind—schools don't want people for whom work or school is the only relevant thing in their lives. Hyper-focused automatons with invisible personalities and zero interests are the opposite of the good community members and ambassadors that most schools are interested in. Only in rare cases, such as at schools with distinct cultures that focus on specific talents, is being well-rounded less important.

Beyond wanting to know that you are engaged in interests outside of school and work, schools will be curious to know the nature of your interest. What you like doing will tell them more about you, and hopefully, will confirm some self-reported qualities you have already placed on your application. Perhaps you described yourself as disciplined in a short answer or essay, or even in an interview. If you list distance running under extracurricular activities, you've just corroborated your own story since distance running requires discipline. You're not being graded on your extracurricular activities alone, yet admissions committees are always looking for connections between what you have said about yourself and what you can show. In addition to helping to get to know you better, your list of extracurriculars has the potential to add credibility to your application.

A common red flag on a high-schooler's application is an overfocus on academics. If a child goes to school full-time, and attends an every-weekend science program as well as math camp in the summer, the absence of non-academic activities would raise serious questions as to whether the child's life is "balanced," and whether he could thrive within the community as a whole, instead of just in the classroom. It's important to show balance, and it's easy for parents hell-bent on seeing their children succeed to oversubscribe kids in academic activities and also be mistaken in believing that a show of extreme dedication to academics strengthens an application. Extracurriculars get at the richness and fullness of a candidate's life.

COMMUNITY INVOLVEMENT

At the most basic level, schools want to know about community involvement for the same reason they want to know about extracurriculars: they want to see that you have interests and commitments outside of academic and professional arenas. They may view your current or past activities as a proxy for how you might contribute to the school's own community if you were to attend. Finally, how you choose to participate in your community often indicates your values. As with other resume elements, what you place in this section will help your application if your activities seem to align with other things you have said.

Let's debunk a common myth: community involvement doesn't need to be "community service." You don't need to feed the homeless on Thanksgiving or pick up litter on the side of the highway in order for it to count in a section like this. Putting in hours in a community garden, volunteering at polling places during elections, and taking tickets at the tilt-a-whirl for your school's (or town's) fundraising carnival all show part of what the committee will be looking to see: that you don't opt out of participating in the world around you, and that you contribute in areas you care about (such as promoting the use of locally-grown produce, supporting civic life, and helping keep local organizations alive).

The strongest examples of community involvement will be ones clearly driven by you. In other words, it will reflect well upon you if you participated in the random community service project organized by your school, church, or company, but it will look *better* if you took a proactive role in arranging self-selected, long-term community activities on your own behalf. Long-term community activities show true commitment, by demonstrating consistency and dedication. They also tell a more cohesive story about the types of things you care about.

AWARDS AND HONORS

Being able to cite awards and honors helps your application in at least two ways: primarily, it shows that you excel at *something*, and based on the area in which the award or honor was given, it shows that you possess superior talents related to that focus. For example, winning a chess tournament shows not only that you were the best among a number of other talented chess players, but also that your strategy and scenario analysis skills are probably also above average. Say it's a speed chess tournament—now, the committee knows that you're a quick thinker who remains effective under pressure. In this respect, awards and honors are doubly beneficial, given their propensity to highlight both excellence and skill.

The caliber of the honor also matters. Winning an Olympic gold medal in a swimming event is clearly different from winning a gold medal in your local Master Swim Club meet. How impressive your accomplishment is will have a lot to do with how important it is in the grand arena of the activity. Is it an honor within a private circle? At a local, state, or national level? Is it world-class? Generally, the more important on a large scale, the better.

The mere presence of any award or honor will usually be a mark in your favor—not all candidates will have them. But if you're feeling a bit light on the awards front, don't grasp for just any old thing you've ever been recognized for in order not to leave the section blank. Finally, don't confuse awards and honors with accomplishments: awards and honors represent something that you won competitively or were specifically selected for. Accomplishments that were self-driven usually don't warrant mentions under awards and honors.

WHEN RESUME ELEMENTS REALLY MATTER

Resume elements, if genuine, well-crafted and thoughtful, can be a great asset to your application. In general, however, I believe that their importance is overstated and misunderstood. Parents who pressure their high school children to spend hours a week (starting in freshman year!) to build up their extracurriculars are extreme, and their behavior probably won't make for the best adult relationships between those parents and children. Building resume elements with only admissions goals in mind is empty—it's far better to find things that you're truly interested in and to carve out time in your schedule for consistent participation. If you find yourself tempted to pander to what schools want, you are completely missing the point—and missing the chance to have the most fruitful and important life that you can.

> *Questions are never indiscreet.*
> *Answers sometimes are.*
> -Oscar Wilde

CHAPTER XV
MASTERING THE ART OF THE INTERVIEW

For many, the interview is the most anxiety-producing element of the application. It is seen as a sort of test, where the answers can either be right or wrong. The intimidation factor—fear of being written off instantly, for lack of sufficient time to craft carefully-worded answers—can take on a life of its own, and many candidates worry about failing. In reality, interviewers rarely intend to grill you or to pepper you with trick questions. But they do want to get a sense of who you are and how you (or your child) would fit into the rest of the class. Interviews afford the opportunity to assess your fit with the school in ways that only a personal interaction can achieve.

The same is true for you. It's fine to read what a school says about itself on its web site, but an in-person visit is needed to confirm or deny your early hunches about fit. Just as most candidates don't accept offers from schools they have never personally visited, many schools don't extend offers to students or families they have not seen. An in-person meeting will enhance the committee's understanding of how your personality, goals, and interests align with and complement the personality, goals and interests of the school. And don't forget: they also create a chance for you to ask questions that will help you decide whether, if given an offer, you could be happy as a student at the school.

ALL INTERVIEWS WANT THE SAME THINGS

Since it's neither useful (nor accurate) to frame the interview as a test, let's view it from another angle. After speaking with you, there is a specific set of new, important information that an interviewer will feel that he knows:

Did the person who showed up for the interview match the person described on paper?

Interviews can either help or hurt your candidacy, by confirming or denying qualities gleaned from your written application. If you describe yourself as fun-loving and outgoing on your application, but barely crack a smile during your interview, you will have raised the red flag of incongruity. But if you describe yourself as serious on paper and you don't smile much in the interview, your self-description and personal presentation will be in alignment. This is a great example of how there is no right or wrong; it's not "right" to smile and "wrong" not to. Much of the judgment rendered during the admissions process has less to do with others and more to do with how clearly, consistently, and candidly you describe yourself. Seeming different in person than you do on paper will always damage some credibility, even if your personal presentation is much better than your application might imply.

Did you share logical, convincing facts that help make a case for offering you a spot at the school?

> *If you describe yourself as fun-loving and outgoing on your application, but barely crack a smile during your interview, you will have raised the red flag of incongruity.*

The "Why this path? Why this school?" duo is likely to come up during the interview, even if it is not asked overtly. As always, your ability to directly answer (or slip in answers to) these questions in a clear, logical, convincing manner is critical.

How well did you interact and respond to questions, compared to your peers?

If you are interviewed by a member of the admissions committee or by a staffer who is exposed to a large number of candidates each year, your interviewer will have a sense for how your overall presentation compares to that of your peers. Were you fantastically confident? Mature? Articulate? Were you exceptionally shy? Immature? Inarticulate? Falling into one extreme or another will get attention, while falling somewhere in the middle is unlikely to help or hurt your application. If you are interviewed by an alum or by anybody who does not have that kind of exposure to many prospective students, your perceived performance vis à vis that of your peers may be arbitrary, if noted at all.

Do you seem like somebody who would represent the school well?

Based on your overall presentation, are you somebody the interviewer would be proud to introduce as a member of the school community? Do you dress and act in socially acceptable ways? Are you pleasant to be around? Do you embody the values of the school? As with the peer comparison dimension, this is unlikely to influence your application in any meaningful way, unless your behavior leans toward an extreme.

How motivated are you to attend this particular school?

How motivated you are to attend a particular school answers two questions for your interviewer. For one, if you seem extremely motivated, it signals that you view the school as an excellent fit. This opinion may be taken at face value if you have established yourself as credible and logical throughout the admissions process; if you meet academic standards, and show that you feel a special affinity for what the school has to offer and its culture, schools will be more inclined to admit you.

Assessing motivation also helps interviewers predict yield. They'll be looking for a sense of whether, if you were made an offer, you would accept. This may not be discussed directly during the interview or elsewhere during the process, but your apparent motivation always comes into play.

WILL YOU BE ASKED TO INTERVIEW?

Whether you will be asked to interview will depend mostly on the type of school to which you're applying. Some schools receive more applications than they have the infrastructure to support, preventing them from arranging an interview for every applicant. In these cases, interviews are extended by invitation only. Some schools that invite students to interview want to see their entire short list of finalists. Other schools will admit and deny the strongest and weakest applicants without interviews, and invite only a list of "maybes" to be seen and compete for final spots. Many schools with invitation- only policies disclose information about how they choose which applicants they want to see, allowing you to know where you fall in early standings via interview status alone.

Other schools require interviews for all applicants, believing them to be critical in assessing the candidate's qualifications. This is especially true of preschools and primary schools, for which preliminary testing and prerequisites can be arbitrary and inconclusive. Yet, the interview requirement is not limited only to those—some schools at every education level extend an interview to every applicant. A school's interview policy is usually a good indicator of how competitive the school is, and how much relative value it places on personal presentation.

Finally, some schools state that interviews are optional. Particularly, ones with geographically dispersed applicants recognize that the expense of traveling to a school for an interview may be prohibitive. In the absence of alumni interviewers covering every corner of the earth, schools simply cannot offer all applicants a practical option for being interviewed. However, if it is reasonable and practical to accept an offer of interview, always take it.

HOW WILL INTERVIEWS BE APPLIED?

Typically, the person who interviews you will fill out a report that is added to your file. This report is usually in the form of a template that asks the interviewer to score the candidate on a specific set of criteria, and to compose answers to other specific open-format questions. Once all elements of your application have been received, the entire packet will be submitted for review, and that interview report will appear alongside all other elements. Your entire application may be read in one sitting, and readers will take the interview report into account before making a recommendation to admit or deny.

WHO WILL CONDUCT THE INTERVIEW?

If you are applying to a local or regional school, and can travel to the school, you have a good chance (but not a 100% chance) of being interviewed by a member of the admissions committee. Those who serve on admissions committees may have interacted with hundreds or thousands of prospective students over the course of their careers. The advantage to being interviewed by a committee member, bluntly, is that they are a less risky choice than a number of others who may queue up to pitch in during admissions season. Committee members are pros who know how to structure a good interview, manage their time, and get what they need to craft a balanced review.

When schools are in the thick of admissions season, teachers, staff, and other members of the administration may pitch in. Though not as skilled as admissions committee members, others within the school community are, generally, not a bad option. They have a current understanding of what's going on at the school, and if they are enthusiastic about you, they may have ample opportunity to talk you up to admissions committee members.

> *Alumni are the riskiest group to interview with because they may be many years removed from the school and the admissions process.*

Some schools also allow students to pitch in with interviews. Most common at the graduate school level, student interviewing is not a universal practice. If a student interviews you, she will ask herself: would I want this person to be my classmate? Also, as a direct, near-term beneficiary of the school's brand equity, she will be committed to maintaining a high standard of quality.

A final group—alumni—may also engage in interviewing. This is typical in two situations. In some cases, schools offer students living in faraway locations interviews by pairing them with willing alumni who live close by; in other cases, alumni located close to campus may be called upon to help out on big interview days. Alumni are the riskiest group to interview with because they may be many years removed from the school and the admissions process. They my not be as skilled at building robust, thorough interview reports that are consistent with reports written by other interviewer groups. They may not be able to answer all of your questions, and in any case, their recollections may be outdated. They may not have a sense for how you stack up next to your peers because you may be the only candidate, or one of a few candidates they will interview in the season in which you apply. Their sense of where "the bar" is, is more likely than with any other group to be too high or too low.

This could work to your advantage — an alum who has no frame of reference for how a typical candidate presents might rave about you on her report, not knowing that you are quite average compared to your peers. By contrast, you could easily get an interviewer who is not impressed by meeting you, even if, by comparison to your peers, you are normally perceived as quite impressive. Interviewer variability proves again that when it comes to admissions, there are no guarantees.

PRESCHOOL AND PRIMARY SCHOOL INTERVIEWS

Nearly all private preschools and primary schools will require interviews with both parent and child. This is because younger children are exposed to different learning opportunities during their first few years and may have wide variances in baseline academic and social skills. A child who has been raised at home by a parent or nanny until the age of five, with no or little everyday exposure to other children, may be vastly different from a child who has been in a day care environment since infancy, or a child who attended preschool prior to kindergarten.

Birth timing also makes a difference. A child whose birthday is very close to the cutoff date may be nine months younger than a child who is well within range. Nine months of development can make a large difference for toddlers and young schoolchildren, once again rendering the skillsets among children bound for the same class year potentially different. Private schools can also be more selective about the age at which they are willing to admit a child. Children younger than the standard age may be admitted if they are judged to have the appropriate academic and emotional maturity. Similarly, children who meet the standard cutoff but who do not meet aptitude or skills standards may be asked to apply in a subsequent year.

Finally, in the absence of useful tests, it is difficult to distinguish individual performance and potential based on what parents or caregivers say about a child on a written application. Many private schools ask that parents of children who have been in a learning-based environment furnish references from day care or preschool teachers or other caregivers. Of course, individual caregiver standards are different, and some early learning programs are more rigorous than others. Consequently, a major goal of the child interview is to allow experienced screeners to assess a child's aptitude against internal benchmarks and with respect to other children.

THE PARENT INTERVIEW

For many families, preschool and primary school will be the first return to academia in a number of years. Therefore, one big goal of the parent interview is to screen for whether the parents know what to expect, understand their role in their child's development, and know what it will take in order for their child to be successful. At this young age, the schools need the parents' full engagement in help their child adjust to a new environment and to develop good habits with regard to learning, studying, and being a good citizen at school. Parents of young children need to genuinely understand these issues and make sure to let their thoughtfulness shine through in the interview. Also, especially at the primary school level, parents need to be well-prepared to answer the two core questions and especially, to explain why they have chosen private vs. public school.

> *One big goal of the parent interview is to screen for whether the parents know what to expect, understand their role in their child's development, and know what it will take in order for their child to be successful.*

Schools will also want to get a sense for how the family as a whole will complement the school community. Private schools are not impersonal places where parents simply drop off and pick up their children every day. Small school communities can be tight-knit and it's important to get a sense for whether the family fits in comfortably at the school and vice versa. Bad fit between the families of young children and schools can be particularly difficult, since a young child is so deeply reliant upon her parent's ability to help her participate in the community and be connected. Therefore, primary schools in particular are very conscious of thinking through whether the relationship feels good and will work out. When parents don't connect well with other members of the school community, it hinders the child.

THE FAMILY INTERVIEW

Most "interviews" of young children tend to be behavioral and play-based and don't follow the same structure as one-on-ones. The younger your child, the less directly he or she will be asked about his or her candidacy for the school. Yet your child may interact with an admissions committee member while you remain in the room. This is, more accurately, a kind of family interview during which everyone casually engages—you in chatting with the committee and your child engaging in some light play. The admissions officer may gently lead the child in playing with several deliberately chosen toys that provide a glimpse into your child's fine motor skills, language, and logic, as well as her knowledge of some fundamentals about the world around her.

Different schools have different expectations, but a preschool interview might gauge your child's ability to:

- count objects
- recognize numbers
- say the alphabet
- know the difference between letters and numbers
- identify colors
- identify shapes
- understand and use words that show position (e.g., up, down, over, under, beside, behind, and below)
- follow directions

The format for kindergarten interviews can be similar, with play-based activities that might include indications of a child's ability to:

- write numbers 0 through 5

- write one's own name

- read and write several three-letter words

- make sets of objects (e.g., eight blocks)

- sort objects by color, size, and shape

- begin to understand patterns and create a two- to three-member pattern

- use pairs of "opposite" words such as short and tall, noisy and quiet, big and little, hot and cold

- understand the idea of more and less

- begin to understand time concepts like days of the week

- use numbers that have personal meaning to them (e.g., phone numbers, birthdays, etc.)

Again, the interviewer will not be quizzing or interrogating your child. Skills the interviewer cares about may be observed after quite a few minutes of play in which the interviewer interacts with your child much in the same way that you might at home.

In some cases, applicants are asked to have independent development assessments completed by an early childhood specialist. In this case, interviews are conducted at the family's leisure and the results of the tester's observations are sent to the school.

You can help your child do his best in interviews like this by taking care to schedule the interview at a time of day when your child is at his best. For many children, this is early in the morning or just after a nap. In the days preceding the interview, make sure he gets plenty of rest at night, plenty of good food that doesn't impact his mood (e.g., no ice cream, birthday cake, or other sweets that might create a "sugar high" and change his behavior for the worse), and begin to speak with him (and get him excited about) going on a fun date with Mommy and Daddy where he will get to play some games.

THE CHILD GROUP BEHAVIORAL INTERVIEW

Often, preschool and kindergarten-age children may be asked to participate in a play-based group interview during which your child will be observed alongside similarly-aged children. These tend to be closed-door interviews that parents may not attend. Typically, you will drop your child off for half an hour to an hour, and several teachers will lead the children in play and/or let play develop organically, while they observe the group dynamics.

Schools want to learn a few things through interviews like this: first, how well does your child separate from you? Your child's ability to separate speaks to her level of maturity and independence, comfort with strangers, and maybe even her intellectual curiosity. For example, when confronted with a classroom full of new, exciting things to explore, does she all but forget you exist, or is she paralyzed by fear of leaving you? Once she does separate, does she take long to bounce back if the separation was hard? Does she play nicely with the other children? Does she listen to and respect the adults? All of these factors will reveal your child's readiness for learning and ability to adapt to a school environment.

THE INTERVIEW AS AN OPPORTUNITY

The best way to approach and prepare for any target school interview is to treat it as an opportunity to improve your application. This means understanding any gaps or other factors that may make you less competitive, and thinking of ways to address whatever reservations an admissions committee might have about you. This may also mean reinforcing other messages you want to get across to the committee, and sharing additional information that was not directly requested in the application. Finally, the interview creates space for you to express final thoughts to punctuate your candidacy and reinforce your interest in target schools.

Opportunity #1: Address weaknesses in your application

If you have performed badly on an admissions test, have lackluster grades or recommendations, or anticipate that something else in your application might be hurting your chances, you will want to think about what evidence to counteract your perceived weakness can be presented to the admissions committee. Since you may not be given the opportunity to guide the conversation, consider common questions you may be asked and look for ways to discuss some of the points you would like to get across.

For example, if you are asked to name strengths and weaknesses, you could choose to bring up a weakness that represents a gap in your application. By bringing up a weakness that you suspect is a red flag for the admissions committee, you put the topic on the table, creating a chance to share your opinion about the red flag, and to make a case in support of your candidacy. Addressing weaknesses like this head-on and effectively may make a big difference to your application.

Opportunity #2: Tell them things about yourself you wish they had asked

If the questions on the application didn't give you a chance to showcase some of your most impressive features, think of ways to work (some of) them into the interview conversation. Your insertion of said discussion shouldn't be overly contrived (e.g., don't respond to "How are you?" with "Not as well as I was that time I rescued a Sherpa from on top of Mt. Everest"), but do walk in with an idea of any additional information about yourself that you want to convey.

Opportunity #3: Get your questions answered

Though not always regarded as such, admissions really is a two-way street. This means you should be mining for information that helps you assess fit to a similar degree that the school will be assessing you. Over-focus on getting accepted is a common mistake. Students who have not done enough of their own vetting end up with no idea what schools they like the most or are the best fit. Use the interview as an opportunity to discover additional information that will help you make your decision down the road.

RED FLAGS

Any admissions officer who's being honest will admit that some percentage of applicants take themselves out of the running based on the interview alone. Contrary to applicants' fears, however, it rarely has to do with "wrong" answers to questions or difficult-to-impress admissions officials. Interviewers are human, and most professional admissions staff truly enjoy meting new candidates and getting to know them. Even alumni interviewers once stood in the interviewee's shoes and want to see candidates succeed. That said, it's hard to "fail" an interview unless something egregious—a serious warning signal—is seen.

So, what raises these red flags? Two things: behavior that calls into question the integrity of the overall application, and behavior that signals the candidate would be a disruptive presence in the school or adversely impact the school's reputation. Inevitably, some handful of applicants who looked promising on paper will fail this test every season. Here are a few red flags to avoid.

Red Flag #1: You're not who your application says you are

Applying to private school is often treated a bit like creating a profile on Facebook or an Internet dating site. In an effort to garner attention and be seen in the most favorable light, people overstate their strengths, downplay their flaws, and post photos of themselves that their own mothers might not even recognize.

On private school applications, some small percentage of candidates will (consciously or subconsciously) exaggerate facts to enhance their prospects for admission. Part of what the interview achieves is a necessary reconciliation of the person portrayed on paper and the person now sitting inside the room.

In some cases, the interview reveals that the candidate has lied on the application. While I was involved in MBA admissions, a common problem was finding that certain non-native English speakers who had listed themselves as fluent in English and had done reasonably well on the TOEFL (Test of English as a Foreign Language) seemed to lack the oral communication skills to survive the program. Beyond the revelation that a basic prerequisite was not met, the fact that the candidate had self-reported his skills incorrectly created another strike against him for lack of integrity. This situation created other doubts: when interviewees were seen grasping hard-to-recall simple vocabulary, it became questionable as to whether someone struggling so desperately with basic conversation could have possibly written a high caliber essay without assistance. Glaring discrepancies such as these can immediately disqualify applicants.

Other subtler discrepancies may relate to a distorted self-image, and may also send red flags. This may come in the form of including favorable but outdated qualities on an application, qualities which, when mentioned in an interview, can't really be backed up. For example, an applicant who writes an essay about how important volunteerism is to her may logically be asked about volunteer activities in the interview. What if the volunteer activities mentioned in the essay concluded five years before, and the applicant has done no volunteer work since? Situations like this—in which the application boasts a certain quality or trait that can't be demonstrated as currently relevant—may call the whole application into question. In the mind of the interviewer, the question becomes: if the applicant has exaggerated this aspect of her application, in what other areas is she stretching the truth?

> *Don't say anything about yourself or your child in an application that you are not reasonably certain can shine through, or wouldn't be overtly contradicted, during a personal interaction.*

A final mistake is the one made by parents who view their child through rose-colored glasses, and say things about them that the child can't possibly live up to in an interview. This is tricky, since every parent is proud of his child, has memories of said child demonstrating his finest qualities, and understands and accepts his child's flaws. When writing applications, parents must be realistic about their child's current developmental state. It may be difficult to convince an admissions committee that your fourteen-year-old boy is joyful, outgoing, and conscientious if he spends most of his time glued to his smartphone, headphones-in-ears, tuning everybody out. Certainly, your sweet boy is in there somewhere, but if his current demeanor is introverted—even sullen—you must infuse balance, awareness, and candor about his current personality into your application.

The lesson is clear: don't say anything that is patently untrue, and when promoting yourself, err on the side of balance. Don't say anything about yourself or your child in an application that you are not reasonably certain can shine through, or wouldn't be overtly contradicted, during a personal interaction.

Red Flag #2: Rudeness or aggression

You probably think this goes without saying, but plenty of candidates fail to demonstrate decorum in interview situations. At times, inappropriate behavior may be driven by lack of awareness of cultural norms, or some general lack of self awareness. At other times, the pressure and stress of school admissions brings out the worst in people, causing them to act out in ways that don't reflect well on them. Chances are that if you are prone to rude or aggressive behavior, you have been given this feedback before. If you know you have a short fuse, schedule interviews for a time of day when you are at your best.

Red Flag #3: Lack of research

Between school web sites, official marketing materials, events, and independent guides, it's easier to learn about schools than ever. There's no excuse for lacking basic information. It's appropriate to ask meaty questions if there are new things you would like to know about the school, but simple questions that are easy to research should be undertaken before the interview. Don't make yourself look like a slacker by skipping the basics.

Red Flag #4: Blatant disrespect for the process

Being late, dressing inappropriately, or any general lack of decorum will signal a disregard for the process and in some cases, insult the interviewer. With that in mind, it's better to be thirty minutes early than five minutes late; better to be overdressed than dressed too casually; better to use formal, respectful language throughout an interview than to follow the lead of a highly colloquial interviewer. It's fine to be yourself, to engage in humor, and to be relaxed and confident. But it's not fine to do so at the expense of propriety, or to forget that you are the one being interviewed.

PART V:
DECISION TIME

> *When you come to a fork in the road, take it.*
> -Yogi Berra

CHAPTER XVI
CHOOSING FROM MULTIPLE OFFERS

Before you open that thick or thin envelope (or, more likely, hit the refresh button a thousand times on your target school's decision page), give yourself credit for taking a risk and pursuing a competitive school in this challenging environment. Reading this book is part of taking a thorough, circumspect approach to the admissions process. Many otherwise qualified applicants will not earn spots at target schools because of squandered opportunities to learn, and master, the art of building well-targeted, persuasive applications. By virtue of your thoughtful, disciplined approach to the process, you have already increased your chances for success.

CHOOSING FROM MULTIPLE OFFERS
However desirable it may be to have multiple offers, choosing isn't always easy. Mixed feelings, inadequate information, and new information about financial fit may influence your decision to attend a given school. This section discusses opportunities to further evaluate your decision while highlighting common dilemmas experienced by those receiving multiple offers.

REFERENCE YOUR ORIGINAL APPLICATIONS

The first place to seek guidance when deciding which school to attend is in your own recorded thoughts and words. If you have followed the advice in this book, you have already done some good thinking about which school will be best for you. To the extent that many weeks or months have passed between the time that you wrote your application and the time that you received your decision, go back and look at the case that you, yourself, built for wanting to attend certain schools.

This hails back to thinking you did about the "Why this school?" question. If you made early notes or lists about the pro and cons for each school, it's time to pull that list out. If you had to directly or indirectly answer this question through essays and short answers about this school, look back at those answers. As you reread them, pay attention to which of your statements ring the most true.

> " *It's time to be honest with yourself about what the real downsides of attending a given school are, and about whether you can really live with those downsides for x number of years. Time can feel as if it's moving very slowly if you're unhappy at a school.* "

Examine your own remarks with a bit more scrutiny—when you were looking to get into schools, you were selling yourself to the schools, but now that you've gotten in, you are the buyer. You must accurately assess your interest in the experience that is now being sold to you.

LET CONCERNS BUBBLE TO THE SURFACE

When applying, you may have been so focused and hopeful about just getting into a school that you took an "I'll cross that bridge when I come to it" approach to concerns and reservations. Once you've gotten into the school, you have arrived at that bridge and need to be candid with yourself about any concerns. This is about taking a more balanced view than the optimistic one that was portrayed in your application. It doesn't matter whether anybody other than you thinks these concerns are legitimate. Ultimately, you are the one who has to live with your choice.

These concerns could relate to anything. Maybe you're a parent deciding between a school that's very close to where you live and work, and another that would require an additional hour of commute time every day. You didn't want to rule out any good options while you were applying, but now that you have an offer, the prospects of driving that extra hour every day feel very real. It's time to be honest with yourself about what the real downsides of attending a given school are, and about whether you can really live with those downsides for x number of years. Time can feel as if it's moving very slowly if you're unhappy at a school.

GO TO SELL EVENTS

Once you've been admitted to a school, you may be invited to an event designed to "sell" you on accepting your offer. These are marketed as half-congratulatory, half-utilitarian events designed to let you celebrate your acceptance among potential future classmates while school officials answer any final questions you may have. The school's purpose in holding events like these is to close the deal with you. They want you to meet people you like, have fun, and feel at home so that you will accept their offer, and not some other school's.

Sell events are most common among elite schools, particularly at the university and graduate school level. Elaborate "sell weekends" (sometimes called "accepted students weekend" or a similar title) involve days' worth of programming, including in-depth school tours, FAQ sessions, and a long line of the school's most impressive faculty, staff, and students showing up to remind you of what a great choice that school would be.

At the preschool and prep school levels, these events are more scaled down. A luncheon or "cake and punch" reception may be more common in this arena. The intention is the same. Schools have gone to a lot of trouble to choose an excellent incoming class, and they don't want to lose you to a competitor.

VISIT THE SCHOOL AGAIN

If convenience and budget permit, it's not a bad idea to revisit the schools to which you were admitted, particularly if you can go at a time that allows you to experience everyday student life. You might even want to observe campus life as an unannounced visitor (an option that may be feasible on an open college or university campus, but not so feasible at a private preschool, elementary, middle, or high school). One parent of young children I know parked outside the schoolyard of a K-12 school to which her child had recently been admitted. Before making a final decision, she wanted to see whether the teachers looked engaged and the children looked happy.

A final visit will achieve a few things: it will allow you to absorb new information that you might not have seen the first time you visited; it will allow you to integrate new insights about what fits for you (particularly if you visited a school to which you received an acceptance relatively early in the process). When visiting the school, do you feel at home on campus? Do you see yourself reflected in the student body? Do you feel a sense of energy and excitement? These are all indicators of good fit potential for a given school.

It can be prohibitively expensive or time-consuming to visit a school campus during college and graduate school admissions. In these cases, students may be admitted to schools which they have not visited. I do not recommend accepting an offer at any school you haven't visited at all.

TAKE ADVANTAGE OF SPECIAL OUTREACH

The most highly desired candidates may receive special outreach from school officials that goes beyond general sell events, such as personal calls from the Dean of Admissions, a School Director, Headmaster or Dean of Schools. The size of the school should serve as an indicator of whether you are indeed receiving special outreach. At very small schools it may be customary to get a personal call from a school official; at large schools, personal outreach can definitively be considered an extraordinary event. If you become aware that you are receiving outreach that is not being replicated for other admits, it's likely that the school in question is very eager for you to attend.

This is a good position to be in, particularly if there are any conditions or other information that would influence your decision to attend the target school. This isn't to say that you should put on your hard negotiation hat the moment you learn that a school is highly interested in you—rather, if you have a genuine concern or holdback about attending the school, you should take advantage of the opportunity to receive a personal response to your concerns.

COMMON DILEMMA: BEST NAME CACHET VS. BEST FIT

This is the most common dilemma experienced by students choosing from multiple offers. Here is an exaggerated example: you get into the Harvard-equivalent in whatever school universe you are applying, but you think you would be much happier at the Pomona-equivalent. So, what do you do? Go to the school that will render you most impressive in everybody else's eyes, or the school that will be more enjoyable and engaging for you?

The answer isn't simple, because what other people think will have a tangible impact on your future prospects. Perceived quality of a given school matters when it comes time to apply to the next level of school, or to apply for a job. But happiness matters too. And even if you could tolerate or be somewhat happy at better-name-cachet school, there's a good chance that you will thrive and be a better performer at better-fit-school. This may be the difference between graduating as a 3.2 GPA student with few friends or happy memories at better-name-cachet school vs. a 4.0 GPA at better-fit-school with a network that will be personally and professionally fulfilling for life.

Happiness is non-negotiable. This should go without saying, but I will say it anyway: don't go to any school where you don't think you'll be happy. School will be a lonely, depressing place if you hate the teaching style, can't make friends, and don't gel with the culture. There is a very good chance that if you hate a school, your grades will suffer, you will end up transferring, or you will drop out. Disturbing college suicide rates and statistics on acts of violence committed on college campuses also speak to the serious consequences of forgoing fit and potential for happiness. A 2010 joint study by the Johns Hopkins Children's Center, the University of Maryland, and other institutions found that 12 percent of college freshmen had considered committing suicide, and cited isolation, depression, and lack of social support as prime contributors to tragic outcomes. If you are a parent, please do not force your child to go to a school in which he or she will not be happy. If you are a student, please do not write off the importance of going to a place where you can see yourself fitting in comfortably, if not happily.

Consider magnitude. How large is the gap in status perception between the schools you are considering? If the gap is narrow, it's a no-brainer: go with the best fit. For example, if you get into Yale, Princeton, and Harvard, and Harvard is two spots higher in the rankings on the year you happen to apply, but Yale is the best fit, go to Yale. The two schools are on the same level in terms of name cachet, so you won't be sacrificing anything. However, if the schools you get into are Yale and Georgetown, and Georgetown is the best fit, recognize that the difference in rankings (of maybe fifteen to twenty spots) may be considered significant by some. If you are already aware of desired career paths, and know that your next steps after the schools in question will also be highly competitive and sensitive to pedigree, it may be better to go with the school with the more illustrious name—if you feel you could be reasonably happy there.

Consider long-term impacts based on your career aspirations. Let's stay with the Yale vs. Georgetown example. Yale may have a consistently higher overall ranking, but if you want to work in politics, you can't beat the location—or network—afforded by Georgetown. If a better-fit school ranks more highly in terms of career or future goals, go to the better-fit school. However, before you make the decision, check in with yourself on how solid your future goal or aspiration is. If you think there's a decent chance you might change your major or focus area somewhere along the line, the higher-profile school may ultimately be the better choice.

COMMON DILEMMA: UNSOLICITED ADVICE FROM FRIENDS AND FAMILY

Major life milestones such as choosing a partner or buying a house tend to attract the attention and unsolicited advice of family and friends. Choosing a school is no different—throughout the process you are likely to hear feedback and opinions, whether you have asked for them or not.

There is a time and a place for soliciting advice and taking different viewpoints into account; ideally, most of this should have come during your research phase. After your applications have been submitted, your primary objective should be to keep your head clear and remain as connected as possible to your own authentic, previously-outlined criteria for knowing which school is the best fit.

The problem with listening to the advice of others—no matter how well-meaning they might be—is that most people unintentionally introduce their own preferences, values, and insecurities into their advice. Being pregnant, a condition which almost seems to come with a "Talk to me about your pregnancy, childbirth and labor" sign on a woman's head, is somewhat similar to this school decision process, in that people somehow feel "invited" to give unsolicited advice.

However innocuous these conversations seem, and even if some part of you wants to talk about the process, you might learn too late that when it's time to actually decide, the opinions of others can create confusion. If you sense that your plans are inviting excessive or unwanted attention, think through ways you that you can stop the conversation. Ultimately, you're the one who will attend the school. You're the one who has to approve your decisions.

> *Of all the hardships a person had to face, none was more punishing than the simple act of waiting.*
>
> -Khaled Hosseini

CHAPTER XVII
BEING WAITLISTED OR DEFERRED

Congratulations—and condolences—if you find yourself on a waiting list or deferred. It's nice to know that a school thinks well enough of you to keep you under consideration. But it's also frustrating to wait in the wings with the knowledge that even though you "almost" got in, there's still a good chance you will not. If you've been waitlisted or, in the case of early admissions, deferred, there are certain circumstances under which you can take action to improve your candidacy.

HOW WAIT LISTS AND DEFERRALS WORK

Schools set up waiting lists in order to offer spots to candidates they like, but who didn't make the first cut. Spots open up along the way when a school predicts that the class of candidates it did make offers to will be undersubscribed. Predicting yield (the percentage of students who will accept an offer) is tricky business; rates can vary significantly from year to year. By maintaining waiting lists, schools hedge against oversubscription (the opposite problem of low yield) by signaling strong interest in a candidate without committing a spot that it might not be able to give if yield is high. Though some schools accept waiting-list students on a rolling basis, others wait until the enrollment deadline before releasing many spots at once.

Deferrals are different—they relate specifically to undergraduate admissions and the early decision option. Historically, all students who could not be offered early decision spots were "deferred" for consideration in the mainstream applicant pool. This meant that students who stood a chance during the main application period were issued the same status as students who might have stood virtually no chance at all. Increasingly (but not universally), schools are outright rejecting early decision applications they feel will stand no chance of admission in the general applicant pool. This trend makes things more transparent for deferred students who traditionally had no sense of whether a school considered them a reject candidate vs. being a candidate who remained in the running.

> *The unsatisfying truth is that there is no definitive way to gauge your chances. Like the rest of the admissions process, waiting list decisions are not linear.*

Waiting lists and deferrals are different because getting off of the waiting list is contingent upon being chosen after yield proves itself to be too low, while getting an offer after being deferred is contingent upon being able to distinguish yourself against the general applicant pool. In the case of the former, you have already passed the test, but won't be offered a spot unless space permits. In the case of the latter, you have yet to pass muster compared to the large group of candidates.

YOUR CHANCES OF GETTING IN OFF THE WAITLIST

Some experts say that landing a waiting-list admit is nothing short of impossible. On grounds of logic and personal experience, I disagree. The waiting list is the natural product of uncertainty relating a school's ability to know how many admitted students will accept its offer. In a year in which that number is lower than the school expected, waitlisted students stand a better chance. Conversely, a year in which yield is higher than expected may give waitlisters no chance at all.

The unsatisfying truth is that there is no definitive way to gauge your chances. Like the rest of the admissions process, waiting list decisions are not linear. That is, students may be accepted off the waiting list in the order in which such acceptances allow the class to shape up to the desired class mix. For example, if a certain group of accepted candidates from the original admit pool (women, for example) seem to be declining offers at a higher-than-expected rate, the admissions committee may be inclined to accept more women than men off the waiting list in order to help round out the class. Many candidates wonder what number they are on the waiting list, but being accepted "in order" is not necessarily how it works.

WHAT TO DO IF YOU ARE WAITLISTED

If you find yourself on the waiting list of one or more schools, take an assessment of deadlines and dates. Supposing that you have hard offers from other schools, you may be required to send in responses and enrollment deposits at hard-offer schools before you know whether you've made it off of other waiting lists.

In this case, you must be willing to meet the deadline and send in the deposit for the most desirable school to which you do have an offer. This doesn't mean that you can't go to a school that is more desirable if you get off of that school's waiting list eventually; only that if you do, you may find yourself withdrawing enrollment from the first school and being on the hook for yet another enrollment deposit.

Some candidates wonder whether there is anything they can do to improve their chances of getting off of the waiting list. Generally speaking, you have little control over whether you will make it off of the waiting list for reasons already mentioned. However, if the waitlisted school is your first choice, and you would attend if offered, there is one gesture that must be undertaken very carefully but that I nonetheless recommend:

Sending a short note to the admissions committee that reiterates your interest signals that the school in question is high on your list. The note should ideally be sent to an admissions committee member with whom you have made a personal connection, the person who has come to know you best and who is most likely to root for you. Since schools are constantly gauging which students would attend if accepted, identifying yourself as strongly interested can elevate you from a question mark to a contender. Some percentage of students on the waitlist will have gotten into schools that were higher on their lists. Since not all waitlisted students remain highly interested, distinguishing yourself as someone who would accept if given the offer is an appealing idea to admissions committees eager to close the door on admissions season and have the final class roster in hand. Issuing offers to candidates who may take weeks to decide is not an appealing thought late in the admissions season.

Some advisors recommend presenting admissions committees with new information that will distinguish you as a more appealing candidate. The problem is that in the case of most waitlisted candidates, little new information will have had time to surface. That is because candidates are only placed on waiting lists after the final round of initial offers has been made, creating a very narrow window for changes and new developments between the time of waitlist notice and final notification. It is difficult to improve test scores or correct any other perceived weaknesses in such short order. In the rare event that something that should truly change the game for your application comes forth (winning an award, receiving a promotion at work, etc.), it is appropriate to say so, but don't grasp at straws to find some new information to present if nothing substantive is really there. In the latter case, a simple reiteration of interest will do.

YOUR CHANCES OF GETTING IN AFTER A DEFERRAL

You have far more control over getting into a school after a deferral than you do getting in off of a waiting list. That is because, as a high school senior whose academic performance is still taking shape, new information about your current performance is considered a relevant and timely addition to your application. Even schools that admit students early require that additional transcripts follow, sometimes mid-year as well as post-graduation. Colleges want to make sure that admitted students maintain similar academic performance that was sufficient to earn them a spot; and, for borderline students, they may want to see whether performance sufficiently improved in the most recent semester. If anything, students who are deferred from early decision or early action may have an advantage over general pool applicants. If their application passes the test, they have the added advantage of having shown early, serious interest in the school.

WHAT TO DO IF YOU ARE DEFERRED

If you have been deferred from early action or early decision, it's time to queue up new information that can help your application. This can be anything that speaks to new academic, extracurricular, or community achievements. If you perceived a weakness or flaw at the time of your original application, you may already know or suspect why the admissions committee may have had reservations about your candidacy. However, asking the admissions committee for feedback on the reasons for your deferral is also recommended.

As always, when approaching the admissions committee for feedback, be humble and respectful, and ask in the spirit of a personal commitment to self-improvement. It is best to approach the member of the committee with whom you have the best connection, and who you believe is most likely to speak with candor about the committee's decision. Be prepared for the possibility that the feedback you receive may not be very specific or very helpful, if the committee is willing to give you any feedback at all. Pay close attention to exactly what was said, and if the feedback seems vague or cryptic, read between the lines.

Once you have integrated feedback with self-evaluation, make your case for being extended an offer of admission. If your junior year math grade was low and it improved in the first semester of senior year, say so—this is quantified evidence of improvement. If you have no hard evidence of improvement, show evidence of commitment (e.g., Because of my commitment to build my skills in math, I have spent the past three months working with a tutor). Now is also a good time to mention any awards you have won, honors you have received, community work you have done, etc., but be sure to place the most emphasis on filling any application gaps. Communicate this new information by sending the committee (again, to the attention of the person with whom you have connected the most if that person's role is appropriate) a well-written letter.

CHAPTER XVIII
HANDLING REJECTION

Rejections are never easy to stomach, but almost everybody gets them. The following section offers guidance on what you might conclude (and what not to read too deeply into) based on your results.

HOW MANY REJECTIONS?

Before launching a more comprehensive discussion of rejections, let's start with a basic truth: the number of rejections matters. If you got rejections from two-thirds or more of the schools you applied to, you made a major miscalculation. Most applicants in this situation either targeted the wrong schools or failed to effectively communicate otherwise good reasons why the target school is an excellent fit. In a smaller number of cases, the applicant lacks critical self-awareness about some flaw in his application or persona and needs candid feedback about the flaw in order to be successful.

If you have received rejections from a third or fewer schools to which you applied, don't be hard on yourself, even if you didn't get in to your first choice(s). I don't know a single person who has gotten into every school to which he has applied, and sometimes getting in or not getting into a school comes down to factors that are beyond any reasonable measure of control. The fact that you got into two-thirds or more of the schools on your list is a signal that you targeted appropriately—if you followed my advice on fit, you should be able to find a school where you will be happy.

What if you got into closer to half of the schools you applied to? This shows that you've done some good targeting, but particularly if you did not get into schools you think you should have, some self-evaluation could be warranted if the rejections are bugging you. Again, a 50 percent acceptance rate is very good, and should give you plenty of schools to choose from if you did your targeting right.

The important thing to remember is this: a few rejections are par for the course, but a lot of rejections are not. If you're closer to the latter, get ready to do some difficult work.

THE ORDER OF REJECTIONS

Some rejections are easier to interpret than others—for example, you might be rejected from the four most competitive schools you applied to, but accepted by the four least competitive ones. Or, you might have been accepted by the four programs with the best fit, and gotten rejections from others. Such situations provide us with at least the comfort of logic to help make the decision more palatable. More frustrating are situations in which rejections show little logic, such as getting accepted at a highly competitive school and rejected from two significantly less competitive ones. It is common among those applying to many schools to receive at least one or two decisions that feel counterintuitive.

One reason for counterintuitive rejections could be an applicant's "over-qualification." If a school thinks that you are so well-qualified to attend that you consider it a safety school, it may narrow its offer pool to students who it believes are genuinely interested in attending. Think of the issue from the school's perspective: accepting only the most qualified students is a risky strategy if other schools with higher rankings are also likely to admit those students. In other words, schools admit students who are not only qualified, but for whom they can reasonably predict yield. They may "reach" for students they hope will choose their school over a competitor that is one tier above, but this will be a relatively small focus of a more holistic strategy.

In many cases, there will be no apparent order to the acceptances and rejections you receive. For example, I was admitted to the #1, #5, and #8 MBA programs (according to Financial Times rankings) in the year that I applied, and rejected from #2, #3, #4, and #9. If nothing else, results like this underscore the non-linear nature of the process and the tenuous relationship between acceptance expectations and rankings. Ultimately, you will be accepted to schools only if you can prove academic aptitude and solidly demonstrate fit. If results seem out of order, the fit factor must be seriously considered.

SELF-EVALUATING REASONS FOR A REJECTION

If you have been denied by most schools to which you applied, wait a few days (or a week or two) for the sting of rejection to subside. When you reach a point at which you can take a calm, objective-as-possible look back at whether you really met the baseline requirements and followed the best practices for targeting and crafting your story as outlined in this book, honestly assess whether you made any bad decisions or missed any opportunities along the way. If it sounds as though I am suggesting that you go back and skim chapters you already read, you're reading this correctly. Being a few months removed from the process might give you perspective. Pay special attention to areas in which common mistakes are specifically discussed. Understanding what might have gone wrong will help shape your decision about whether to attend a school where you were accepted or wait a year and reapply to targets you like more.

Beyond submitting the application itself, think also about other opportunities you may have had to supply a good or bad impression to the committee. You should already have a sense for whether you aced (or bombed) the interview or presented well during other interactions like campus visits, meet and greets, and open houses. Factor virtual interactions into your equations as well. Did you have positive e-mail and social media interactions with committee members? Did you ever get the sense that you made a misstep in a personal interaction at a school from which you received a rejection? Did you feel a sense of belonging at schools from which you received a rejection? If you never got the sense of being at home at a given school, maybe the committee got that sense, too.

You might also want to inspect your rejection letter. Was it a "nice" deny? That is, did it encourage you to apply again in a future year or say anything else that seemed like a genuine expression of interest instead of a platitude? One admissions officer I interviewed said her school had two admissions letters, one for students they genuinely hoped would beef up their applications and try again, and another letter for students they'd be just as happy not to hear from again.

SOLICITING DIRECT FEEDBACK

Particularly if you received many rejections, it's a good idea to approach the admissions committee for feedback. And if you are committed to getting helpful, constructive feedback, you may want to wait a few days until call and e-mail volume from similar requests has died down. Think about it: you don't want the person giving you feedback to be rushed, busy, or overwhelmed. You want real, constructive feedback, and in order to receive it, you must give the committee space.

One admissions officer recommended submitting requests for feedback exclusively by e-mail, citing two rejected applicants who subverted their own desire for feedback by going about it in the wrong way. "One person walked into my office and asked why he had been rejected. Another called me and wanted to talk about it right then. I'd rather have had time to look back at their applications and give thoughtful answers rather than be put on the spot," she said.

In terms of how to ask, keep it simple. Say something like: "I was excited by the prospect of attending XYZ school and was disappointed not to have been extended an offer. Is there anything you can share about why my application was rejected?" Schools will generally be very candid about telling you that academic aptitude was an issue, if that is the real problem. However, it is less likely that other true reasons will be candidly shared with you. In many cases, you will hear a sanitized (if not completely whitewashed) version of why you did not get in.

This cleansing of the truth may happen for one of two reasons. The first reason relates to our litigious society—even if the rejection is defensible and justified, some schools won't want to expose themselves to litigation risk. If an admissions officer tells a rejected applicant that he was not admitted because he was not a good fit, the applicant could sue for discrimination. Don't believe me? Consider a February 2012 investigation in which the U.S. Department of Education's Office of Civil Rights probed Harvard and Princeton following allegations that the schools discriminate against Asian-Americans in undergraduate admissions. The story made national news less than one year after a different admissions discrimination suit was heard in the Supreme Court.

Another reason you might not get the straight story on why you were rejected is because the real reason is awkward or uncomfortable to mention; many people in a position to give you feedback may be inclined to avoid discomfort and confrontation.

THE FEEDBACK NOBODY WANTS TO TALK ABOUT

It's not pleasant to discuss, but it would do certain applicants a disservice to pretend that students (and indeed families) don't get rejected because of personality. If you have a 4.0 GPA, perfect test scores, and a perfect resume of extracurriculars and you still didn't get into a school, I am talking to you. In fact, I'm talking to any applicant who looks great on paper for whatever grade level to which he's applying, but who has received multiple rejections. If this is the case, you have found the enemy, and he is you.

This type of rejection goes past cultural fit straight to ambassadorship. Did you present yourself as somebody the school would want to have as part of its community? Did people find you likable and pleasant to be around? Applying to school is stressful and can be very competitive, and the truth is, it doesn't always bring out the best in people. Did you come off as collaborative, or competitive? Accommodating, or pushy? Humble, or condescending? No admissions officer will tell you that you didn't get an offer because you came off as overly competitive, pushy or condescending, but every admissions officer has rejected applicants for showing these qualities.

The other ground on which an applicant who looks flawless on paper might be rejected is lack of personality. Some students are indisputably smart and capable, but aren't able to impart compelling personal qualities that distinguish them from their record of high achievement. This type of applicant has done all the right things to look good on paper, but fails to be interesting or dynamic in person. Often, hard "quantifiable" skills are on target, but soft skills leave something to be desired. This relates to being well-rounded. You're smart, but are you dynamic and relatable?

REAPPLYING

If you are certain that a particular path or school is integral to your future plans, and you are not satisfied with your current options, you may decide to wait a year and reapply. Depending on the type of school to which you are applying, this may defer the start of school altogether (some parents delay a child's start in kindergarten to help their chances of getting into a desired school; prospective graduate school students may spend an extra year in the work force before reapplying to targets). In other cases, students will attend a less desirable school for the interim year and pursue a transfer to the target school in a future year. This is the case with primary or secondary schoolchildren who must move forward in their education, regardless of acceptance status.

There are pros and cons to reapplying. If you are eventually accepted to your target school, you will feel the extra time, effort, and stress were worth it. If you aren't, you may find that you've put your life on hold for a year (and your hopes and dreams on the line once again) for a goal that didn't come to fruition. If you find yourself in the latter situation, you may wish you had let go of your dream and moved on after receiving the first rejection.

Little information is known about whether re-applicants stand a better chance across the board, though some schools say they do. In a March 2008 BusinessWeek article, Wharton MBA Admissions director Thomas Caleel said re-applicants had a 5–10 percent higher acceptance rate than first-time applicants. Former Dean of Admissions at the University of Chicago Booth School of Business, Rose Martinelli, was not specific on how much more successful re-applicants were, but echoed the sentiment that, on average, they fare better.

It's important to put these numbers into perspective. At the time, Wharton's re-applicant rate stood at ~25 percent. That means that even though a higher than average number of re-applicants were granted admission, some 75 percent were not. This means that three-quarters of applicants who've been through the process at least once before miscalculated their chances of getting in a second time.

That said, I recommend re-application only if you are strongly dissatisfied with your current choices and if the path to getting an offer the second time around is relatively straightforward. If you know that grades and test scores were the primary holdback, or that you did well across nearly every dimension but bombed an interview or some other known factor…if you can isolate and fix what prevented you from getting admitted before, you are an excellent candidate for reapplication.

> *If you are eventually accepted to your target school, you will feel the extra time, effort, and stress were worth it. If you aren't, you may find that you've put your life on hold for a year (and your hopes and dreams on the line once again) for a goal that didn't come to fruition.*

But if you don't really know why you were rejected and suspect you weren't given the candid truth, and you're not committed to soliciting an expert opinion, recognize reapplying under these circumstances for the huge risk and emotional roller coaster that it will be — one you may not want to take without confidence that you will prevail the second time around.

ENGAGING A CONSULTANT AFTER A REJECTION

If you received multiple rejections are considering reapplying, or don't feel that you have a firm grasp on what went wrong the first time and/or how to fix it, you may want to hire an admissions consultant. In this situation, it's best to find somebody who is experienced in reapplication and who is oriented toward problem-solving and candid feedback. Less fitting to the task is a consultant who focuses more on the front-end strategy and planning phases. You want somebody who spends more of her time addressing unique issues for individual clients than explaining the basic elements of the process to newcomers.

The value that a consultant can add is candor about what an admissions committee member wouldn't tell you. A committee member will not tell you that your resume seems to stretch the truth and that your essays sound self-aggrandizing, but if that's the case, a good consultant will not be afraid to tell you the truth.

> *If your outgo exceeds your income,*
> *then your upkeep will be your downfall.*
> -Bill Earle

CHAPTER XIX
FINANCIAL AID

Earlier in the book, I cited not applying to a school for reasons of affordability as a common application mistake. The fact is, you will not find out exactly how affordable a school is until you learn about your financial aid package. A school's ability to offer financial aid may vary from year to year, and class to class; the availability of funds from secondary sources is also subject to change. Now that you know what to expect, it's time to factor finances into your decision. This section will expose considerations, common dilemmas, and mistakes made by those on the hook to pay for school.

STEP #1: UNDERSTAND THE "ALL-IN" ANNUAL COSTS
For some schools, tuition is only one of many areas of financial obligation. Even starting as early as preschool, "fees" to cover books, uniforms, electives, field trips, miscellaneous learning materials, before- or after-school care, or any other kind of additional expense may add to your overall financial responsibility. Some schools (particularly prep schools) explicitly ask for a fundraising commitment or an annual donation to the school's endowment. Schools increasingly make all-in costs transparent, but some research is still required since the way in which financial information is presented varies from school to school.

Similarly, if you (or your child) are off to grad school or college, anticipate how much you will budget for incidentals. It's important to be realistic about how much you or your child will need to live on in order to maintain a practical, socially healthy lifestyle. Even if you buy a meal plan for an undergrad student, he won't want to eat in the dining hall all the time. It's easy to arbitrarily set allowances of discretionary funds, but they should be rooted in how much it actually costs to do normal things that are vital to basic social participation and making friends. If you are from Tennessee and you are sending yourself or your child to school in New York City, take differences in cost of living between each geography into account. It may be appropriate to multiply your normal food and entertainment budgets in a situation like that.

Even if you can afford to pay out-of-pocket, now's the time to document the full set of costs involved. Now's also the time to understand payment schedules and whether there is any advantage to paying a portion of tuition and fees on a specific schedule or in advance. Many primary and secondary schools give parents who pay annual tuition up front a slightly lower cost.

STEP #2: UNDERSTAND THAT FINANCIAL AID EQUALS THE WHOLE PACKAGE, NOT THE GRANT

Most laypeople use the term "financial aid" to describe a tuition reduction or grant amount issued to help cover education costs. When school officials and financial aid officers discuss financial aid, however, they are referring to the total package of grants, scholarships, loans, and in some cases, work study that may comprise your financial picture. This semantic difference has been the source of much confusion. Specifically, at the college and graduate school level, some schools have come under fire for making it difficult to distinguish aggregate aid from tuition reduction and grant amounts on financial aid documents. The result has been legislative debate and an investigation by the Consumer Financial Protection Bureau, which culminated in the passage of a July 2012 Senate bill committed to better transparency in communications.

Important elements of the package include all-in costs (e.g., tuition, fees, books, supplies, housing and meals if applicable, personal expenses), school-sponsored grants, federal or state grants, and scholarships. Grants and scholarships should be deducted from all-in costs to show your total expected contribution. Once you know your own contribution, you can decide whether you can pay the balance out of pocket (as is usually the case for preschool and K-12 schools), or whether you will take out loans (as may be the case at the college and graduate school levels). From there, financial aid extends into whatever federal loans, private loans, and work study agreements you might enter into in order to help you pay for school.

STEP #3: UNDERSTAND TUITION INFLATION AND CHANGES IN GRANT AMOUNTS

The tuition and financial aid package that you receive this year may not be identical to that which you receive next year. To the extent that schools try to keep it predictable, large swings in tuition or aid are unlikely, but a few percentage points each year over a number of years will start to add up.

Suppose you enroll at a school that costs $10,000 in tuition, and it raises its cost by 2 percent each year. In Year Two, you would pay $10,200; in Year Three, you would pay $10,404; by Year Four, $10,612; by Year Five, $10,824. By the end of five years, you will have paid $2,040 more than if tuition had stayed flat. Financial aid may be similar. Colleges in particular are sometimes willing to subsidize students only for the amount beyond that which the student can borrow. Therefore, if the amount of federally subsidized loans a student can borrow increases, the grant provided by the school may decrease.

> *The tuition and financial aid package that you receive this year may not be identical to that which you receive next year.*

In the case of K-12 schools, grant amounts may be guaranteed for several years or reviewed annually. Both methods will yield mixed results as the ability of an individual family to pay may change from year to year. For example, if a working parent in an enrolled family loses a job and combined income drops dramatically, the grant amount to that family may increase in a subsequent year at a school that reviews annually. However, if that same enrolled family experiences no job loss, but ten other families in the school experience job loss that year, the grant amount for the family that experienced no job loss may decrease as the grant amount for families that did experience job loss increases. The annual review method creates upside for families whose financial position weakens at some point during enrollment, while guaranteed aid creates upside for families whose financial position strengthens during the same period of time.

COMMON DILEMMA: BEST PERSONALITY FIT VS. BEST FINANCIAL FIT

Another common problem is finding that the school you are most excited about attending would be financially difficult or infeasible to attend. If you have gotten into a school that you now know (based on new and complete information about financial aid) is outside of what you had hoped or are able to pay, it's time to decide whether to cross it off your list. When making this decision, don't rely on what you believe or think to be true about the return on investment (ROI) of pursuing that particular school. Take the time to sit down and do the math on the financial impacts of all of your options.

If you are applying to preschool, elementary school, or middle school, the opportunity cost of paying more than you can comfortably afford in early years is that you'll be in a worse position to save for college for the same child or children. To the extent that you will earn interest on investments the earlier you start, there is a financial advantage (not to mention peace of mind) in starting college savings early. The multiplier of starting early with private school should also be considered—however many thousands of dollars outside of your budget you might spend in a single year can be multiplied by up to thirteen times if your child is starting in kindergarten, with tuition bumps typically occurring at grade six and grade nine.

Finally, with schools reviewing financial aid annually (which is common at the lower levels of education), there is always the risk that your financial aid package could change. A friend of mine recently pulled her children out of an excellent private school when, after receiving a salary increase, the school lowered her financial aid package by a magnitude greater than the amount of her earnings bump. Prep schools rarely (if ever) guarantee financial aid, and while most schools try to keep things logical and consistent, the reality is that it may vary.

High school, college and graduate school can be a bit of a different story. For one, these higher education levels begin to have a more tangible impact on the student's future prospects for lifetime success. Coming from a strong high school has a tangible impact on getting into a good college; strong undergrad degrees have a tangible impact on getting into a good graduate school. If there is any place you should find wiggle room in your thinking and your budget, it should be here. That isn't to say that you should go outside of your financial comfort zone to pay for any school— only that here it makes more sense to consider the financials in terms of ROI.

Here's a simple example: if College A costs $20,000 per year to attend and will allow you to earn $40,000 per year upon graduation, and College B costs $30,000 per year to attend and will allow you to earn $45,000 per year upon graduation, which school should you attend? With college B, you will pay $40,000 more in the four years you are attending, but your higher salary will place you in a position to pay off the difference in nine years (considering student loan interest) if you take out debt to cover the difference. If College B is a better fit, and if intangible qualities such as College B's name cachet are more appealing, and if you don't mind more student loan debt or sacrificing some other financial goal to pay a premium for College B, it might be a better choice.

Now I'll play the devil's advocate: many people don't attain the projected financial ROI from a given school. Average starting salaries are fickle— the recent recession is a great example of when salary ROI might not pan out. There is also personal preference to consider. The target school might show a high average starting salary only because of a certain population of students who migrate to highly-paid careers. The earnings potential of a computer science major in today's economy can't be compared to that of a liberal arts major, though both students may attend the same school. Finally, a lot can change in the years it may take to pay the incremental cost of the more expensive school. Graduates may leave the work force prematurely in order to start a family, pursue a new level of education, or for some other reason. Also, excessive student loan debt might hinder the graduate's ability to reach other financially sensible goals, such as being able to purchase a home.

IF YOU'RE NOT GOOD WITH FINANCES...

If you're not a math maven and are a bit uncomfortable mapping out financial scenarios, it may be advisable to seek advice from someone who knows their way around numbers. Ideally, this should be someone familiar with school tuition dynamics, someone capable not only of doing the math but also accounting for the risk and handling the assumptions sensibly. The good news is that properly worked-up numbers will hold little ambiguity. At the end of the day, this part is just math, and there will be clear guidance as to what you can and cannot easily afford.

PART V:
DECISION TIME

> "*Success is a little like wrestling a gorilla.*
> *You don't quit when you're tired.*
> *You quit when the gorilla is tired.*"
> -Robert Strauss

CHAPTER XX
EMERGING ISSUES IN ADMISSIONS

The goal of this book has been to frame best practices for applicants in terms of the fundamentals, to represent the set of things that a school is looking for that is the same regardless of the applicant's age or level of education—a set that has remained largely unchanged over time, and how candidates can use this knowledge to their advantage. Yet, though underlying motivations for applying to schools and admitting students stay the same, the processes, decisions, and methods surrounding admissions may be changing.

All of the changes make sense within the framework of the basics. Schools' willingness to admit more international students may relate to basic concepts of self-preservation and diversity as presented in Chapter 2. The use of admissions consultants and the occurrence of application inflation may be on the rise due to market factors as presented in Chapter 1. Technology is changing the way schools screen candidates and vice versa, but not for the first time. The emerging issues that we will discuss are timely, but cyclical. These sorts of shocks to the system happen all the time. All changes to admissions practices can be interpreted vis-à-vis the fundamentals.

ADMISSIONS CONSULTANTS

I am often asked whether it's advisable to hire a consultant to maximize the chances for acceptance. It really depends on what services the consultant offers, and the unique situation of the applicant.

Is Using a Consultant Ethical?

Before discussing consultants in detail, I'll make one thing clear: admissions consultants make most schools uneasy. Objections are twofold: 1) if hiring a consultant really does make for a better application, then only those who can afford to hire consultants will have better applications, which defeats any hope of meritocracy, diversity and a level playing field; 2) some "consultants" are really cheaters-for-hire, individuals willing to write applications for pay. This undermines schools' goals to get to know the real you—not some filtered, engineered, manicured version of you. The methods of many consultants—and the willingness of some candidates to hire such outfits—make cheaters, liars, and plagiarists of the applicants who use them. Be very careful (and clear on your reasons) for hiring a consultant.

It comes down to this: the influence of consultants is not appropriate if it distorts your personality and the true scope of your abilities. Letting somebody else write or edit your short answers or essays (as opposed to giving you feedback on how to improve them), and outsourcing personal decisions such as what activities to participate in or what organizations to join, strips away valuable information about who you are. Colleges can't easily see who you are if others are making decisions. The best consultants aren't the ones who try to fit you into a "successful applicant" mold (whatever that is); rather, the best advisors help peel back layers of self-doubt and misinformation and help you to present your authentic self. A good consultant isn't there to give you the answers, but rather to challenge you to come up with the best answers for yourself.

What Kinds of Consultants are There?

So, let's talk about different kinds of consultants. Some are geared toward giving you an early opinion of how they would assess you or your child if they were on a target admissions committee. These consultants tend to be former admissions officers who are willing to give you candid feedback and recommendations for improvement. They tend to work with you after you have done a significant amount of work on your own, to give you feedback on an element of your application or the whole package that you bring to the table.

> *It comes down to this: the influence of consultants is not appropriate if it distorts your personality and the true scope of your abilities.*

Some consultants would like to be engaged earlier in the process—very popular at the moment are consultants who work with high school kids as early as freshman or sophomore year to discuss college application strategy. These consultants give advice about how to position yourself. Beyond offering a preview of the process and recommending actions that can be taken over months or years to make your application more attractive, they also focus on being organized and gaining advantage through sheer preparation. This type of consultant is with you for the long haul and will probably place herself in a position to eventually review and give feedback on your application as well.

A final group of consultants focuses on a specific element of the application. Essay-writing consultants, interview coaches, and standardized test tutors are all a in that category.

Do I Need a Consultant?

"Need" is a strong word, and if we're going to use it, then the answer is a vehement "no." If you have the academic aptitude and personal qualities a school is looking for in ways that surpass that of the competition, you will be admitted whether you used a consultant or not. It really is as simple as that. If you know what you want, understand the process, and feel confident that you can communicate effectively and present yourself well, hiring a consultant would be a waste of money, not to mention a poor use of your time.

That said, despite not needing a consultant, many people will see a slight benefit to using one. It's a little like hiring an accountant vs. doing your taxes yourself: doing it yourself will take the most time, be the most frustrating, and you may miss a few credits or deductions that could make a difference to your bottom line. By hiring an accountant, you can circumvent reading indecipherable small print on IRS forms and instead have the most relevant items pointed out to you and clearly explained. Hiring an accountant will make you aware of some of your blind spots, and you will ultimately leave the experience with a better plan for presenting your financial picture to the IRS. An accountant cannot change your fundamental financial picture, however. If you would have owed $10,000 by doing the calculations yourself, you will probably still owe in the neighborhood of $9,000 on the consultant-prepared return.

Hire a Consultant If...

In a few special cases, and a very limited set at that, the use of a consultant may be advisable. Having a complicated overall story to tell or a tricky piece of information to convey is one legitimate reason—candidates with non-traditional or uncommon backgrounds vis à vis their target programs may fall into this category. Similarly, if there is something on your application that you feel could kill your chances of getting into your targets, doing some creative problem-solving with a professional is probably a good idea. In all of these cases, the consultant can help you to build confidence around how to package and deliver an out-of-the-ordinary message.

It can also be helpful to hire a consultant if you are considering reapplying, especially if originally you did not get into any of the schools you applied to. In this case, it looks like you have a blind spot in some area and you'd benefit from the kind of extremely candid feedback that an admissions committee will not give you.

Finally, if you are overwhelmed or lost in the process (and I mean really lost, not just nervous and anxious about getting into your top choice school) and you can locate an ethical, high-quality professional to help you find your path, taking advantage of assistance to get your bearings won't hurt.

HELICOPTER PARENTS

High stakes in modern education have driven hundreds of thousands of parents to unprecedented levels of involvement in their children's academic lives. This behavior—dubiously known as "helicopter parenting"—describes ways in which parents "hover" over children, involving themselves actively in previously autonomous areas of their kids' lives. It is clear why so many parents are driven to this point. Lofty goals of being able to attend (and afford) schools that will tangibly help a child's prospects for success in life create a sense of angst, and consequently, internalized stress for parents. Even parents who don't place direct performance pressure on their children may still qualify as "helicopter" parents if they over-insert themselves into interactions that would have been allowed to play out naturally twenty years ago, ones that are better managed by children on their own.

In a study conducted by Arthur Levine, president emeritus of Teachers College at Columbia University, and Diane R. Dean, a higher education policy professor at Illinois State University, interviews with deans and students at more than thirty U.S. colleges found that overparenting is at an all-time high. In their book *Generation on a Tightrope: A Portrait of Today's College Student*, parental involvement was rated as the number one change introduced to the college environment in recent years, with reports of parents advocating on their children's behalf with admissions committees, administrators, teachers, and even roommates! Forty percent of interviewed students reported to speaking with their parents at least once a day. One school even admitted that it had set up an unofficial "dean of parents" position to handle the heightened volume of interactions.

> *Overparenting in the admissions process can be a red flag for schools—unwarranted interactions and any tone of impatience or indignation will identify you as pushy, high-maintenance, and perhaps aggressive.*

"Parents are just so nervous in this process, and in their nervousness, they lose sense of boundaries, they lose appropriateness, and they certainly lose perspective," said Gabriella Rowe, head of New York's Mandell School. Rowe was discussing the admissions process in a 2008 radio interview and drew this conclusion after telling a story about a parent who approached her in the shower at the gym with a plea to receive one of only a small number of applications. Overparenting in the admissions process can be a red flag for schools—unwarranted interactions and any tone of impatience or indignation will identify you as pushy, high-maintenance, and perhaps aggressive. Even if a school is excited about your child, you may lose an offer of admission if the school decides it doesn't want to risk x number of years of dealing with you. If you're a nuisance before your child has been offered a spot, there's a good chance you will be as much or even more of a nuisance as the parent of an enrolled student.

Beyond your direct interactions with the admissions committee, schools may also react to signs of overparenting elsewhere on the application. Remember—schools want students who can be happy, grow and thrive, but kids can crash and burn when parents apply too much pressure and are generally too involved in engineering their children's educations. The more that parents appear to be running the show, the harder it is for schools to understand what is genuinely of interest to the child. Parents must be engaged and committed to their children's success, but not so involved that they hinder the growth and learning, and obscure the personality of the child.

THE NEW FACE OF CHEATING

Cheating isn't new, but several methods of procuring and creating false credentials are. It is frighteningly easy to purchase essays, forge recommendations, and falsify other supporting documents using everything from paid services to sophisticated computer software that makes rendering fake documents straightforward, even for amateurs. Even standardized tests are subject to cheating: the College Board flags approximately 2,500 scores per year for suspicion of fraud, and "withholds" 1,000 of those flagged by refusing to send suspect scores to colleges. Technology also plays a role in standardized test cheating trends: anyone who knows how to use Google or YouTube can do a simple search for cheating instructions or tips.

The Harvard Crimson followed the case of Adam Wheeler, a former student who was indicted in May of 2010 for plagiarizing essays and letters of recommendation, and submitting false transcripts and fake SAT scores to Harvard College, as well as other institutions and scholarly programs including Fulbright and Rhodes. Charges of larceny, identity fraud, falsifying an endorsement or approval, and pretending to hold a degree culminated in a conviction of a one-year prison sentence and a $45,000 fine. The *Yale Daily News* profiled three of its most egregious cheaters in a lengthy April 2008 article, detailing "a chain of admissions-fraud cases at Yale, dating back at least to 1977." In the case of the Yale frauds, perpetrators were charged with many of the aforementioned offenses, often with larceny elements tied specifically to stealing financial aid. In September of 2011, seven teenagers in Great Neck, New York, were charged with hiring stand-ins to take college admissions tests for them.

High profile cases like these only scratch the surface. Other practices, such as coaches colluding with underperforming athletes to bolster test scores and get help with other application elements, have also been prevalent. *The Chronicle of Higher Education*, in a November 2011 article that specifically discussed an influx of Chinese applicants to American universities, reported "widespread fabrication on applications, whether that means a personal essay written by an agent or an English-proficiency score that doesn't jibe with a student's speaking ability." The article framed the phenomenon as a new issue in admissions, asserting that American colleges "struggle to distinguish between good applicants and those who are too good to be true." How widespread this issue is, is certainly up for debate; yet, the breadth and depth of media coverage related to cheating is telling.

Technologically-enhanced cheating, in particular, means a few new things for applicants: first and foremost, schools are fighting fire with fire. Just as it has become easier for candidates to cheat, it is also now easier for schools and other official organizations to track such deception using technology. The College Board screens for collaborative cheating by observing the scores of students sitting near one another and correlating the occurrence of identical answers to find anomalies in right/wrong answer patterns. It also uses an algorithm to determine unlikely score changes among students who take the test more than one time. Even the portion of the test in which students are asked to copy an integrity statement by hand has been analyzed in suspected cases of cheating. Planned security enhancements to the SAT in particular include the placement of student photos on the testing ticket, to be cross-referenced against the standard identification required to take the test. Beyond controls on standardized tests, schools are using everything from IP address indexing and login-tracking, biometric signature profiling, and anti-plagiarism software to flag inconsistent and suspect markers on submitted works.

If you are the parent of a technologically-apt child or teen (a description of most kids nowadays), it's a wise idea to discuss this issue openly. Even responsible parents who have encouraged their children not to cheat may find that the influence of peers may cloud your child's judgment (and let's face it—teenagers are not known for perfect judgment). Recent cases of students found cheating on their homework assignments by logging onto friends' accounts and using their work resulted in serious consequences (expulsion) for the kids who are charged. Smears on a child's disciplinary record will not help his chances of earning a spot at the next competitive school.

Lying on any part of your application goes beyond impacting you—the more schools see this as a problem, the harder it becomes for everyone to be taken at their word. The current environment is so controlled in part because schools have added extra safeguards and precautions over the years to defend against people who try to cheat the system.

INTERNATIONAL STUDENT ENROLLMENT

An influx of international students to U.S. schools has been a topic of recent attention, as the deepening of the international candidate pool has become a significant contributor to overall application growth. In a survey conducted by the Institute of International Education that polled international enrollment on 750 U.S. college campuses in the fall of 2011, 52 percent of responding institutions reported an increase, compared to only 23 percent reporting a decline and 25 percent reporting flat enrollment. A 2011 Council of Graduate Schools report showed that foreign student applications increased 11 percent over the previous year, marking the seventh consecutive year of growth. These numbers are significant, but whether and how much you will be impacted by these trends will have more to do with the individual set of schools you apply to than anything else.

First and foremost, a school that already receives a large volume of international student applications and that has well-established internal targets for international vs. domestic student mix may not view an increase in international applicants as a reason to change anything. Schools like this have already thought through how they want to target international vs. domestic enrollments, and may view a growing international base as business as usual. If you are a U.S. student applying to such schools, increases in international applicant volume won't impact you as much as increases in domestic student enrollment. The only candidates impacted by the rise in international applications, in these cases, are international students—a larger number of them will compete for a relatively smaller number of spots.

Conversely, increasing application volume from international students may have a large impact on admissions at schools in which a desire for greater international diversity is being pursued. Every school is conscious of its target class mix and its own goals in terms of the culture and community it wishes to build. In some cases, schools without much of an international base may be looking to grow it.

There are other reasons why schools might want to change their target mix to include more international students. The controversial practice of admitting more international students for financial reasons (since international students usually pay out of pocket, putting less financial pressure on a school to help pay for student education) is alive and well on some campuses. So, while a rise in international candidate applications may have indeterminate implications for the overall market, significant changes may manifest given decisions made by individual schools.

It's really all about target mix. Even in cases in which more international students are admitted year-over-year, it is unlikely that a simple rise in international candidate applications drove the change. Maybe a certain school isn't looking to grow its international base but it cares very much about growing its base of science prodigies. If most science prodigy applicants that year are international candidates, a school's targeting goal for science aptitude may overrule its adherence to earlier percentages of international students. Suggesting that schools are so heavily influenced by the mix of students they receive attention from (rather than the mix of students they have consciously decided they want) is illogical. Though changing applicant demographics may cause slight shifts in admitted student distribution from year to year and more significantly over time, most schools are conscious about managing their target mix and do so quite deliberately.

SOCIAL AND EMERGING MEDIA

Chapter 6 discussed leveraging social media and blogs to research individual schools; indeed, the universe of media used for school admissions is expanding. From densely-populated web sites that are rich with previously obscure information, to virtual campus tours and video channels, schools are providing greater visibility into their vision, programs, student life, and culture than has ever been seen before. The prevalence of online applications discussed in Chapter 11 has streamlined interactions and processes as well. In this sense, technology isn't desirable merely because it is easier, cheaper, and more far-reaching—it has introduced a quality and transparency to the process that holds benefits for all involved.

> *Your focus should be resourcefulness (e.g., using technological tools to learn what you need) without using them to replace personal interactions.*

Part of making the most of the admissions process is using technology to better understand and assess fit with your target school. Yet the unprecedented use of technology has also created the risk of relying on technology at the expense of other important ways of receiving and extending information. Your focus should be resourcefulness (e.g., using technological tools to learn what you need) without using them to replace personal interactions. *Remember: the ultimate goal of the admissions committee is to get to know you.* The wise use of social and emerging media will strike a balance between virtual self-service and personal interactions that build the relationships critical to truly understanding and becoming important to a school.

As we've discussed, it is no longer acceptable to use admissions events and printed marketing materials as the primary sources of information about a school. Most schools expect you to have read their web site, viewed multimedia, and conducted some other research prior to initiating meaningful conversations with them. Independent research using current media (virtual self-service) is simply a baseline expectation—yet it is not acceptable to use technology to get all that you need. An e-mail is not the same as a phone call, and a phone call is not the same as a visit. Memorability is critically important, and to be memorable, it's best to cultivate as many personal interactions as possible.

What about interactions that seem to straddle this line? Posting a question on the Facebook wall of an admissions committee, for example, is not anonymous. It is interactive, yet the interaction is virtual. Such actions are fine, yet interactions of this nature should not be the only ones. To the extent that so many interactions have been shifted to virtual media, don't squander any opportunity to have as many real person-to-person touch points as possible.

APPLICATION INFLATION AND YIELD GAMES

Though the cycle of application inflation is described briefly in Chapter 1, it is now so prevalent that it merits another mention here. This phenomenon occurs when candidates and schools both take measures to hedge against uncertainty in the process, but in ways that ultimately serve to create less certainty for all parties involved, which in turn creates inflationary pattern in the market.

Candidates, believing in stiff competition, apply to more schools as a hedge against rejections. Growing application volumes are reported by schools each year, adding to the perception of increasing competition, causing candidates to apply to even more schools as time goes on.

What this means for schools is that more students than ever are applying—and more students than ever, if admitted, probably will not attend. That's because achieving the goal of pocketing multiple offers lowers the probability that a student will attend any individual school. For example, if you have offers from two schools, each school may have a 50/50 shot at enrolling you; but if you have offers from four schools, that possibility drops to 25 percent. This creates a need for schools to be especially careful about who, when and how they admit candidates; if they miscalculate the number of offerees who will actually attend, it could throw off an entire class.

Numerous tactics to mitigate yield risk are becoming more prevalent. Early decision is attractive to colleges because it allows them to lock in a percentage of highly desirable admits early on. Any known increase in early decision enrollments at a school may be a sign that the school has lost some of its ability to predict yield, and wishes to secure more high-quality enrollments earlier in the process. Advanced waiting list strategies may also be employed to give schools space to let more students in if yield is looking low. However, most schools want to seem more, not less, competitive, so it is not ideal for schools to admit an excessive number of students to hit its desired yield. What schools really want is to admit students who are highly desirable and also likely to attend.

Given these concerns, showing serious interest in a school will probably increase your chances for admission. The problem with this advice, of course, is that if everybody took it, the act of showing such interest would become meaningless, effectively neutralizing any influence such information might have had on a given school. So, here is my caution: do express interest, but don't be disingenuous, and save your strongest expressions of interest for your most desired schools.

OUT-OF-STATE APPLICANTS

Sweeping budget cuts at many state-funded universities during recession years has changed admissions dynamics. In some cases, policies on preferred enrollment for state residents has even gone awry. Absent benefits of preferred admissions and deep tuition savings, it has become more logical for students across the board to consider schools outside of their own states. For those applying to state schools (whether their own or anybody else's), a seismic shift may be occurring in the applicant pool.

No state schools have received more media coverage on this issue than those in the University of California system, which caused quite some controversy when they admitted that severe budget troubles compelled new policies of giving priority to out-of-state and international students based on their higher tuition obligations, and therefore, the desperately needed revenue they could bring to the schools. Following these announcements, the number of out-of-state freshman applications for entry in fall 2012 rose 56 percent over the previous year to about 33,000, an unprecedented 26 percent of the applicant pool. About 93,300 in-state student applications represented a 9.8 percent jump in freshman applications despite fewer opportunities for in-state students and flat high school graduation volumes within the state. Overall, freshman applications to the university rose 19 percent, to 126,300. Within this state school system, the admissions market changed drastically in just one year.

It's not just California. Changes to the enrollment pool are being reported in state school systems across the country, with similar financial concerns cited as the biggest drivers. Thirty-five percent of University of Missouri freshmen are now from out-of-state (compared to nearly half that number almost ten years ago). During the same time frame, the University of Kansas system reported a 14 percent increase in out-of-state enrollments and a 33 percent rise in enrollments from international students. Therefore, if you're looking at state schools, and you're trying to assess your chances for admission, research any changes that have occurred in the pool. Also, recognize that enrollment stats that were relevant even a couple of years ago may not be relevant anymore.

> *One day your life will flash before your eyes.*
> *Make sure it's worth watching.*
> -Robert Strauss

FINAL THOUGHTS

As you continue on your journey, feel free to review the specific pages of admissions wisdom that are pertinent to wherever you are in the process. Here, I'll leave you with a few thoughts to return to should you ever feel insecure or lost. It's easy to become so immersed in the process itself that you can lose sight of what you're really trying to do: take the next step on a path that will lead you to your best life. It's also easy to become influenced by other candidates (recall earlier comments about the blind leading the blind), or sidetracked by other information and advice that may be disorienting, distracting, or just wrong. If you ever sense a need to find your bearings again, begin right here:

Don't just check the boxes. Building a strong application isn't about having the highest tally of facts that speak to your credit. Every year many well-credential candidates fail to get offers from schools because despite being able to show that they are smart and capable, they miss opportunities to build personal connections, and they don't make a compelling case for why they should attend a certain school. Schools want smart people with the potential to do great things in life, but they don't want mindless automatons who only know how to fit a mold. Be authentic when you craft your story, when you interact with others, and when you choose how to spend your time. Don't underestimate admissions committees (or your competitors, for that matter). It's easy to distinguish those who are passionate and engaged from those who are simply following a formula to get in.

Be clear, consistent, and candid. Admissions committees respond to authenticity and repetition. They want to be anchored to your core story and see evidence that reinforces what you've told them again, and again, and again. The best applications find things you've said about yourself in one element of the application echoed in another. This builds critical connections and credibility. For example, admitting that you struggle with public speaking is most credible if a recommender says the same thing and if one of your extracurriculars includes membership in Toastmasters. Never mind that you may have positioned this fact as a weakness—the important thing here is that multiple threads of the same truth identify you as credible and strengthen your application. The more credible you seem, the more likely a school will be to believe you when you say you deserve an offer.

Practice resourcefulness without replacement. This is about utilizing all of the new tools and technologies available to you to research and interact with schools without sacrificing opportunities to have real, one-on-one interactions with people in your target school community, and without sacrificing opportunities to visit target schools. Leverage technology, but only to the extent that it gets you closer to substantive experiences that help you—and the committee—get to know each other. Also, take what you read from unofficial sources with a grain of salt. Don't let your research wander so far afield that you are forming opinions many degrees away from primary sources.

Hedge your bets on happiness. It's wise to apply to some schools that you are confident you can get into, but unwise to choose "safety" schools based solely on your chances of admission. Don't let the fear of being left without options cloud your judgment and compel you to apply to schools that are simply not a good fit. Schools that don't make you feel motivated or excited during a visit may come to feel only marginally better if you actually had to attend. Even a single semester can feel excruciatingly long if you're at a school where you are neither socially nor academically happy. Apply to schools where you can study what you're passionate about, where you see yourself making friends, and where you're confident that you can perform well.

Don't miss seeing the forest for the trees. In the thick of the application process, you may feel—very acutely—that getting in to one of your top choice schools is the only thing that matters. Whether you end up with your first choice or your last choice, it is the experience you have as an officially enrolled card-carrying student on campus that will determine the impact of this path on the trajectory of your life. Chances are, you are preoccupied with getting into certain schools that seem to hold the most promise of helping you to achieve, of setting you up for success. The truth is, schools don't make people successful—people make themselves successful. No individual school will make or break your chances in life. Learn about yourself, learn about the schools that will fit you best, and then put the two together. Good luck!

For ongoing discussion and tips, visit the book's official web site, www.getintoanyschool.com.

REFERENCES

CHAPTER I: UNDERSTANDING THE MARKET

Mead, Sara. "Find Success in Early Childhood Education," *American School Board Journal*, November 2008, http://www.asbj.com/MainMenuCategory/Archive/2008/November/FindSuccessinEarlyChildhoodEducation.html?DID=270212.

"Why Waldorf Works: FAQs About Waldorf Education," Association of Waldorf Schools of North America, accessed August 15, 2012, http://www.whywaldorfworks.org/02_W_Education/faq_about.asp.

Simon, Marc H. *Nursery University.* VOD. Directed by Marc H. Simon and Matthew Makar. 2008.

"Is It Really Easier To Get Into Harvard Than An NYC Nursery School?," *New York Family*, July 24, 2012, accessed July 15, 2012, http://www.newyorkfamily.com/is-it-really-easier-to-get-into-harvard-than-an-nyc-nursery-school.

Broughman, Stephen P. "Characteristics of Private Schools in the United States: Results From the 2009–10 Private School Universe Survey: First Look," National Center for Education Statistics, U.S. Department of

Education, May 2011, accessed June 15, 2012,
http://nces.ed.gov/pubs2011/2011339.pdf.

"The Condition of Education: Participation in Education", National Center
for Education Statistics, U.S. Department of Education, 2010, accessed
June 15, 2012,
http://nces.ed.gov/programs/coe/tables/table-pri-1.asp.

"Preschool: First Findings From the Preschool Follow-up of the Early
Childhood Longitudinal Study, Birth Cohort (ECLS-B)", National Center
for Education Statistics, U.S. Department of Education, October 2007,
accessed June 15, 2012,
http://nces.ed.gov/pubs2008/2008025.pdf.

"Grade 4 National Mathematics Results – 2011 Report," National
Assessment of Educational Progress, accessed June 15, 2012,
http://nationsreportcard.gov/math_2011/gr4_national.asp?tab_
id=tab2&subtab_id=Tab_4#chart.

"Grade 8 National Mathematics Results – 2011 Report," National
Assessment of Educational Progress, accessed June 15, 2012, http://
nationsreportcard.gov/math_2011/gr8_national.asp?subtab_
id=Tab_4&tab_id=tab2#chart.

"Grade 4 National Reading Results – 2011 Report," National Assessment
of Educational Progress, accessed June 15, 2012,
http://nationsreportcard.gov/reading_2011/nat_g4.asp?subtab_
id=Tab_4&tab_id=tab2#chart.

"Grade 8 National Reading Results – 2011 Report," National Assessment
of Educational Progress, accessed June 15, 2012,
http://nationsreportcard.gov/reading_2011/nat_g8.asp?subtab_
id=Tab_4&tab_id=tab2#chart.

"Grade 8 National Reading Results – 2007 Report," National Assessment
of Educational Progress, accessed June 15, 2012,
http://nationsreportcard.gov/writing_2007/w0011.asp.

"Grade 8 National Civics Results – 2010 Report," National Assessment of Educational Progress, accessed June 15, 2012, http://nationsreportcard.gov/civics_2010/g8_national.asp?subtab_id=Tab_4&tab_id=tab2#chart.

"Grade 8 National Geography Results – 2010 Report," National Assessment of Educational Progress, accessed June 15, 2012, http://nationsreportcard.gov/geography_2010/g8_nat.asp?subtab_id=Tab_4&tab_id=tab2#chart.

"Grade 8 National Science Results – 2011 Report," National Assessment of Educational Progress, accessed June 15, 2012, http://nationsreportcard.gov/science_2011/g8_nat.asp?subtab_id=Tab_4&tab_id=tab2#chart.

"Grade 8 National History Results – 2010 Report," National Assessment of Educational Progress, accessed June 15, 2012, http://nationsreportcard.gov/ushistory_2010/g8_nat.asp?subtab_id=Tab_4&tab_id=tab2#chart.

Chilcott, Lesley. *Waiting for Superman*. VOD. Directed by David Guggenheim. 2010.

Sackler, Madeleine, James Lawler, and Blake Ashman-Kipervaser. *The Lottery*. VOD. Directed by Madeleine Sackler. 2010.

Strauss, Valerie. "Report: Rise in college applications hurts low income students," *The Washington Post*, November 19,2010, accessed July 15, 2012, http://voices.washingtonpost.com/answer-sheet/college-admissions/report-rise-in-college-applica-1.html.

Monks, Kate. "Grad School applications soar," *The Brown Daily Herald*, February 2, 2010, accessed July 15, 2012, http://www.browndailyherald.com/grad-school-applications-soar-1.2146361#.UAGKc8omb3E.

Fischer, Karin. "Admissions Offers to Foreign Students at U.S. Graduate Schools Climb at Faster Pace," *The Chronicle of Higher Education*, August 16, 2011, accessed July 15, 2012, http://chronicle.com/article/Admissions-Offers-to-Foreign/128700.

Aronson, Emily. "Graduate School applications rise almost 10 percent," Princeton University Press Release, accessed July 15, 2012, http://www.princeton.edu/main/news/archive/S27/29/04Q48/index.xml?section=newsreleases.

Ruiz, Rebecca. "Recession Spurs Interest in Graduate, Law Schools," *The New York Times*, January 10, 2010, accessed July 15, 2012, http://www.nytimes.com/2010/01/10/education/10grad.html?_r=1&pagewanted=print.

Weinstein, Deb. "Jobless Gen Ys Turn To Grad School," *Forbes*, December 21, 2009, accessed July 15, 2012, http://www.forbes.com/2009/12/21/mba-law-journalism-gre-gmat-personal-finance-grad-school-applications-up.html.

Smith, Mitch. "Foreign Grad Applications Up Again," *Inside Higher Education*, April 23, 2012, accessed July 15, 2012, http://www.insidehighered.com/news/2012/04/03/chinese-students-lead-increase-international-graduate-school-applications.

Woods, Belle. "International Graduate Applications Rise for Seventh Consecutive Year; China, Mexico, and Brazil show largest gains," Council of Graduate Schools, April 3, 2012, accessed July 15, 2012, http://www.cgsnet.org/international-graduate-applications-rise-seventh-consecutive-year-china-mexico-and-brazil-show-large.

Pérez Peña, Richard and Jenny Anderson. "As a Broader Group Seeks Early Admission, Rejections Rise in the East," *The New York Times*, January 13, 2012, accessed July 15, 2012, http://www.nytimes.com/2012/01/14/education/early-admission-applications-rise-as-do-rejections.html?pagewanted=all.

Ruiz, Rebecca. "Early Applications Flood Harvard," *The New York Times*, November 21, 2011, accessed July 15, 2012, http://www.nytimes.com/2011/11/22/education/early-applications-flood-harvard.html.

Hoover, Eric. "Appliction Inflation: When is Enough, Enough?," *The New York Times*, November 5, 2010, accessed July 15, 2012, http://www.nytimes.com/2010/11/07/education/edlife/07HOOVER-t.html?pagewanted=all.

CHAPTER II: ALL SCHOOLS WANT THE SAME THINGS
"Tuition & Fees," The Bentley School, accessed August 15, 2012, http://www.bentleyschool.net/podium/default.aspx?t=114776.

CHAPTER III: THE ONLY TWO QUESTIONS THAT MATTER
Lawrence, Mark, Katie Ford, and Caryn Lucas. *Miss Congeniality*. VOD. Directed by Donald Petrie. 2000.

CHAPTER VI: BUILDING YOUR LIST OF TARGET SCHOOLS
Lytle, Ryan. "10 Colleges With Highest Freshman Retention Rates," *U.S. News & World Report*, August 16 2011. Accessed August 15, 2012, http://www.usnews.com/education/best-colleges/articles/2011/08/16/10-colleges-with-highest-freshman-retention-rates.

U.S. Department of Education Database of Accredited Post-Secondary Schools and Programs, http://ope.ed.gov/accreditation/.

University of Chicago Class of 2015 Profile, accessed March 12, 2012, https://collegeadmissions.uchicago.edu/apply/classprofile.shtml.

Selingo, Jeff. "The Rise and Fall of the Graduation Rate," *The Chronicle of Higher Education*, March 2, 2012, accessed July 26, 2012, http://chronicle.com/article/The-RiseFall-of-the/131036.

"The 50 Most Stressful Colleges," *The Daily Beast*, April 4, 2010, accessed July 26 2012, http://www.thedailybeast.com/articles/2010/04/04/the-50-most-stressful-colleges.html.

Sudikoff, Natalie. "High College Suicide Rates Stem From Depression, Isolation: Study," *The Huffington Post*, July 6 2010, accessed July 26 2012, http://www.huffingtonpost.com/2010/07/06/high-college-suicide-rate_n_636878.html.

"Cornell Putting Nets Over Gorges to Stop Suicides", August 20 2012, accessed August 20 2012, http://www.cbsnews.com/8301-201_162-57496230/cornell-putting-nets-over-gorges-to-stop-suicides/

"Net installations to begin on campus area bridges," The Ithaca Journal, August 16, 2012, accessed August 20 2012, http://www.theithacajournal.com/article/20120816/ NEWS01/308160041/Net-installation-begin-campus-area-bridges?odysse y=tab%7Ctopnews%7Ctext%7CFRONTPAGE&gcheck=1&nclick_check=1.

DeVise, Daniel. "Nearly half of doctorates never completed," April 29 2010, accessed August 20, 2012, http://voices.washingtonpost.com/college-inc/2010/04/nearly_half_of_ doctorates_neve.html.

CHAPTER IX: INDIVIDUAL SCHOOL PREREQUISITES

"Honors and AP Courses," The College Board, accessed August 15, 2012, http://professionals.collegeboard.com/guidance/prepare/honors-ap.

CHAPTER XI: COMPLETING THE APPLICATION FORM

"All Members," The Common Application, accessed August 3, 2012, https://www.commonapp.org/CommonApp/Members.aspx.

"Benefits of Applying Through the Consortium," The Consortium for Graduate Study in Management, accessed August 3, 2012, http://www.cgsm.org/students/benefitsofapplying.asp.

CHAPTER XII: GATHERING RECOMMENDATIONS

"Application Process," The Trinity School, accessed August 3, 2012, http://www.trinityschoolnyc.org/podium/default.aspx?t=143358.

CHAPTER XVI: CHOOSING FROM MULTIPLE OFFERS

"Depression, Lack of Social Support Trigger Suicidal Thoughts in College Students," Johns Hopkins Childrens Center, June 28, 2010, accessed July 26, 2012, http://www.hopkinschildrens.org/Depression-Lack-of-Social-Support-Trigger-Suicidal-Thoughts-in-College-Students.aspx.

Chapter XVIII: Handling Rejection

Golden, Daniel. "Harvard Targeted in U.S. Asian-American Discrimination Probe," *Bloomberg News*, February 2 2012, accessed July 27, 2012, http://www.bloomberg.com/news/2012-02-02/harvard-targeted-in-u-s-asian-american-discrimination-probe.html.

Dizik, Alina. "Bouncing Back from Rejection," *Bloomberg BusinessWeek*, accessed July 27, 2012, http://www.businessweek.com/stories/2008-03-06/bouncing-back-from-rejectionbusinessweek-business-news-stock-market-and-financial-advice.

CHAPTER XX: EMERGING ISSUES IN ADMISSIONS

Spak, Kara. "Book: College kids today are coddled, entitled, tech savvy," *Chicago Sun Times Post Tribune*, August 21 2012, accessed August 28 2012, http://posttrib.suntimes.com/news/14613764-418/book-college-kids-today-are-coddled-entitled-tech-savvy.html.

Cohen, Steve. "SAT's Legacy of Cheating," *The Daily Beast*, September 28 2011, accessed August 27, 2012, http://www.thedailybeast.com/articles/2011/09/28/sat-cheaters-college-admissions-exam-has-history-of-fraud.html.

Jan, Tracy and Milton Valencia. "Trust-based admissions process leaves elite colleges open to fraud," *The Boston Globe*, May 19 2010, accessed August 27 2012, http://www.boston.com/news/local/massachusetts/articles/2010/05/19/wheeler_case_shows_flaws_in_college_application_process.

Yu, Xi and Julie M. Zauzmer. "Wheeler Sentenced to One Year in Prison After Violating Probation," *The Harvard Crimson*, December 23 2011, accessed August 27 2012, http://www.thecrimson.com/article/2011/12/23/wheeler-prison-sentencing.

Yu, Xi and Julie M. Zauzmer. "Ex-Harvard Student" Adam Wheeler Pleads Not Guilty to Charges of Fabricating Academic History," *The Harvard Crimson*, December 23 2011, accessed August 27 2012, http://www.thecrimson.com/article/2011/12/23/wheeler-prison-sentencing.

Arenson, Karen w. "Yale Student Is Accused of Lying on Application," *The New York Times*, April 10 2008, accessed August 27 2012, http://www.nytimes.com/2008/04/10/education/10yale. html?pagewanted=print.

Arnsdorf, Isaac. "Yale no stranger to application fraud," *Yale Daily News*, April 10 2008, accessed August 27 2012, http://www.yaledailynews.com/news/2008/apr/10/yale-no-stranger-to-application-fraud.

Bartlett, Tom and Karin Fischer. "The China Conundrum: American colleges find the Chinese student boom a tricky fit," *The Chronicle of Higher Education*, November 3 2011, accessed August 27, 2012, http://chronicle.com/article/The-China-Conundrum/129628/

Kossman, Stephanie. "New York SAT cheating scandal urges new rules," *Wellesley News*, April 6 2012, accessed August 27, 2012, http://www.wellesleynewsonline.com/opinions/new-york-sat-cheating-scandal-urges-new-rules-1.2841343#.UDvXFMhSSYk

"eduKan Adds Biometric Technology to Deter Student Cheating," accessed August 28 2012, http://www.edukan.org/2012/05/18/edukan-adds-biometric-technology-to-deter-student-cheating.

"Fall Survey Data: Continued Growth in International Students Enrollments in the U.S.," Institute of International Education, November 14 2011, accessed August 28 2012, http://www.iie.org/en/Who-We-Are/News-and-Events/Press-Center/Press-Releases/2011/2011-11-14-Open-Doors-Fall-Survey-International-Students.

Gordon, Larry. "Higher numbers of out-of-state foreign students apply to UC," Los Angeles Times, January 13 2012, accessed August 28 2012, http://articles.latimes.com/2012/jan/13/local/la-me-uc-apply-20120113.

Steinberg, Jacques, Daniel E. Slotnick and Rebecca R. Ruiz. "Applications Surge to Berkeley and Virginia," The New York Times, January 23 2012, accessed August 29 2012, http://thechoice.blogs.nytimes.com/2012/01/23/regular-admission-tally-2012.

Zimar, Heather. "Missouri and Kansas Universities See Rise in Out-of-State Applicants," American Association of Collegiate Registrars and Admissions Officers, August 16 2012, accessed August 29 2012, http://www2.aacrao.org/transcript/index.cfm?fuseaction=show_view&doc_id=5556.

"The Increasing Impact of Mobile Trends on College Admissions in 2012," Report, Cappex Inc.

Ezarik, Melissa. "Now Try This: A Mobile (Admissions) App," University Business, November 29 2011, accessed August 27 2012, http://www.universitybusiness.com/article/now-try-mobile-admissions-app.

ABOUT THE AUTHOR

Kim Palacios is an alumna of the Baldwin School, the New York University Gallatin School of Individualized Study and the University of Chicago Booth School of Business, where she was a Robert W. Fogel Distinguished Fellow. She began writing professionally in 2009, after a lifetime infatuation with the craft; her writing on travel, entertainment, and finance has won recognition including a 2009 Book Passage Travel Writers and Photographers Conference 2nd Prize for her essay "I Dreamed of Africa", and syndication of her columns for various news outlets on dozens of sites, including *The Huffington Post*. She is quadrilingual, a studying Sommelier, and an epicurean zealot. While not mourning the death of free markets and the tax treatment of Californians, she enjoys film.

Made in the USA
San Bernardino, CA
22 December 2012